BENGAL PEASANT LIFE

BENGAL PEASANT LIFE

By

THE REV. LAL BEHARI DAY,

CHINSURAH, BENGAL.

Let not ambition mock their useful ton.
Their homely joys and destiny obscure
Nor grandeur heart with a disdainful smile.
The Short and simple annuls of the poor — Gray

GYAN

Published by

Gyan Publishing House
5, Ansari Road
Daryaganj, New Delhi-110002
Phone: 011-47034999, 9811692060
E-mail: books@gyanbooks.com

Distribution Network
gyanbooks.com
India, USA, Canada, UK, Australia, France

ISBN : 978-81-212-6288-0 (PB)
First Published, 1916

2nd Impression 2022

Printed at: Gyan Press, Delhi.

BENGAL PEASANT LIFE
Author: The Rev. Lal Behari Day

THE FIRST EDITION OF THIS BOOK WAS PUBLISHED UNDER THE TITLE

OF

GOVINDA SÁMANTA,

OR

THE HISTORY OF A BENGAL RÁIYAT.

BENGAL PEASANT LIFE

BY

THE REV. LAL BEHARI DAY,

CHINSURAH, BENGAL.

> Let not ambition mock their useful toil,
> Their homely joys and destiny obscure
> Nor grandeur hear with a disdainful smile
> The short and simple annals of the poor —*Gray*.

1916

TO

BABOO JOY KISSEN MOOKERJEA,

ONE OF THE MOST ENLIGHTENED ZEMINDARS IN BENGAL,

AND

THE DONOR OF THE PRIZE OBTAINED BY THE FOLLOWING PAGES,

THIS LITTLE BOOK

Is Inscribed,

WITH SENTIMENTS OF ESTEEM AND REGARD,

BY THE AUTHOR.

PREFACE.

EARLY in the year 1871 Baboo Joy Kissen Mookerjea, of Uttarapara, a zemindar in Bengal, offered a prize of £50 for the best novel, to be written either in Bengali or in English, illustrating the "Social and Domestic Life of the Rural Population and Working Classes of Bengal." The essays were sent in to the adjudicators early in 1872; but, owing to the absence of two of the adjudicators in England, and to other causes, the award was not made till about the middle of 1874, when the following pages, written in English, obtained the prize. It is proper to state that the original book, to which the prize was adjudged, wanted the last three chapters; these chapters have now been added, in order to bring down the narrative to the present day.

I cannot let this book go to the world without

expressing the obligations I am under to several English gentlemen who have taken an interest in its publication. First of all, I have to thank Mr. Gordon Robb, of Messrs. G. C. Hay and Co., of Calcutta, for taking a kindly interest in the book, and putting me in the way of the publishers. I have to thank Dr. George Smith, lately editor of the *Friend of India*, and now editor of the *Edinburgh Daily Review*, for reading the book in manuscript, and expressing a favourable opinion of it. I have to thank the Honourable J. B. Phear, one of Her Majesty's Judges in the High Court of Judicature in Calcutta, for not only reading the manuscript, but proposing verbal alterations and suggesting other changes. And last of all, I have to thank Professor E. B. Cowell, of Cambridge, for revising the proof-sheets, and for bringing to bear upon the book his ripe scholarship, his sound judgment, and his fine taste.

LAL BEHARI DAY.

Hooghly College, Chinsurah,
November 27th, 1874.

CONTENTS.

BENGAL PEASANT LIFE.

CHAPTER I.

PREMISES WHAT THE READER IS TO EXPECT, AND WHAT HE IS NOT TO EXPECT, IN THIS AUTHENTIC HISTORY.

> The village life, and every care that reigns
> O'er youthful peasants and declining swains;
> What labour yields, and what, that labour past,
> Age, in its hour of languor, finds at last;
> What form the real picture of the poor,
> Demand a song—the Muse can give no more.
>
> *Crabbe.*

GENTLE READER, in case you have come with great expectations to the perusal of this humble performance, I deem it proper to undeceive you at the very outset; lest after going through it, or through a good bit of it, you are disappointed, and then turn round and abuse me as a fellow who, with a view to attract customers, has put a misleading sign-board over the door of his shop. I therefore purpose, like a tradesman who, though anxious to turn a penny, wishes to obtain it in an honest way, to tell you at once, in all sincerity and good faith, what you are to expect, and what you are not to expect, in this hall of refreshment; so that after being acquainted with the bill of fare, you may either begin to partake of the repast or not, just as you please, and thus save yourself the trouble of sitting down to a dinner not congenial to your taste, and me the abuse justly merited by a man who holds out expectations which he cannot fulfil: and, after the approved manner of the popular preachers of the day, I shall treat first of the second point. The first head, then, of this preliminary discourse, or—to use a still more learned word—of this prolegomenon, is what the schoolmen would call the negative point, namely, what you are not to expect in this book.

And *firstly*, of the first point. You are not to expect anything marvellous or wonderful in this little book. My great Indian predecessors—the latchet of whose shoes I do not pretend to be worthy to unloose—Válmiki, Vyás, and the compilers of the Puránas, have treated of kings with ten heads and twenty arms; of a monkey carrying the sun in his arm-pit; of demons churning the universal ocean with a mountain for a churn-staff; of beings, man above and fish below, or with the body of a man and the head of an elephant; of sages, with truly profound stomachs, who drank up the waters of the ocean in one sip; of heroes as tall as the lofty towers of the golden Lanká; of whole regions inhabited by rational snakes, having their snake-kings, snake-ministers, snake-soldiers hissing and rushing forth to battle. And some of my European predecessors, like Swift and Rabelais, have spoken of men whose pockets were capacious enough to hold a whole nation of diminutive human beings; and of giants, under whose tongue a whole army, with its park of artillery, its pontoon bridges, its commissariat stores, its ambulance, its field post, its field telegraph, might take shelter from the pouring rain and the pitiless storm, and bivouac with security under its fleshy canopy. Such marvels, my reader, you are not to expect in this unpretending volume. The age of marvels has gone by; giants do not pay now-a-days; scepticism is the order of the day; and the veriest stripling, whose throat is still full of his mother's milk, says to his father, when a story is told him: "Papa, is it true?"

Secondly, you are not to expect in this authentic history any thrilling incidents. Romantic adventures, intricate evolutions of the plot, striking occurrences, remarkable surprises, hair-breadth escapes, scenes of horror, at the recital of which the hair stands on end—the stuff of which the sensational novels of the day are made—have no place here. Thrilling incidents occur but seldom in the life-history of ninety-nine persons out of a hundred, and in that of most Bengal ráiyats never. If you, gentle reader, choose to come in here, you must make up your mind to go without romantic adventures and the like; and, as for horrors, this country inn has not the means to make you sup off them.

Thirdly, you are not to expect any love-scenes. The English reader will be surprised to hear this. In his opinion there can be no novel without love-scenes. A novel without love is to him the play of Hamlet, with Hamlet's part left out. But I cannot help it. I would fain introduce love-scenes; but in Bengal—and for the matter of that in all India—they do not make love in the English and honourable sense of that word. Unlike the butterfly, whose courtship, Darwin assures us, is a very long affair, the Bengali does not court at all. Marriage is an affair managed entirely by the parents and guardians of bachelors and spinsters, coupled with the good offices of a professional person, whom the reader may meet with in the course of this narrative. Of dishonourable, criminal love, there is no lack; but I do not intend to pollute these pages with its description.

Fourthly, you are not to expect here "grandiloquent phraseology and gorgeous metaphors." Some of my educated countrymen are in love with sonorous language. The use of English words two or three feet long is now the reigning fashion in Calcutta. Young Bengal is a literary Bombastes Furioso; and Young Bengalese is Johnsonese run mad. "Big thinkers may require," as old Sam Johnson said, "big words;" but we, plain country-folk, talking of fields, of paddy, of the plough and the harrow, have no sublime thoughts, and do not, therefore, require sublime words. If, gentle reader, you have a taste for highly-wrought, highly-seasoned language, for gorgeous similes, for sesquipedalian phraseology, for sonorous expression, making a maximum of noise with a minimum of sense, and for such other comfits, I advise you to go elsewhere and not to come to this country confectionery.

I now come to the second point of this preliminary discourse, which is, what the reader *is* to expect in this book. Remembering that brevity is the soul of wit, I despatch this part of the subject in one short sentence. The reader is to expect here a plain and unvarnished tale of a plain peasant, living in this plain country of Bengal—I beg the pardon of that sublime poet who sung in former days of the "hills of Hooghly and the mountains of the Twenty-four Parganás"—told in a plain manner. Such, gentle reader, is my bill of fare. If you think it will suit you, I bid you welcome; if not, please pass on to some other quarter.

CHAPTER II.

INTRODUCES AN OLD WOMAN TO THE READER.

Sche cowde moche of wandryng by the weye,
Gat-tothed was sche, sothly for to seye.
Prologue to Canterbury Tales.

It was considerably past midnight one morning in the sultry month of April, when a human figure was seen moving in a street of Kánchanpur, a village about six miles to the north-east of the town of Vardhamána, or Burdwán. There was no moon in the heavens, as she had already disappeared behind the trees on the western skirts of the village; but the sky was lit up with myriads of stars, which were regarded with superstitious awe by our nocturnal pedestrian, as if they were the bright eyes of men who once lived on the earth, and had since passed into the realms of Indra. Perfect stillness reigned everywhere, except when it was interrupted by the barking of dogs, or the yells of the village watchmen, two or three of whom often join in a chorus, and send forth those unearthly shouts which so often disturb the sleep of the peaceful inhabitants. The human figure, which was moving with rapid strides, had no other clothing than a *dhuti*, wrapped round the waist, and descending to the knee-joints; and he had a thick bamboo-stick in his hand. As he was rounding a corner of the street, he saw dimly a man sitting at the door of a hut, who shouted out—

"Who goes there?"

"I am a ráiyat," exclaimed the moving figure.

"What ráiyat?" rejoined the village watchman, for it was none other.

"I am Mánik Sámanta," was the reply.

"Mánik Sámanta, at this late hour!" said the watchman.

"I am going to fetch Rupá's mother."

"Oh! I understand: come, sit down and smoke—tobacco is ready."

"You smoke—I am in haste!"

So saying, Mánik Sámanta walked on faster than before, passed that part of the street which was lined on both sides with houses, and came to the outskirts of the village, where there were a great many mango orchards, sprinkled here and there with a few huts.

Before one of those huts Mánik stood and called out: "Rupá's mother! Rupá's mother!" At the first call Mánik perceived, from whispers inside the hut, that Rupá's mother was awake; but he received no answer to his call. He called a second time, but no answer was returned; he called a third time, no answer yet. It was only after he had bawled out the fourth time that the call was responded to. The reader may suppose that Rupá's mother was deaf; but it was not so. She had a meaning in not answering the call till it was repeated the fourth time. It is the invariable custom of the rural population of Bengal never to respond to a call at night, especially after midnight, till it is repeated three times. It is believed that *Nisi*, that is Night personified, has often stood at night at the doors of simple folk, called them out of their beds, and decoyed them to pools and tanks, where they were drowned. The sable goddess never calls, it is believed, more than three times; and in order to be sure that it is the voice of a human being, and not of *Nisi,* no answer is given till after the fourth time. The superstition has doubtless its origin in the perils incurred by those who are afflicted with somnambulism. But to proceed with the narrative. The door was opened. Mánik told Rupá's mother that she was wanted immediately. Rupá's mother told Rupá, her daughter, to strike a light. Rupá brought from a corner a small gunny bag, and poured out its contents, which were two or three pieces of flint, an iron striker, and some pieces of *solá,* the Indian cork-plant. In a moment the flint gave out a spark of fire, which fell into the *solá;* the sulphur match was applied; and an earthen lamp, containing a small quantity of mustard oil and a cotton wick, was lit.

Let us take a hasty glance, by the dim light of the lamp, at Rupá's mother and her hut. On the floor of the hut, surrounded on all sides by mud walls and over-topped by a straw thatch, lay a coarse mat of palmyra-leaves, which served as a bed for the mother and the daughter. In the four corners were some *háṇḍis* (earthen pots) which contained all their stores, consisting chiefly of rice, a few vegetables, and some culinary condiments like turmeric, salt, mustard oil and the like. There was no furniture. Rupá's mother, who was of the *bágdi* caste, appeared to be a woman of between forty and fifty years of age, of rather below the average height of Bengali women, and had a slender figure;—indeed, her limbs seemed to be as thin and shrivelled as the dry stalks of the lotos. For some reason or other she had very few teeth in her head, and those few at a great distance from one another; in consequence of which she spoke like a woman eighty years old. We have used the circumlocutory phrase, Rupá's mother, instead of mentioning her own name; but the fact is, we never heard her name mentioned by anybody in the village; and though we have made laborious inquiries into the matter, our exertions have proved fruitless,—every one insisting on calling her Rupá's mother. Rupá herself appeared to be a young woman about twenty years old, and the fact that she had not on her wrist the usual iron circlet, nor the vermilion paint on the top of her forehead, where the hair was parted, showed that she was a widow.

Rupá's mother had no great preparations to make for accompanying Mánik. She had no bundles to make up of her clothes, for she usually carried about with her on her person the whole of her wardrobe, which consisted of one long *sári* and one short one; the latter of which she put on every day after bathing, while the former one was being sunned, and both of which she used to whiten once a month by steeping them in a solution of ashes and *cows' urine*—the cheap soap of the peasantry of Bengal. She uncovered one of the *háṇḍis*, took out some drugs, put out the light, and ordered Rupá to lock the door and follow her. But as Rupá was putting the padlock on the door, a lizard, which was resting on the eaves of the thatch, chirped. The *tik, tik, tik,* of the lizard is always regarded as a bad omen by all classes of the people of Bengal, so the journey was delayed. The door was re-opened, the lamp was again lit, and they sat for half an hour in pensive meditation, though Mánik vented no little wrath against the audacious reptile. At last, however, they set out. They went the same way through which Mánik had come, went nearly to the middle of the village, and entered a house. By this time the stars had disappeared from the heavens, excepting the kingly *Sukra* (or regent of the planet Venus), which was shining above the eastern horizon, and proclaiming to an awakening world the cheerful approach of day.

As I already perceive people passing in the street, smoking as they are walking on, and coughing over their hookahs, I do not intend going into the house into which Mánik and the two women have just entered, but purpose taking a stroll through the village, and trust my reader will give me the pleasure of his company.

CHAPTER III.

SKETCHES A VILLAGE IN BENGAL.

> Sweet Auburn! loveliest village of the plain,
> Where health and plenty cheer'd the labouring swain.
>
> *The Deserted Village.*

KÁNCHANPUR, or the Golden City, is a considerable village in Parganá Sáhábád, in the district of Vardhamána, and lies about six miles to the north-east of the town of that name. It has a population of about fifteen hundred souls, belonging to most of the thirty-six castes into which the Hindus of Bengal are generally divided, though the predominating caste in the village was the *sadgopa*, or the agricultural class. Why the village has obtained the name of the "golden city," I have not been able exactly to ascertain; some of the oldest inhabitants maintain that it has been so called on account of the wealth accumulated, and comforts enjoyed by the peasantry in general; while others are of the opinion that the village has been called "golden," on account of the residence in it of some rich families of the *suvarna-vanikas* (literally, traders in gold), usually called the banker caste. However this may be, Kánchanpur is a large and prosperous village. There is a considerable Bráhmana population, the great majority of whom are of the *srotriya* order, often called *rádhi*, from the fact of their living in *Rádh*, the name by which the country lying on the western side of the

Bhágirathi river is usually designated. The *káyasthas*, or the writer caste, are comparatively few in number. *Ugra-kshatriyas*, or *Aguris*, as they are called in common parlance, who are all engaged in agricultural pursuits, though less numerous than the *sadgopas*, are an influential class in the village; while there is the usual complement of the medical caste, of blacksmiths, barbers, weavers, spice-sellers, oilmen, *bágdis*, *doms*, *hádis*, and the rest. Strange to say, there is hardly a single Muhammadan family in the village—the votaries of that faith being less numerous in western than in eastern Bengal.

Kánchanpur, like most villages in Bengal, has four divisions agreeably to the four cardinal points of the compass—the northern, the southern, the eastern, and the western. The village lies north and south, and the northern and southern divisions are much larger than the eastern and western. A large street runs north and south, straight as the crow flies, on which abut smaller streets and lanes from the eastern and western divisions. The bulk of the houses are mud cottages thatched with the straw of paddy, though there is a considerable number of brick houses, owned, for the most part, by the *káyasthas* and the banker caste. The principal street, of which I have spoken, is lined on both sides by ranges of houses, either of brick or of mud, each having a compound, with at least a tree or two, such as the plum, mango, guava, lime, or papaya, and the invariable plantain. Outside the village, the main street is extended nearly a quarter of a mile at each end, with rows on either side of the magnificent *asvatha*, the *Ficus religiosa* of botanists. In the centre of the village are two temples of Siva, facing each other; one of them has a large colonnade, or rather polystyle, as there are no less than four rows of columns; and the intervening space between the two temples is planted with the *asvatha.* There are other temples of Siva in other parts of the village, but there is nothing about them worthy of remark. In the central part of each of the four divisions of the village there is a *vakula* tree (*Mimusops Elengi*), the foot of which is built round with solid masonry, raised three or four feet above the ground, in the form of a circle, in the centre of which stands the graceful trunk. As the diameter of this circle is seldom less than twelve feet, a good number of people can easily sit on it, and you meet there, of an afternoon, the gentry of the village, squatting on mats or carpets, engaged in discussing village politics, or in playing at cards, dice, or the royal game of chess.

There are not more than half-a-dozen shops in the village; in these are sold rice, salt, mustard, oil, tobacco, and other necessaries of Bengali life. The villagers, however, are supplied with vegetables, clothes, cutlery, spices, and a thousand knick-knacks, twice a-week, from a *hát,* or fair, which is held on Tuesdays and Saturdays, on a plain on the south-western side.

To a person coming towards the village, from whatever point of the compass, Kánchanpur presents a most striking view. In addition to the usual topes of mangoes and clumps of bamboo which skirt most villages in the country, our village is nearly encircled with some of the finest and most picturesque tanks in a district which is noted for its fine and picturesque tanks. These tanks, often covering forty or fifty acres of land, are surrounded by lofty embankments. On these embankments wave hundreds of the stately *tála (Borassus flabelliformis)*, which look from a distance like so many gigantic warders posted as sentinels on the high battlements of some fortified castle. Two of these tanks are worthy of description. On the south-east skirt of the village lies the *himságara*, or sea of ice, so called from the excessive coldness of its water. It has, like most tanks, two bathing *gháts*, one for men and the other for women, at a good distance from each other. The steps of the landing-place are made of marble. At the head of the *ghát*, on either side, is a sacred *tulasi* plant *(Ocymum sanctum)*, placed on a high pedestal of masonry; a little higher up stand on two sides two *sriphal* trees *(Ægle Marmelos)*, and in front of the *ghát* is a temple containing a statue of Chaitanya, of the size of life. The other tank is called *Krishnaságara*, or the black sea, from the fact of its water appearing black from a distance; indeed, the people say that its water is as black as the eye of a crow. The *gháts* of this great reservoir are not so grand as those of the *himságara*, but it is said to be the deepest tank in the village; indeed, some people believe that it has subterranean communication with *pátála*, or the infernal regions. It is also believed that in the bottom of the tank there are jars of untold treasures, in the shape of gold *mohurs*, in custody of a demon of the *Yaksha* species. The *krishnaságara* is therefore looked upon with mysterious awe. The oldest inhabitant does not remember its having been drained of its fish, the drag-net having been invariably cut on such occasions in the middle of the tank. Scarcely any one bathes in it, though scores of women may be seen every morning and evening drawing water from it for drinking. As the tank has never been cleansed since it was excavated, it is filled with aquatic plants of a hundred species; yet its water is beautifully transparent, and unquestionably wholesome. The other tanks of the village, though not so large, contain equally good water, and their embankments are all covered, more or less thickly, with the heaven-pointing *tála,* with its long trunk and its leafy crown; while below the embankments, on all sides, are groves of the mango, the tamarind, and the *Kathbel (Feronia eléphantum).*

The reader must not suppose that this display of the glories of the vegetable creation is confined to the outskirts of the village. Inside the village, around the homesteads of the people, are to be found innumerable clumps of the bamboo, and trees of every description; while there are not a few gardens in which fruit-trees are carefully tended. In these orchards a cocoa-nut tree may be occasionally seen, but that tree does not take kindly to the soil of Parganá Sáhábád. At Kánchanpur there are three curiosities of the vegetable kingdom. One is a row of two dozen *palása* trees *(Butea frondosa)* in the southern division of the village. When these are in flower, they present a most imposing spectacle. The whole of every tree, branches, trunk and all, becomes covered with gorgeous flowers; and to a spectator looking at them from a distance, it is a truly enchanting vision. The second curiosity is a gigantic *Vakula* tree, which has a leafy circumference of several hundred feet, and which affords shelter every night to thousands of birds. The *Vakula* tree is a great favourite of the people of Bengal; it is one of the most graceful of all trees; it has a small flower of delicate sweetness; and its head, naturally large, is so smooth and rounded in shape that a foreigner would suppose that the pruning-knife had been used. But the remarkable feature of this particular *Vakula* tree is its size. I have not seen its equal in the whole district of Vardhamána. The third curiosity of the vegetable kingdom at Kánchanpur is a magnificent *vata* tree (*Ficus Indica*) which grows near the *hát* to the south-west of the [village; it covers many acres of ground; it has sent forth hundreds of branches downwards, which have taken root in the soil, and become separate trees. It affords not only shelter to thousands of the feathery race at night, but grateful shade at noon to scores of peasant boys tending their cows in the adjacent meadows. Milton must have had one of these trees in his mind's eye when he sang of the big tree which

> In Malabar or Deccan spreads her arms
> Branching so broad and long, that in the ground
> The bended twigs take root, and daughters grow
> About the mother-tree, a pillar'd shade
> High over-arch'd, and echoing walks between:
> There oft the Indian herdsman shunning heat
> Shelters in cool, and tends his pasturing herds
> At loop-holes cut through thickest shade.

Sir Henry Maine, in his ingenious and thoughtful work entitled "Village Communities in the East and West," adopting the language of the Teutonic township, speaks of three parts of an Indian village:—*first* the village itself or the cluster of homesteads inhabited by the members of the community; *secondly*, the "arable mark" or lands under cultivation surrounding the village; and *thirdly*, the "common mark," or waste lands for pasturage. Of the first we have already spoken. The second, or the arable mark, of Kánchanpur consists of some thousands of *bighás* of land, encompassing the village, and forming a circle of cultivation the radius of which is about half a mile. Paddy of various kinds is the staple produce of the bulk of the land, though there are not wanting different species of pulse, rye, barley, cotton, tobacco, hemp, flax, and sugar-cane. As almost every inch of the land around the village was under cultivation, there was no "common mark" or waste connected with it. Nor were waste lands needed for pasturage, as there was not a single flock of sheep in the village; and the cows and bullocks, of which there was a large number, grazed on the verdant spots on the roadside, on the sloping sides of tanks with high embankments, on the green balks separating one field from another, on the grass-covered areas of mango topes and tamarind groves, and on those patches of untilled land situated near pools of water which ever and anon relieve the eye amid the infinite expanse of never-ending paddy.

CHAPTER IV.

DESCRIBES A RURAL SCENE, AND USHERS OUR HERO INTO THE WORLD.

Young elms, with early force, in copses bow,
Fit for the figure of the crooked plough:
Of eight feet long, a fastened beam prepare—
On either side the head, produce an ear;
And sink a socket for the shining share.
Georgics.

IT was midday. The cruel sun, like a huge furnace, was sending forth hot flames all around. There was hardly any breeze, the broad leaves of the tall palmyra hung quite motionless; the cows were resting in the shade of trees, and were chewing the cud; and the birds were enjoying their mid-day siesta. At such a time, when all Nature seemed to be in a state of collapse, a solitary husbandman was seen ploughing a field on the eastern side of the village of Kánchanpur. In the previous evening there had been a shower, accompanied with a thunderstorm, and Mánik Sámanta was taking advantage of that circumstance, to prepare the soil for the early crop of *Áus dhán,* so-called from the fact of that sort of paddy ripening in less time than is taken by the *Áman,* or the winter paddy. As some of our readers may not have seen a Bengal plough, it is as well to describe it here; and we do not think the object is too low to be described, especially when we remember that it exercised in antiquity the genius of two such poets as Hesiod and Virgil. The Calcutta cockney, who glories in the Mahratta Ditch, despises the scenery of the country, and plumes himself upon the fact of his having never seen in his life the rice-plant, may well be addressed in the language of the poet of the "Seasons":—

> Nor ye who live
> In luxury and ease, in pomp and pride,
> Think these last themes unworthy of your ear:
> Such themes as these the rural Maro sung
> To wide imperial Rome, in the full height
> Of elegance and taste, by Greece refined.
> In ancient times the sacred plough employed
> The kings and awful fathers of mankind.
> And some, with whom compared your insect tribes
> Are but the beings of a summer's day,
> Have held the scale of empire, ruled the storm
> Of mighty war; then with victorious hand,
> Disdaining little delicacies, seized
> The plough, and, greatly independent, scorned
> All the vile stores corruption can bestow.

What, then, is a Bengal plough? The Bengal plough is very much the same as the Greek and the Roman one, though it has not the mechanical adjustments of its English namesake. For the ilex oak of the Theban bard, and the elm of the Mantuan, the Bengali husbandman substitutes the *bábul,* or rather *bábla,* as the Vardhamána peasant calls it—the *Acacia Arabica* of botanists. The wooden coulter is shod with iron, which serves the purpose of the "shining share." The plough-tail, which is inclined to the plough-share at an acute angle, is furnished with a short handle, by means of which the peasant guides the share and presses it into the earth. At the meeting-point of the share and tail is a hole, through which passes a beam, to the end of which is attached the yoke. When the machine is set a-going, it is kept tight by ropes attaching the yoke to the plough-tail. With such a plough Mánik is tilling the ground. But he is not making much head. Look at him. Floods of perspiration are pouring in copious streams down his swarthy cheeks as he holds the plough by both his hands and scolds the bullocks at the top of his voice. The bullocks do not apparently like the idea of working. Every now and then they stand stock-still. Mánik catches the tails of the oxen, twists them with all his might, and abuses the poor animals as if they were pickpockets. "You sálá" (wife's brother), "why don't you move? Don't you see it is getting late? Do you want a bambooing on your forehead, you brother-in-law of a brute?" Seeing that threats prove unavailing, he has recourse to flattery, and addresses the team thus—"Get on, my treasure, my father, my child; get on a little further, and the whole will be over." But in vain. The jaded, thirsty, hungry brutes, who had been tugging at the plough since early dawn, refuse to stir. Not far from this scene of alternate scolding and coaxing were observed two men under the shade of an *asvatha* tree situated near a pool of water. One of them was lying down on the grass, and the other, who seemed to be the older of the two, had his hookah in his hand.

Let no one grudge the Bengal ráiyat his hookah It is his only solace amid his dreary toil. The English peasant has his beer and his spirits to refresh and cheer him up, but the Bengal husbandman drinks neither. Should the Legislature be so inconsiderate as to tax tobacco, the poor peasant will be deprived of half his pleasures, and life to him will be an insupportable burden. No ráiyat in Bengal ever goes to his field without the hookah in his hand and a quantity of tobacco wrapped up in a fold of his *dhuti;* and as lucifer matches are unknown to him, he keeps fire in a rope of straw made for the purpose. We may remark, for the benefit of the foreign reader, that the Bengal ráiyat never chews tobacco: he invariably smokes it. He either raises the refreshing leaf in his own field, or buys it in a dry state in the village shop. He cuts each leaf into small pieces, pours into the mass a quantity of treacle and a little water, kneads it as the baker kneads his dough, and thus reduces it to a pulpy substance. It is then fit to be smoked. The machinery he uses for smoking is altogether of a primitive character. A hollow tube is inserted into a cocoa-nut shell through the opening at the top; a small hole is bored between the two eyes of the shell: the shell is more than half filled with water; a small earthen bowl called *kalki*, filled with the prepared tobacco and fire, is put on the top of the hollow tube; to the hole between the eyes of the cocoa-nut is applied the mouth, which thus draws in the smoke through the tube, making that gurgling noise of the water inside the shell—*bhroor, bhroor, bhroor*—which to the overworked ráiyat is more refreshing than the music of the *tánpurá* or the *viná.* The whole smoking apparatus, which may last for years, need not cost more than a penny; and to a peasant who smokes hard half a farthing's worth of tobacco is sufficient for twenty-four hours. And what infinite comfort and solace does this simple and inexpensive instrument afford to the husbandman! It dries up the sweat of his brow, pours vigour into his muscles, takes away from him all sense of languor, restores lustre to his sunken eyes, recruits his fading energies, and alleviates the pains of his toilsome life. "What a glorious creature," said the Homer of English novelists, "was he who first discovered the use of tobacco! The industrious retires from business; the voluptuous from pleasure; the lover from a cruel mistress; the husband from a cursed wife; and I from all the world to my pipe." Let Government impose any tax it likes—income tax, license tax, succession tax, salt tax, feast tax, or fast tax, but let it have a care that it does not tax that precious weed, which is the Bengal ráiyat's balm of Gilead—his only solace amid the privations of his wretched life.

But to return: when the older of the two men, sitting and smoking under the tree, saw in what a plight Mánik and his bullocks were, he bawled out, "Ho, Mánik! you had better loosen the oxen, they are tired; and you yourself come and rest here." The moment the bullocks were loosened from the plough, they rushed towards the pool, and putting their fore feet into the water, took a long draught. Mánik himself, with the plough on his shoulders came to the tree, and began smoking with his companions. The eldest of the party said to the other two, "Brothers, let us all bathe and get ready for *bhát* (boiled rice), as Málati must soon be here." Mánik replied, "Very well, Gayárám," addressing the youngest of the three, "you had better rub your body with oil." Gayárám replied, "Let brother Badan begin."

I need scarcely tell the reader that these three persons were brothers. The eldest, Badan, who was about thirty years old, was the head of the family. Mánik, the second brother, was about twenty-five years of age, and the third, Gayárám, about twenty. Gayárám had charge of the cows which were grazing, and the two elder brothers had come to work with the plough. They had no other clothing than a simple *dhuti*, about four yards long and a yard broad, wrapped round their waists, and descending a little below the knees. The rest of the body was quite bare; they had nothing on their heads, and as for shoes, they had never used any since the day of their birth. The poet Hesiod advises the Boeotian peasant to sow naked, to plough naked, and to reap naked, but this exhortation of the Theban bard hardly applies to the Bengal ráiyat, as he is always in a state of semi-nudity. Each of the three brothers, however, had a spare piece of cloth called *gámchhá*, or bathing towel, about three cubits long and a cubit and a half broad. The *gámchhá* is indispensable to every Hindu peasant of Bengal, as he bathes every day in the year. But besides its use in bathing, it serves a variety of purposes. It acts as a wrapper for the head, to protect it from the sun; sometimes it serves the purpose of a *chádar*, or sheet, when it is placed on the shoulder; sometimes it does duty for a belt round the waist, and it is always handy for tying up anything in it, as the Bengal peasant has no pockets.

Badan was of the average height of a Bengali, strong-built, had a rather high forehead, and large, bright eyes, and his body, especially his chest, was thickly covered with hair. Gayárám resembled Badan in features, though they had not become so hard through toil.

Mánik was quite different from the other two; and no one that did not know him could ever suppose from his look that he was the brother of Badan and Gayárám. His complexion was much darker than that of the other two, it was deep ebony, or rather, glossy Day and Martin; indeed, he had the darkest complexion of anyone in the village, and it was in consequence of this circumstance, that, although his name was Mánik, or the jewel, he was universally called Kálamánik, or the Black Jewel. He was taller than the average run of his countrymen, being upwards of six feet high; he had a large head of hair which was not parted, which never had come in contact with a comb, and which stood erect like the bristles of a porcupine; his mouth was wider than that of most men, and, when open, discovered two rows of ivory-white teeth, so big in size that his friends compared them to the hoe with which he was so familiar as an implement of husbandry. His arms were of such length that when he stood bolt upright the tips of his fingers reached his knee-joints. On each shoulder there was a hump, not unlike that of a Bráhmini bull, an aggregation of flesh generally owned by *Pálki* bearers and other persons accustomed to carry heavy loads on their shoulders. His feet were not straight, but took the shape of an arc of a circle. The toes, which closely stuck to one another, were all bent towards the big toe; and he could never move two paces, but some of his toes cracked and gave out a peculiar kind of music. It may be easily conceived that a gigantic figure, upwards of six feet in height, of ebony complexion, wide-mouthed, hoe-toothed, high-shouldered, long-armed, and splay-footed, was not "a thing of beauty," and therefore not "a joy for ever." He was an object of terror to all the children of the village, who, when fractious, used invariably to be quiet when they were told that Kálamánik was coming. Nor had the maidens of the village better regard for him. Badan was anxious that Kálamánik should enjoy connubial felicity: but though he easily succeeded in getting a wife for his youngest brother Gayárám, no parents in wide Kánchanpur, or in any village twenty miles around, could be persuaded to bestow the hand of their daughter on the Black Jewel. Kálamánik was more simple than most of his class—indeed, it was generally asserted that he was somewhat silly; but this mental defect was amply compensated by his great physical strength and courage. He was the swiftest runner, the fastest swimmer, and the best wrestler in the village; he could stop a huge Brahmini bull, when running in fury, by catching hold of its horns; he could carry on his head a whole stack of paddy sheaves; and in every village fray he always stood in the fore-front, and manipulated his club with the strength of Hercules and the unerring precision of Yama himself. Such was the Black Jewel of the Golden City, the uncle of our hero.

After the short conversation given above, Badan took hold of a bamboo phial which was lying on the ground, poured from it on the palm of his hand a quantity of mustard oil, and besmeared with it every part of his body, the hair not excepted, not forgetting at the same time to push a little of the oil into the nostrils and the ears. Kálamánik and Gayárám followed suit. They then bathed in the adjoining pool. Kálamánik enjoyed a swim. He plunged headlong into the water:—

> His ebon tresses and his *swarthy* cheek
> Instant emerge; and though the obedient wave,
> At each short breathing by his lip repelled,
> With arms and legs according well, he makes,
> As humour leads, an easy-winding path.

Having well wrung the water from the *gámchhá*, they wrapped it round their loins, and washing their *dhutis* in the pool, spread them on the grass for sunning. They then sat down under the tree and began chewing a small quantity of rice which, tied in an extra *gámchhá*, had been soaked in water. The chewing over, they went to the pool for a drink, and as they had no vessel with them, they extemporised one by joining together the palms of both hands in the shape of a cup—a primitive and inexpensive mode of drinking universally resorted to by the Bengal peasantry when no vessel is at hand.

Thus refreshed, Badan and Kálamánik went to their plough, while Gayárám sat watching the cows. After the lapse of an hour or two, a little girl was seen approaching the tree under which Gayárám was sitting, with a small bundle in her hand. On seeing her, Badan and Kálamánik loosened the bullocks, and joined the party under the tree.

Badan said, "Well, Málati, so you have brought *bhát*. All right at home?"

The little girl replied, "Yes, *Bábá* (Papa); a *khoká* (male child) has come into the house."

The three simultaneously exclaimed,

"A *khoká!* good! when was it born?"

"At noon," was the reply.

After replying to a few more enquiries, Málati

opened her bundle and brought out the dinner, which consisted of a large quantity of boiled rice, and some vegetables cooked with fish. The dinner service consisted of three pieces of plantain-leaf and a brass *ghati* (a small drinking vessel). The little girl dealt out the dinner, and her father (for she was Badan's daughter) and uncles did full justice to it. It is superfluous to say that they ate with their fingers; they drank from the same *ghati*, which was replenished every now and then from the pool, though in the act of drinking their lips did not touch the vessel. After they had gargled their mouths and washed their hands, they again began to smoke. They then resolved, on account of the joyful news they had heard, to discontinue the labours of the day, and go home; Gayárám, however, stayed behind, as the cows could not well be brought home before sunset.

CHAPTER V.

PHOTOGRAPHS A RÁIYAT'S COTTAGE, AND THOSE WHO LIVE IN IT.

Behold the cot! where thrives th' industrious swain,
Source of his pride, his pleasure, and his gain.

The Parish Register.

When Kálamánik with the plough on his shoulders, and Badan in charge of the yoke of oxen, reached home, they found the yard of their house crowded with a number of women, who had come to congratulate the family on the birth of the new-born babe. One old Bráhmani (a Bráhman woman), said to the happy father—"Well, Badan, the gods have given you a male child; may he live for ever." Another old woman said—"It is a fine child; the gods give him long life; may he always find plenty to eat and to put on; may his granary be ever full." Badan's mother could hardly speak to him, for her heart was overflowing with joy. Rupá's mother—for she was the village midwife—was in all her glory. From the door of the lying-in room, into which no one, not even the father of the newly-born child, might enter—for it is regarded as ceremonially unclean—she was every now and then showing the baby with evident pride and satisfaction, as if the new comer were her own son or grandson. While the young husseys and the old gossips are pouring forth congratulations, let us, my gentle reader, take a look at Badan's cottage.

You enter Badan's house with your face to the east, through a small door of mango wood on the street, and you go at once to the *uthán*, or open yard, which is indispensable to the house of every peasant in the country. On the west side of the yard, on the same line with the gate of which I have spoken, stands the *baṛa ghar*, or the big hut. This is the biggest, the neatest, and the most elaborately finished of all Badan's huts. Its walls, which are of mud, are of great thickness; the thatch, which is of the straw of paddy, is more than a cubit deep; the bamboo frame-work, on which the thatch is laid, is well compacted together—every interstice being filled with the long and slender reed called *śará* (*Saccharum sara*) alternating with another reed of red colour; the middle beam, which supports the thatch, though it is neither of the costly teak or *sál*, is made of the pith of the palmyra; and the floor is raised at least five feet from the ground. The hut is about sixteen cubits long and twelve cubits broad, including the verandah, which faces the yard, and which is supported by props of palmyra. It is divided into two compartments of unequal size, the bigger one being Badan's sleeping room, and the smaller one being the store-room of the family, containing a number of *háṇḍis*, or earthen vessels, filled with provisions. The verandah is the parlour or the drawing-room of the family. There friends and acquaintances sit on mats. In Badan's sleeping-room are kept the brass vessels of the house and other valuables. There is no *khát* or bedstead in it, for Badan sleeps on the mud floor, a mat and a quilt stuffed with cotton interposing between his body and mother earth. There is not much light in the room, for the thatch of the verandah prevents its admission, while there is but one small window high up on the wall towards the street. I need scarcely add that there is no furniture in the room—no table, no chairs, no stools, no almirah, no wardrobe, no benches; there is only in one corner a solitary wooden box. In one side of the room two whole bamboos are stuck into the walls on which clothes are hung, and on which the bedding is put up in the day. Such is the *bara ghar*, or the big hut.

On the south side of the yard, and at right angles to the big hut, is a smaller hut of far inferior construction, which serves a variety of purposes, and which is used by the women of the family when in an interesting condition. When not required for that purpose it is used as a lumber-room, or rather as a tool-room, for keeping the implements of husbandry. On the present occasion it was occupied by Badan's wife and Rupá's mother. In the verandah of this little hut is placed the *dhenki*, or the rice-husking pedal. From this circumstance the little hut is called *dhenkiśálá* (pedal-house), or more familiarly *dhenskál*.

In the south-east corner of the yard, and at right angles to the *dhenkisálá*, is another hut of somewhat better construction, inside which Gayárám sleeps, and the verandah of which serves the purpose of a kitchen. From this latter circumstance it is called *páksálá* (cooking-house), but Badan and his family always called it by the more familiar name of *ránnághar*. The only other hut on the premises is the cow-house, called *gosálá*, or more familiarly *goál*. It is situated to the north of the yard, nearly parallel to the big hut, only the cow-house is much longer than all the other huts.

Several large earthen tubs, called *nánds,* which serve the purposes of troughs, are put on the floor, half buried in small mounds of earth, near which are stuck in the ground tether-posts of bamboo. In one corner is a sort of fire-place, where every night a fire, or rather smoke, of cow-dung cakes is made, chiefly for the purpose of saving the bovine inmates from the bite of mosquitoes and fleas.

The eastern side of the premises opens on a tank which supplies the family of Badan, as it does other families in the neighbourhood, with water, not, indeed, for drinking, but for every other purpose; the drinking water being obtained from one of those big tanks of which I have spoken in the preceding chapter, and which are situated on the outskirts of the village. On the edge of this tank are a few trees belonging to Badan. There is a tall palmyra tree near the *ghát,* or landing-place, surrounded by a bush, which prevents the women, when they go to the water's edge, from being seen. There is a *jam* tree *(Eugenia jambolana)* not far from it, and at no great distance is a date tree, which is so situated that its fruit, when it drops, falls into the water.

About the middle of the *uthán,* or yard, and near the cow-house, is the granary of paddy, called *golá* in other parts of the country, but in the Vardhamána district invariably called *marái.* It is cylindrical in shape, made entirely of ropes of twisted straw, with a circular thatch on the top. It contains a quantity of paddy sufficient for the consumption of the family from one harvest to another. Not far from the granary is the *pálui,* or straw stack, which is an immense pile of paddy-straw kept in the open air, to serve as fodder for cows and oxen for a whole year. Behind the kitchen, and near the tank, is the *sárkuḍa,* or the dust-heap of the family, which is a large hole, not very deep, into which the sweepings of the yard, the ashes of the kitchen, the refuse of the cow-house, and all sorts of vegetable matter, are thrown. This dust-heap, though somewhat hurtful in a sanitary point of view, is essentially necessary to our ráiyat, as it supplies him with manure for his fields.

In other respects, our Mofussil villages are better supplied in regard to sanitary arrangements than Europeans might suspect. Their great sanitary officers are the wild village pigs, who easily, instantaneously, and inexpensively remove all obnoxious matter from the neighbourhood.

We may remark that the huts which we have described were originally built by one of Badan's ancestors; that the thatching was slightly repaired every year, and replaced every five or six years; that Badan paid nothing for their use, as they were his own property; and that the only sum he paid to the zamindár for his homestead was one rupée, or two shillings, a year as ground-rent.

As we have said so much of the dwelling-place of our peasant family, we must say something here of its inmates. With Badan, Kálamánik, and Gayárám, our readers have already formed acquaintance. It is necessary, however, to give the full names of the three brothers. They were as follows: Badan Chandra Sámanta, Mánik Chandra Sámanta, and Gayárám Sámanta. They were not of the *sadgopa* caste, as most of the peasants of Kánchanpur were, but of the *ugra-kshatriya* or *águri* caste—a class of men abounding chiefly in the Vardhamána district, and noted for their courage, personal strength, and independence. The other members of the family were Badan's mother, Alanga; his wife, Sundari; his daughter, Málati; and Gayárám's wife, Áduri. Alanga, forty-six years old, was the *grihini* or mistress of the household. Her son Badan paid her boundless respect, and always agreed to every domestic arrangement she made. Nor were her other sons and her daughters-in-law less obedient to her. Badan's wife, Sundari, might be expected, according to English notions, as the wife of the head of the family, to feel aggrieved at her being deprived of her rightful authority as the mistress of the house. But such a notion is never entertained by a Bengali wife while her mother-in-law is living. And the idea never occurred to Sundari. She deemed it her duty, and esteemed it a privilege, to be under the guardianship of her husband's mother. She was thankful that all domestic affairs were under the management of one so much older, wiser, and more experienced than she. As the eldest daughter-in-law in the house, Sundari was the cook of the family, in which work she was assisted by Gayárám's wife, Áduri. Now that Sundari was confined, the work of the kitchen devolved chiefly on Badan's mother, Alanga, as Áduri was too young to be wholly trusted with that important department.

Unlike Sundari, Áduri was somewhat peevish and often showed temper, especially when, as on the present occasion, she had a great deal to do. She was naturally of an imperious disposition, and therefore hated the idea of playing second—or rather third—fiddle in the family. Amidst the general harmony which prevailed in Badan's house, she was the only cause of discord. With Badan and Kálamánik she, of course, never exchanged a single word in her life; for it is reckoned a piece of the greatest indecency on the part of a woman even to look at the face of her husband's elder brothers, though with his younger brothers she is permitted to be quite familiar. Áduri had therefore not only not spoken to Badan and Kálamánik, but they had never seen her face, she being always completely veiled when going about in the house in their presence. She often gave cross answers to her mother-in-law, for which she got curtain-lectures from her husband at night—indeed, now and then something more substantial than lectures, namely, a slap or a cuff, in consequence of which the whole of the following day she gave sullen looks and peevish answers.

Málati, Badan's daughter, was a girl of about seven years of age. Though her complexion was by no means fair, her features were far from disagreeable. She had the gentleness of her mother's disposition, and though as the first, and for a long time the only child in the house, she was made too much of, her head never got turned. She never did a rude thing, nor uttered a cross word. She was the joy of Badan's life. After the fatiguing labours of the day in the field, he would of an evening sit cross-legged on the open yard of the house, and, with hookah in hand, would listen to her sweet prattle, reciting the incidents of the day in the little family. Nor was she less useful than agreeable. She assisted her mother and grandmother in fifty little things in the house; and also in going on errands, bringing from the village shop mustard oil, salt, and other little articles for daily consumption; and taking to the fields the dinner of her father and her uncles.

The description of a farmer's household would be imperfect if, besides treating of the *homines*, it did not also include what the Romans, who paid so great attention to agriculture, called the *adminicula hominum*, those domestic cattle without whose assiduous and disinterested co-operation the husbandman could not reap the fruits of his industry. As Badan had about thirty-six *bighás*, or nearly twelve acres, of land, he had only one plough, and therefore two bullocks. One of these bullocks was of black complexion, and therefore called Kele, and the other being brownish was called Sámlá. They were between seven and eight years of age; had seen good service, and as they were far from infirm, many years of useful industry lay before them. As they were, in a manner, the support of the family, particular care was bestowed on them. Gáyárám, every morning and evening, filled their tubs with chopped straw, well soaked in a solution of water and oil-cake. But Kele and Sámlá were not the only inmates of the cow-house. There were three milch-cows with their calves, two young steers in the process of training for the plough, and a heifer. The oldest cow, named Bhágavati, gave only three quarters of a *seer* of milk in the morning, and half a *seer* in the evening; the next in age, called Jhumri, gave a *seer* and a half in the morning, and one *seer* in the evening; and the last, though not the least in value, called Kámadhenu (the cow of desire) gave every morning three *seers* of milk, as thick as the juice of the fruit of the *Ficus Indica*, and two *seers* in the evening.

The two young steers were called by no particular names; but the heifer, the favourite of Málati, about two years old, was called Lakshmi. These cows were all attended to by Gayárám, who was the neat-herd of the family. Besides grazing on the fields nearly the whole day, they had their *nánds*, or tubs, filled every evening with chopped straw and mustard oil-cakes, and they chewed dry straw in the morning; while Kámadhenu, the best cow in the house, in addition to ordinary fodder, had every now and then *bhusi* (husk of pulse), and occasionally a gourd boiled together with *khud*, the refuse of rice. Every morning after the cow-house had been cleansed, Málati used to visit Lakshmi while she was in the act of chewing her dry straw, stroked her body, caught hold of her little horns, and played with her; and the gentle creature seemed really to have affection for Málati. The reader may ask what Badan did with so much milk. I answer that all the three cows did not give milk at the same time; that some was drunk by the women, especially by Málati: that some quantity was sold every day to a Bráhman family in the neighbourhood; that some was made into cream and then into *ghi*, or clarified butter; and some into curds for home consumption. It was a happy day when the cream was churned, and *ghi* made by old Alanga, as it gave the family the benefit of a large quantity of sour milk, of which they were all fond.

Besides the bullocks and the cows, Badan had no other domestic animals. He had no poultry, for fowls, ducks, and geese are abomination to the majority of Hindus, and to that particular caste to which Badan belonged. He had one more animal besides those we have mentioned, and that was a dog. But dogs are not cared for in Bengal; they are not even touched by their masters, being reckoned unclean. Bághá, or Tiger—so the dog was called, either on account of his ferocious disposition or on account of some fancied resemblance to a tiger—used always to lie about the door and in the open yard, and had for his meals a handful of boiled rice from each male inmate of the house, who, after finishing breakfast or dinner, carried it to him on his way to the tank to wash his mouth and hands. Besides this stated provision, Bághá procured whatever he could from the houses in the neighbourhood and from the streets.

CHAPTER VI.

FIXES THE FATE AND NAME OF OUR HERO.

The destyné, mynistre general,
That executeth in the world over-al
The purveiauns, that God hath seyn byforn;
So strong it is, that though the world hadde sworn
The contrarye of a thing by ye or nay,
Yet somtym it schald falle upon a day
That falleth nought eft in a thousend yeere.
The Knighte's Tale.

In the *sútikágriha*, or lying-in-room, the sixth day after the birth of a child is an important day. Besides the worship of the goddess Shashṭhi, the protectress of children, which takes place in the day, the destiny of the child is fixed on that night by Vidhátá Purusha, the Creator, and written in indelible characters on its forehead. As Vidhátá is not expected to bring with Him writing materials, an inkstand and a reed pen are put at the door of the room; but neither Badan nor his brothers have ever been initiated into the mysteries of reading and writing, and there was neither pen nor ink in the house. Alanga, therefore, who took more interest in the affair than any other member of the family, borrowed writing materials from a neighbour, and put them at the inner threshold of the lying-in-room. There is no fixed time for the appearance of Vidhátá; he may come at any time in the night; and as it is important that some one should be awake at the time, the duty of sitting up devolves on the midwife.

Rupá's mother did not close her eyes that night. As everyone else in the house was asleep—only old Alanga's sleep was greatly disturbed through excitement—no one knew what happened at night except Rupá's mother, who next morning related the whole story. For the benefit of the reader we here give a translation of her account:—

"After two *praharas* of the night were over," said Rupá's mother, "I heard the sound of footsteps at the door, especially on that side where the pen and ink were. The same sound of footfall was heard all along the passage from the door to where the baby was sleeping by the mother. Immediately after I heard a sound similar to that which is made by a man when writing, but I saw no figure. By the light of the fire, however, I saw a smile playing on the lips of the baby. Shortly after I heard the sound of retreating footsteps, and I rushed towards the door and said, '*Thákur* (god)! I hope you have written favourably.' The god knew me well, as he has often seen me, and told me what he had written on the forehead of the child, but on condition of the strictest secrecy. I dare not disclose it to you, for if I disclose it Vidhátá will be angry with me, and kill me outright by twisting my neck. But, oh! mother Alanga, rejoice, for your grandchild's *kapála* (forehead) is good." I cannot take upon me to assert that Badan and his brothers credited the story, but I am certain that all the women of the house believed that Vidhátá Purusha had revealed to Rupá's mother what he had written on the child's forehead.

Two days after—that is, when the infant was eight days old—a ceremony called the *Átkouḍiyá* (eight cowries) was performed. Alanga and Áduri were very busy all that day. They fried paddy, and made it into *khadi*, and eight sorts of pulse. Badan also brought from the village money-changer a large quantity of shells called *kaḍi* or cowries. About sunset a number of boys of the village, chiefly of the peasant class, came to Badan's house, and, standing in the yard, made a great noise with winnowing fans which they carried in their hands, and, approaching the door of the lying-in room, bawled out: "*Atkouḍe! bátkouḍe!* is the baby well?" The little urchins perpetrated many jokes at the expense of Alanga and the midwife—they laughed, they danced, they made noises with the winnowing-fans. Alanga, in the meantime, came to the yard with a basket in her hand, and scattered over the heads of the boys the shells and the fried paddy and pulse. The boys scrambled for these treasures, trod upon one another's heels, threw down one another, and made infinite fun. Thus merrily went off the *Áṭkouḍiya* of Badan's child; and Alanga's joy knew no bounds.

On the twenty-first day of her confinement, Sundari was bathed for the first time, came out of the *sutikágriha*, and joined the family after the worship of the goddess Shashṭhi. She did not, however, at once after her purification, commence to discharge the duties to which she had been accustomed, as a good deal of her time was taken up with the baby. But the baby was no great burden to her; it was constantly attended to by its grandmother and aunt, while Málati always sat by it and watched the movements of its little hands and fingers with the liveliest interest. Baby had no clothing of any sort. In Bengal, unlike England, there is no fear of babies catching cold; all babies are therefore allowed to revel in unfettered nakedness. Besmeared with mustard oil—a large quantity being especially put in the hollow of the chest—Sundari's baby used every day to be laid on a piece of plank, called *pindá,* and exposed to the sun for some hours. European doctors will perhaps hold up their hands in astonishment, and declare that such exposure is calculated to result in infanticide. But Bengali peasant women know better. They consider that a good sunning of this sort is an admirable preparation for the child's duties in after life. Thanks to this grilling during infancy, there are scarcely any cases of *coup de soleil* amongst Bengal peasants, though they live in one of the hottest countries in the world, and are incessantly exposed, bare-headed, to the scorching rays of a fierce sun. The head gets sun-hardened, and defies the fiery god of day to do his worst.

When the child was seven months old, and after the *áus* crop had been gathered in, came the ceremony of *Annaprásana,* or the Feast of Rice, generally called by women *bhujno* (that is, *bhojana*), or the feast when rice is for the first time put into the mouth of the infant. The feast of a child's first rice is celebrated by wealthy Hindus with great pomp. Badan, being a poor man, could not afford to spend much; still, being an orthodox Hindu, and diligently observant of the customs of his forefathers, he thought it his duty to spend something. The goddess Shashṭhi was first worshipped; this ceremony was followed by a feast to a select party of Badan's kinsmen. A Bengal Hindu peasant's feast is by no means an expensive affair. The bill of fare consisted of the following dishes:—*bhát,* or boiled rice; *dál,* of the pulse called *kalái; chhenchki,* usually called *tarkári* in the Vardhamána district, a sort of hodge-podge, consisting of potatoes, brinjal, and tender stalks of the creeper *pani;* fish fried in mustard oil, fish cooked with tamarind; and, last of all, curds. The small party, consisting only of males—for the women eat separately—sat in two rows on the floor of the verandah of the big room; a piece of plantain leaf was placed before each on the ground; a brass *ghati* filled with water was put on the left-hand side of each guest, and a small quantity of salt on the right-hand side. Alanga, who alone attended on the guests, appeared on the scene with a large dish of boiled rice, and put a quantity on each of the plantain-leaves. She appeared again with a large *háṇḍi* of *dál,* and put a quantity upon the rice on each of the plantain-leaves. She next came with *tarkári,* and dealt out a little to each. Then commenced the business of eating, during the progress of which, the fish cooked in tamarind, the most prized of all the dishes, was distributed. As two large *rohita* fishes, each weighing ten or twelve seers—that is twenty or twenty-four pounds—caught in Badan's own tank, had been cooked, there was a superfluity of that delicacy. Badan, happy in celebrating the *annaprásana* of his son and heir, pressed his guests to eat heartily; and Alanga, in the overflow of her joy, put on every plantain-leaf heaps of the cooked fish, though the guests shouted out at the top of their voices, "Give no more; give no more; we shan't be able to eat half of what is on the leaf." In the end, however, not a particle of the fish remained on any of the plantain-leaves. Last of all, Alanga brought out a large *háṇḍi* of *dadhi*, or curds. As the curds were not very thick, one would have thought it impossible to eat, or rather drink them off a plantain-leaf, on which the liquid could hardly find a *locus standi*. The ingenious guests, however, had cleared off in the middle of the leaf a circular space, encompassed by a wall of rice, which prevented the curds from flowing out on the floor. The eating over, each one took hold of the brass *ghati* with the left hand—the right hand having become dirty with eating—and poured its contents down the throat, in such a manner, however, that the vessel did not touch their lips. The guests then hastened to the tank to wash their hands and mouths; after which, they chewed *pán* leaves, together with a mixture of quick-lime, betel-nut, coriander-seed, catechu, cloves, cinnamon, and cardamums. They then sat on a mat in the yard, and smoked to their hearts' content. On departing, the guests pronounced a thousand blessings on the head of the child, who had that day been named Govinda Chandra Sámanta.

CHAPTER VII.

THE PROTECTRESS OF CHILDREN.

And are there then celestial habitants
Whom a kind Father's care around us plants,
Sent to walk with us in our earthly trance?

Keble.

THE reader will have noticed that in the last chapter allusion was more than once made to the worship of Shashṭhi, the beneficent goddess whose happy vocation it is to take care of children, and protect them from danger and trouble, to which they are so constantly exposed on account of their helplessness; and since we regard this divinity as one of the most amiable creations of Hindu mythology, we trust we shall be excused for dwelling a little on the adoration of the Protectress of Children.

The goddess is called Shashṭhi, or the sixth, because she is believed to be the sixth part of the divine essence of *Pradhána-Prakriti*, the male and female creative principles, by whose influence this universe has been generated. The following legend is related in connection with her worship:—"Priyavrata, the son of Svayambhu-Manu, who had spent many years in enthusiastic and solitary devotion, was at last persuaded by Brahmá to contract the bonds of matrimony. But as his wife did not for a long time present him with offspring, he desired the divine sage Kaśyapa to celebrate the *putreshti-yága*, on the completion of which the sage gave her to eat the sacrificial *charu* (rice cooked in clarified butter), on swallowing which she became *enceinte.* In due time she brought into the world a son 'as bright as gold,' but, unfortunately, still-born. The king (Priyavrata) with a sad heart, took the dead child and laid it on the funeral pile with a view to cremation. On a sudden, however, there appeared overhead in the sky, a goddess of surpassing beauty, radiant as the summer sun. The king, entranced with her heavenly grace, asked her who she was. The goddess said, 'I am the wife of Kártikeya; the Chief of Mothers; and as I am the sixth part of *Prakriti,* men call me Shashṭhi.' So saying, the bright goddess took hold of the child, gave it breath and life, and made a gesture, as if she was going to take it away with her to the realms of glory. The king, petrified with fear, addressed many a fervent prayer, beseeching her to restore the infant to him. The goddess, pleased with the incense of praise, said, 'O thou son of Svayambhu-Mánu, thou art the lord of the three worlds! If thou promise to celebrate my praise as long as thou livest, I will give the child to thee.' The king readily agreed to the condition, embraced the child, and returned home with a joyful heart." As a grateful return for her favour he celebrated the worship of Shashṭhi with the utmost pomp. From that time the worship of Shashṭhi became one of the most popular institutions in the land of *Bhárata.* She is worshipped every month, on the sixth day of the waxing moon, by every Hindu wife who has not been blessed with offspring, on the sixth and the twenty-first day after the birth of a child, and at *Annaprásana,* or the Feast of the First Rice.

The proper image of Shashṭhi is a woman of matronly appearance, painted yellow, riding on a cat, and nursing a child; but usually she is represented by a rude stone, not bigger than a man's head, painted with red-lead, and placed under a *vaṭa* tree (*Ficus Indica*) in the outskirts of the village; while not unfrequently she is worshipped in the form of a branch of the *vaṭa* tree stuck in the yard of a house.

One of the pleasantest sights ever witnessed in a Hindu village in Bengal is the spectacle presented some day in the month of Jaishṭha, under a large banyan tree just outside the hamlet. There the womanhood of the village—matrons, mothers, wives, spinsters—are assembled, dressed in their *púјá's* best, their bodies loaded with ornaments, their faces shining with oil, their veils gracefully hanging over their heads, with offerings in their hands. The priest recites the holy texts, and blesses every woman present; the offerings go, of course, to him; but some of them are given away to those unfortunate women—they are regarded such by Hindus—who have not borne the fruit of marriage. These women receive the gifts eagerly in the skirts of *sáḍis* (women's clothes), while the proud mothers say to them, "The blessing of Mother Shashṭhi be upon you! May you next year come to this spot, not only with offerings, but also with a child in your arms." The ceremony is then concluded, and the women return to their homes.

On the sixth day after the birth of our hero Govinda, the worship of Shashṭhi was, as we have already said, performed. It took place in the open yard, where the branch of a *vaṭa* tree was stuck in the ground. The father of the child presented offerings, and prayers were offered to the effect that, if the beneficent goddess would be pleased to spare the life of the child, more gifts would be offered on the twenty-first day. At the door of the house was placed the skull of a cow, its forehead painted with red-lead, and three *kaḍis* were stuck on three lumps of cow-dung; over the whole, a yellow cloth—the symbol of Shashṭhi—was spread. This was allowed to remain at the door for a whole month, and was regarded as a security of the infant's preservation and welfare.

On the twenty-first day after the birth of Govinda was performed the ceremony of *ekusiyá*, or the Twenty-first. Sundari, coming out of the *sutiká-griha*, bathed and dressed in clean clothes, repaired to the stone under the *vaṭa* tree, adorned it with a garland of flowers, presented offerings to it, and, with the assistance of the priest, went through some religious ceremonies. She made many a vow, and besought Mother Shashṭhi to protect her child. A few sweetmeats which had been offered to the goddess were then distributed to bystanders, and the *pújá* was concluded.

Of the Hindu Lares and Penates, Shashṭhi is by no means an unimportant personage. As the imparter of fecundity to women, as the protectress of children, and the patroness of domestic happiness, Mother Shashṭhi, as she is generally called, is universally regarded, especially by women, with feelings not only of the deepest reverence, but of the warmest affection. Sundari through her whole life manifested the greatest delight in the worship of that divine mother to whose kindness she equally attributed the preservation of her own life during the recent trials, and the safety of her child. May we not regard this amiable fiction of Shashṭhi as an adumbration of the teaching of Scripture, that children are the especial objects of the ministrations of celestial spirits?

CHAPTER VIII.

THE VILLAGE ASTROLOGER.

—Not far from hence doth dwell
A cunning man, hight Sidrophel,
That deals in destiny's dark counsels,
And sage opinions of the moon sells;
To whom all people far and near,
On deep importances repair:
When brass and pewter hap to stray,
And linen slinks out of the way;
When geese and pullen are seduced,
And sows of sucking pigs are chows'd;
When cattle feel indisposition,
And need the opinion of physician;
When murrain reigns in hog or sheep,
And chickens languish of the pip;
To him with questions, and with urine,
They for discovery flock, or curing.

Hudibras.

"Ho, BADAN! are you at home?" said a husky voice at the door of Badan's house one evening, a few days after the celebration of the Feast of First Rice.

"Who are you?" shouted Badan from the verandah of the big room, where he was sitting and enjoying a pull or two of the peaceful hookah.

"I am Surya Kánta," replied the husky voice.

"Come in," said Badan, and jumped out of the verandah towards the door. "Come in, Áchárya Mahásaya; this is an auspicious day when the door of my house has been blessed with the dust of your honour's feet. Gayárám, fetch an *ásan* (a small carpet), for the Áchárya Mahásaya to sit on."

The Ácharya having put off his shoes—I should rather say, slippers, for Bengalis, as a rule, excepting those who imitate English customs, put on only slippers—and taken his seat, said,

"Well, Badan, I hope you are quite well. I was glad to hear that the *annaprásana* of your son went off very well. And why should it not? Your ancestors, though poor, were all good, pious, and God-fearing men, men at whose birth, the sun, moon, the planets, and the zodiacal constellations shed their most benign influences; and, I have no doubt that your son, whom, I understand, you have called Govinda, has been born under similar auspicious influences. This can be owing only to your piety, and the piety of your son in his former birth. Are you not thinking, Badan, of getting a horoscope made of your son?"

"I should like very much to have Govinda's nativity cast; but you know, Ácharya Mahásaya, I am a poor man. I am in arrears already to the jamidár,* and in debt to the *maháján* (money-lender); and what little was in the house has been just spent on my child's first rice."

"Oh, never mind about payment; I can wait; and you know, you and I are old friends, I will not charge you much."

"What will you take for a good horoscope?"

"If you want to know the proper price of a horoscope, I may tell you that I cast, not long ago, a horoscope of the child of a *Bania*, and I got a gold *mohar* for it (thirty-two shillings)."

* Hindu Bengalis always call the zamindár, *jamidár*—the Persian *zamin* (land) being naturalized in the Bengali language in the form *jami*.

"A gold *mohar!* But surely there is a great difference between a *Bania* and a poor ráiyat like myself—as great a difference as between a Bráhman and a *Chandála*. What will you take from me for a horoscope of Govinda?"

"You asked me the proper price of a horoscope, therefore I mentioned one gold *mohar;* but of course I won't charge you that sum. I don't wish to make a bargain with you. Let me first cast a horoscope, and you can pay whatever you like."

"I am a poor man, what can I pay you? I cannot give you a sum of money worthy of your acceptance; but if you make a good horoscope I'll give you, at the next harvest, two *solis* of *áus* and two *solis* of *áman* paddy."

"You are becoming very niggardly, Badan; well, besides the four *solis* of paddy you have promised, give me also half a *man* (maund—that is, about eighty pounds avoirdupois) of molasses at the time of cutting sugar-cane, and I'll cast your child's horoscope."

"You, Ácháryas, are very fond of sweet things. Well, I agree. Set about the matter immediately. What time will you take to complete it?"

"Casting a horoscope, Badan, is not an easy affair; it is no child's play. It requires intricate calculations regarding the position of the heavenly bodies and their influences. I could not do it in less than a month."

"Very well, bring the horoscope after a month, and I'll give you what I have promised at the harvest and at the time of cutting sugar-cane. But see that you make the horoscope a favourable one."

"You speak like a woman, Badan. How can I make a horoscope either favourable or unfavourable?

Everything depends on the position of the heavenly bodies at the moment of your child's birth. If he has been born under auspicious influences his horoscope will be a favourable one; if otherwise, then unfavourable. I can but interpret the heavens and the gods. But I have no doubt that it will be a favourable one, considering that you are a good man, and have faith in gods and Bráhmans."

This Surya Kánta Ácharya, with whom Badan had the above conversation, was the astrologer of Kánchanpur. By his proper name, however, he was not generally known, the villagers insisting on calling him "Dhumketu," or the "Comet," in consequence of his having predicted, some years since, a terrible famine and pestilence, from the appearance in the heavens of a "fiery broomstick," as the people called the comet. It is not every village in Bengal that rejoices in the possession of an astrologer, but Kánchanpur being a large village and inhabited by a considerable number of rich men, it had one. Dhumketu cast the nativities of male children—for girls have no horoscopes properly so called, the dates of their birth and the positions of the heavenly bodies being briefly registered in a small slip of paper—not only of Kánchanpur but of several villages round about. But casting of horoscopes was not his only work. He also pointed out auspicious and inauspicious days by calculating the positions of the heavenly bodies, which trade brought him no little gain, as orthodox Hindus never engage in any important work, like marriage, or even undertaking a journey to a distant place, without first ascertaining from the astrologer the most auspicious day for its performance. He was also, at the beginning of a new year, in the habit of *reading the new almanack,* as it is called, in the house of every respectable orthodox Hindu, which *reading* consisted in a prophetic review, or rather prevision, of the leading astronomical phenomena and astrological events of the coming year, together with the recitation of a few legends connected with the subject; and every person who heard the new almanack read or recited was bound to give some present, however little, to the Ácharya.

But Dhumketu not only cast nativities and recited the new almanack; he pursued the profession of a *ganatkára,* or calculator—that is to say, a diviner. He was so skilful in the manipulation of figures that it might have been said of him—

> In Mathematics he was greater
> Than Tycho Brahe or Erra Pater;
> For he, by geometric scale,
> Could take the size of pots and ale;
> Resolve by sines and tangents straight,
> If bread or butter wanted weight;
> And wisely tell what hour o' the day
> The clock does strike, by Algebra.

This miraculous knowledge of figures Dhumketu turned to a very profitable account. Whenever the cow of a peasant strayed and could not be found; whenever an ornament of gold or silver—a pair of bangles or earrings, for example—was filched from its rightful owner; whenever a plate of Monghyr clay-slate, or of brass, was missing; in all such cases Dhumketu was able, by skilfully handling a bit of chalk, and by tracing hieroglyphical characters on the mud floor of his hut, to tell with infallible certainty the present *locus* of the strayed or missing articles. His humble hut was frequented by the rich and the poor of Kánchanpur and the neighbouring villages, who were anxious to know who had stolen their golden ornaments or where their cows had strayed. Though his predictions often turned out false, the people were not shaken in their belief in his supernatural skill, for sometimes his divination proved correct; and such is human credulity, that, in divination, the failures are forgotten, and the successes carefully remembered. There was one notable case of failure which was remembered for a long time, though it did not permanently injure his reputation as a diviner. Two very respectably dressed gentlemen, natives of a village some miles distant from Kánchanpur, once went to the prophet to ask where one of their cows, which had strayed, was. As peasants only come to the prophet on the errand of strayed cows, he was completely thrown out of his calculations. From the respectable look of the enquirers, Dhumketu never dreamed that they had come to ask about a cow; he shrewdly guessed that they had lost some article of gold, a gold chain, or a diamond ring. Accordingly, as was his custom, after tracing on the floor a world of unintelligible characters, he looked intently at the faces of the two men, and repeated the following words: "You have lost a substance, a substance; of a metallic nature, of a metallic nature; gold, gold, gold; diamond, diamond, diamond; gold and diamond, gold and diamond: yes, it is a gold ring, diamond set. It is wrapped up in a bit of cloth in the eaves of the cottage-thatch of your maid servant." The two men laughed outright in the face of the diviner, and told him that one of their best cows was missing. Nothing abashed, Dhumketu immediately said: "Oh yes, yes, I see that I put a wrong figure there through inadvertence. Of course it is a cow; you will find it in the house of your maid-servant." Such was the village astrologer, who now set about casting the horoscope of our hero.

True to his word, Dhumketu brought Govinda's horoscope after a month. It was a roll of yellow paper measuring, when opened out, about ten cubits long, bristling in every page with figures and the zodiacal signs, and written in Sanskrit from beginning to end. The fortunes of the native were calculated up to the hundredth year, the character of the events of each year being briefly indicated by one or two short sentences. The following words frequently occurred in this prophetic roll of our hero's life—*dhana dhánya vriddhi*, that is, literally, the *increase of wealth and paddy*. Several *phánḍás*, that is, accidents or misfortunes, were mentioned, the most serious of which was predicted to occur about the thirtieth year of our hero's life; the baneful influence of the planet Saturn that year of the native's life would be so great that the astrologer put it down as extremely doubtful whether Govinda would survive the malignant attack. Badan took into his hands the horoscope with the utmost reverence, and locked it up in the wooden box which lay in a corner of the big room, and which was the repository of all valuable documents. The astrologer did not acquaint him with the *phánḍás* or misfortunes which were to befal our hero; he assured him only in general terms that Govinda's life on the whole was to be a career of continual and ever-increasing prosperity. In due time Dhumketu was rewarded for his pains, agreeably to contract, with four *solis* of paddy and half a *man* of molasses.

CHAPTER IX.

AN IMPORTANT DISCUSSION.

But knowledge to their eyes her ample page,
Rich with the spoils of time, did ne'er unroll;
Chill penury repressed their noble rage,
And froze the genial current of the soul.

Gray.

THERE is nothing worthy of notice during the first five years of the life of Govinda, except that one day, while he was crawling in the yard of the house and was left to himself, the little urchin crawled on to the edge of the tank and fell into it. Fortunately at that time Áduri was at the *ghát* scouring the brass and stone vessels of the family. When she saw the child tumble into the water she gave a loud scream; but as the water in that part of the tank was shallow, she easily took him up, and was glad to find that he had received no hurt. Thus grew up little Govin, crawling through the length and breadth of the yard, his naked body covered with dust. Málati was often with him, making him stand on his legs, and teaching him to walk to the sound of the doggerel verse:—

Chali, chali, pá, pá,

that is to say, "Walk, walk, step by step." When the child was five years old, an important conversation was held regarding his future by Badan and Alanga. In order to prepare the reader for understanding the conversation which is given below, it is necessary to remark that in Bengal, in all well-to-do Hindu families, the education of a male child commences in his sixth year, and that the commencement is celebrated by a religious ceremony, in which Sarasvati, the goddess of wisdom, is worshipped and invoked to shed on her young votary her selectest influences. This ceremony is called *háte khaḍi*, that is, "putting chalk into the hands of a child," as the child commences his education by tracing on the floor, with a bit of chalk, the characters of the Bengali alphabet. The question which had been for some time agitating the mind of Badan was, whether he should give his son, Govinda, the elements of education, that is, instruct him in the three R's—Reading, 'Riting, and 'Rithmetic. He had felt his own sad deficiency in this respect, as he could neither read nor write—indeed, he had never learnt the Bengali alphabet, nor any other alphabet in the world. He thought that if his son were initiated into the mysteries of reading and writing he might be more prosperous in life than himself, and prove a match for the wily *gomástá* and the oppressive zamindár. But as he would not undertake a thing of this kind without consulting his mother, whom he highly reverenced, and for whose practical wisdom he had great respect, he resolved at some convenient opportunity to break his mind to her.

Accordingly, one day, in the afternoon, having little to do in the fields, he came home earlier than usual, leaving Gayárám to look after the cows, and Kálamánik to weed the paddy field. He found his mother sitting on the verandah of the kitchen, and busily engaged in spinning. He washed his hands, feet, and face in the tank, and preparing the hookah for a smoke, took it in his hand, went to his mother, and sat beside the *charká* or spinning wheel.

Has the English reader seen a Bengali *charká?* It is not unlike the Jersey or the Saxon spinning wheel still used in the country parts of England and Scotland, though somewhat more primitive in its construction, there being no wheel properly so called, but a rude apology for one. Two planks of wood placed parallel to each other are joined together by driving two sticks into them. Between the planks is suspended a solid ball of wood with spokes on it, supported by sticks, and so placed that it is made to whirl round by turning a handle at the end. The spindle is put upon three supports on the other plank, connected with the wheel, or rather with the wooden ball with spokes, by means of a thong. Carded cotton in the shape of fleecy rollers of the length of half a foot is applied to the point of the spindle by the left hand, while the right hand turns the wheel. One turn of the wheel produces a great many revolutions of the spindle, which twists the cotton and lengthens it out in thread or yarn for the weaver. I may here remark that in Bengal, unlike England, generally old women, and especially widows, spin—the younger women being engaged in more active household duties; so that a Bengali "spinster" is not like her English sister, an unmarried girl, but an old woman. And I cannot but think that the Bengali, in this respect, is wiser than the Englishman; for, sitting down for hours in a bent posture, and drearily turning the spinning wheel, cannot but prove prejudicial to the growth and health of a girl, whereas to an old woman it cannot do much hurt. But however this may be, while Alanga was busily turning the *charká*, Badan sat quietly by her, and began to smoke. Neither of them spoke for some time, enjoying, we presume, the exquisite music which was produced between them. The "*bhroor—bhroor—bhroor*" of the hubble-bubble kept time with the "*ghnan—ghnan—ghnan*" of the *charká*, and the two together evoked a melody which the immortals might have heard with rapture. At last Badan broke the divine harmony.

Badan. "Mother, I have for some time past been thinking of speaking to you on a certain subject."

Alanga. "What subject, Bábá Badan? Has anything happened? Is anything troubling your mind? Do tell me what it is."

Badan. "Nothing has happened, but I wish to speak to you about Govin."

Alanga. "What about Govin, my son? Is the child sick? Is anything the matter with him?"

Badan. "Don't you think, mother, it would be a good thing to give Govin his *háte khaḍi?* It is a great drawback that I cannot either read or write. I cannot read a *páṭá* (pottah) or write a *kabúliyat*; I cannot even sign my name: I am obliged, owing to my ignorance, to put a *ḍheṇḍá* (a cross) for my signature. Though I have eyes, I cannot see. I am at the mercy of every deceitful *gomastá*, and of every tyrannical zamindár. Don't you think it would be a capital thing to teach Govin *lekhá-paḍá* (writing and reading)?"

Alanga. "Oh, Bábá Badan! don't talk of *lekhá-paḍá.* Your elder brother was sent to *páṭhśálá* (school) by your father, contrary to my wishes. And what was the consequence? The gods took him away from us after he had been to school only one year. Reading and writing do not suit poor people like us. I fear the gods will take away Govin also (the son of Shashṭhi! may he live for ever!) if you send him to school."

Badan. "Oh, mother, what an idea! Who ever heard of reading and writing killing a child? Why are not Bráhman and káyastha boys who learn reading and writing also killed?"

Alanga. "The gods do not become angry with Bráhman and káyastha boys for learning, because that is their profession. But our business is to till the ground, and if we become so ambitious as to learn reading and writing, the gods will certainly become angry with us."

Badan. "But do you not know, mother, that some Aguris, men of our caste, know how to read and to write? Does not Naṭavara Sámanta read and write? Is not Madhu Sinha a *moharir* (writer)? Why have the gods not killed them?"

Alanga. "Whatever it may be with other people, writing and reading do not seem to agree with our family. If that be not the case, why did your brother die shortly after he had begun to go to school? Answer that."

Badan. "Why, as to death, mother, that is the decree of fate. Whatever is written on the forehead by Vidhátá Purusha must come to pass. Vidhátá had written on my brother's head that he would die when seven years old, and therefore he died; and he would have died at that age whether my father had sent him to school or not. The quantity of rice with which he had come into the world was finished, and therefore he died. It is fate, mother, it is fate."

Alanga. "Quite true, Bábá Badan, the forehead is the chief thing. Why, then, should you fight against the forehead? We have been born tillers of the ground, and we must remain tillers of the ground all our life. Besides, did your fathers ever learn to write and to read? Why should you wish your son to do what your forefathers never did?"

Badan. "The days in which our fathers lived were days of piety and virtue. That was the *Satya-Yuga.* There was no cheating, no oppression in those days. Writing and reading, therefore, were not essentially necessary. But in our days, men have become very deceitful—they fear neither gods nor men. It is necessary to learn to read and to write, that we may not be cheated and oppressed."

Alanga. "You men can talk a great deal, and bring a great many reasons for what you say. What can a woman say before a man? Do what you think best, Bábá Badan; I am only afraid that he may be taken away by the gods like your elder brother. It is far better for poor Govin to get his daily rice by tending cows in the field, than to learn to read and write and then die."

Badan. "I have told you, mother, that life and death are in the hands of the gods. If it be written on Govin's forehead that he will die (may the gods make him immortal!) on such a day it will come to pass, whether he be sent to school or not, as no one can reverse the writing on the forehead. I beg of you, mother, to agree to sending Govin to the *páṭhśalá* of Ráma Rúpa Sarkár: I prefer his school to the other, as he is well versed in zamindári accounts. Do agree to it, mother."

Alanga. "If you will have it so Bábá Badan,

then send him. May Gopinath preserve him! But if he is to be sent to school, you must wait a few days till I spin some more thread, sufficient to make for Govin a *dhuti.*"

Badan, overjoyed at his mother's consent, readily agreed to the delay.

Gentle reader, allow me here to make one remark. You perceive that Badan and Alanga speak better English than most uneducated English peasants; they speak almost like educated ladies and gentlemen, without any provincialisms. But how could I have avoided this defect in my history? If I had translated their talk into the Somersetshire or the Yorkshire dialect, I should have turned them into English, and not Bengali, peasants. You will, therefore, please overlook this grave though unavoidable fault in this authentic narrative.

CHAPTER X.

THE FIVE-FACED.

> He foams at mouth; and, by-and-by,
> Breaks out to savage madness.
>
> *Othello.*

I SAID in the last chapter that nothing worthy of notice occurred during the first five years of Govinda's life. I beg now to recall that statement, as I have been since informed that a notable event happened when he was about five years old; whether it was towards the end of his fifth year or the beginning of the sixth I have not been able exactly to ascertain, but it did happen about that time. Alanga always remembered that it happened on a Saturday, but the month and the year escaped her memory. I have to throw myself upon the indulgence of the reader for the absence of minute chronological accuracy in this notable event of Govinda's life.

Well, upon a Saturday some time about the fifth or sixth year of Govinda's age, something extraordinary happened to him. He was standing near his mother in the yard when he suddenly fell down, threw his arms and legs about in an extraordinary manner, foamed at the mouth, tore his hair, and seemed altogether to be wrought up into a state of perfect frenzy. Sundari shrieked, which brought Alanga and Áduri to the spot. Alanga, observing Govinda's convulsions, and the contortions which his body was undergoing, at once inferred the cause, and weeping said—"Oh, mother, my child is possessed by *Pencho!*"

What is *Pencho?* the reader will ask. Pencho is a colloquial abbreviation of Panchánana—literally, the five-faced, one of the gods of the Hindu pantheon, a form of the all-destroying Śiva. The image of this divinity, when properly represented, is a monster in the shape of a man with five faces and fifteen eyes—each face containing three eyes. This image of the god, however, is not usually made, owing, we presume, to his hideous appearance. He is generally worshipped in the shape of a stone, painted red at the top, anointed with oil, and placed under a *vaṭa* or *asvatha* tree. There is scarcely a Hindu village in Lower Bengal on the outskirts of which there are not one or more trees, at the foot of which such stones are worshipped under the name of Panchánana. Among the three hundred and thirty millions of Hindu deities of both genders, there is none which is more dreaded by Hindu mothers than this five-faced and fifteen-eyed demon. Though the god has his good points, since he is pleased sometimes to make barren women prolific, he is in general regarded as exceedingly irritable and malignant; and so fiery is he in temperament that, if any children, playing under the tree where the painted stone is placed, happened accidentally to touch it, the demon would immediately possess them, and throw them into convulsions. Alanga concluded in her mind that Govinda must have that day, while playing with other cowboys at the Panchánanatalá (that is, the foot of Panchánana's tree), touched the divinity, or unwittingly shown some disrespect to him; and that therefore the god, by way of punishment, had taken possession of him. Conceiving this to be the case, she asked the child, then writhing in agony, "Father, who are you? Why have you possessed my Govin? Are you a god or a ghost?" The child, or rather the demon in the child, answered: "I am Panchánana; your child put his foot on my image. I am going to break his neck and to suck his blood." The women set up a loud cry, which brought all the women and children of the neighbourhood into the house. Alanga, who had greater presence of mind than the rest, said to the god, "O Thákur! Panchárana! forgive this child and get out of him; for he is but a child, thoughtless, senseless, without any knowledge of what is right or wrong. O Thakur! (god) O Thákur! forgive Govin, and we will do *pújá* (worship) to you." After these words were uttered, the child had a more violent fit than before, and the women set up a louder cry than ever. Notice was sent to the child's father and uncles, who were working in the fields. They came home, running in breathless haste, and saw the child foaming at the mouth, and tearing his hair. What was to be done? Some Bráhmani women, who were present, proposed the immediate celebration of the *pújá* of Panchánana, as the only means of appeasing the incensed deity. Rám Dhan Misri, the family priest, was sent for. When he came, he confirmed the opinion of the Bráhmani women, that Panchánana's *pújá* must be immediately performed. No time was lost in making the necessary preparations. Taking the sick child with them, they went to the outskirts of the village, and stood under a *vaṭa* tree, where was lying a large stone painted red, and anointed with oil. At the moment of their arrival there, Govinda had another of his epileptic fits. The priestly Misri commenced worshipping the demon by the repetition of *mantras* (prayers); flowers, fruit, and sweetmeats were offered, and the women bawled out their loudest—as if the god was deaf—beseeching him to take pity upon them, and to come out of the child. Govinda, too, was made to bow down several times before the stone, and to beat his head on the ground. The god was again and again plied with entreaties, with flatteries, with promises of future presents, and *pújá,* and it seemed that the coaxing had its effect, for the fit suddenly came to an end. The women now thanked the god for his favour, and went away to their house. We state, on the authority of Alanga, that, after this time, Govinda had no return of epilepsy.

CHAPTER XI.

HOUSEHOLD MATTERS.

The *cow-house* yields a stercoraceous heap.

Cowper.

SINCE the conversation which took place between Alanga and Badan on the education of Govinda, the old lady was observed to be busier with her *charká* than usual. All the forenoon she was engaged, along with Sundari and Áduri, in the affairs of the house and in cooking; but she devoted the whole of the afternoon to spinning. What I mean by the affairs of the house perhaps requires a word of explanation. When the women got out of their beds, which they did always at crow-cawing—I cannot say cock-crowing, for there was no cock, not only in the house, but hardly any in the village, as cocks and hens are abomination to Hindus—they went to the side of the tank near the house, which served all necessary purposes. They then made a solution of cow-dung and water, and sprinkled the liquid by the hand on the open yard, which was next swept by a broom made of the stalks of palm-trees. But the rooms and the verandahs require to be cleansed and washed in another fashion. As the flooring was entirely of earth, there being not a single brick or stone in the house, or a plank of wood either, every inch of the floor of every room was besmeared by means of a piece of rag, with the said solution of cow-dung and water, and allowed to dry itself. The reader may think that this is a dirty business, and that the rooms must be the worse for being thus besmeared. But he is mistaken. He may take our word that the floor greatly improves by the process. It becomes smooth and glossy, and no cracks are visible. And as for any disgusting smell, there is nothing of the sort—the smell, if any, being positively pleasant. Hindu peasants besmear their cottages with a solution of cow-dung and water, because cow-dung is regarded ceremonially as a purifier; it is, however, a question why Hindu law-givers should have pitched upon cow-dung as a purifier. Has it any sanitary value? Has it any disinfecting property? From the universal practice of the Hindus of Bengal, I should be inclined to think that cow-dung was a disinfectant; but I prefer to leave the matter in the hands of doctors and chemists.

Our women, however, have not yet done with cow-dung. There is a large heap of it lying in a corner of the yard, partly obtained from the cow-house and partly collected the previous day by Gayárám, whose business is not only to tend the cows, but to collect whatever cow-dung he may find in the fields, either from his own cows or from those of other people, and a basketful of which valuable substance he every evening brings home on his head. On this heap Alanga, Sundari, and Áduri now fell. They put a little water on it, kneaded it as a baker kneads his dough; and each went with a basketful to the sunny sides of the walls of their huts, and covered them with cakes made by the palms of their hands. These cow-dung cakes, when they become dry, are of great use: they are the only fuel of the family. From year's end to year's end they do not buy fire-wood; for cooking and for keeping a fire in the cow-house they use no other fuel than what is afforded by the cow.

To a Bengal peasant the cow is the most useful of all animals. The cow supplies the newly-born infant with food for some years; the cow—or rather the bull, but it is the same thing—tills the ground on which the ráiyat's food grows; the cow brings home on its back that food, when it is ready, from the fields; the cow furnishes the peasant-family with the only fuel they have; The cow provides the peasant with curds, sour-milk, and whey; and the cow gives that *ghi* (clarified butter) which is so grateful to the palate and nostrils of Hindu gods and Bengali Bábus. After this, is it to be wondered that the cow should be greatly respected by Hindus and worshipped as "Mother Bhagavati?"

After the sweeping and cleansing of the house are over, the women have to go through other domestic duties, such as boiling paddy and drying it in the sun, with a view to turn it into rice, and scouring at the tank all the brass and stone pots and pans, and the like. Ablution comes next, after which commences the serious operation of cooking. in which Alanga takes the leading part. After all have eaten, and some food has been sent, if necessary, to the fields for the gentlemen of the house, Alanga sits down to her breakfast, or dinner, or supper, anything you choose to call it, for she, as a widow, takes only one meal in twenty-four hours, and does not seem to be any the worse for it. It was only after this meal, which took place generally about two or three o'clock in the afternoon, that Alanga could sit to her *charká*; but long practice had made her an adept in the craft, so that in the course of a few days she spun a quantity of thread sufficient to make for Govinda a *dhuti* five cubits long, and a cubit and half broad. Alanga did not herself weave the cloth, as she was unacquainted with the art; it was woven by the weaver of the northern division of the village, for which he received his usual fee.

The day on which Govinda was for the first time taken to the *páṭhśálá* was an important day to the family, as well as to our hero himself. Though, unlike the middle and higher classes, who seldom send a child to school for the first time without performing some religious ceremonies, the poorer classes ask not the ministrations of the Bráhman, yet the matter is regarded with the liveliest interest. Ever since his birth, Govinda has not had a stitch of clothing on his person; though more than five years old, he was allowed to revel in the unrestrained freedom of primæval nudity. It was on the morning of that important day that his grandmother wrapped round his waist, in folds, the *dhuti* of which I have spoken, leaving the rest of the body—which was nearly the whole—quite naked. Thus dressed, our little man bowed down to the ground before his grand-mother, his mother, his father, uncles, and aunt, and they all gave him their benedictions. As on the very first day he was expected at the *paṭhśálá* to commence writing, Badan tied in one corner of Govinda's *dhuti,* a piece of chalk, or rather *rámkhaḍi,* and Alanga, ever on the alert to minister to the wants and comforts of every member of the family, put in one of the folds of the *dhuti*, a quantity of *muḍi* (fried rice), in such a way that Govinda could easily dip his hand into it whenever he felt himself hungry. Thus accoutred, our young soldier was ready to begin his attack on the realms of knowledge. Badan took Govinda by the hand, and repeating three times the words, "Śirí Hari! Śirí Hari! Śirí Hari!" left the house for the *paṭhśálá*, a description of which place, and of its presiding genius, we must reserve for the next chapter.

CHAPTER XII.

THE VILLAGE SCHOOLMASTER.

> The village all declared how much he knew,
> 'Twas certain he could write, and cypher too;
> Lands he could measure, terms and tides presage,
> And even the story ran—that he could gauge.
>
> *The Deserted Village.*

THE reader will remember that, in the middle of the village of Kánchanpur, there are two temples of Śiva facing each other, and that one of those temples has before it a colonnade. In this colonnade was held the village *páṭhśálá,* properly so called, where the sons of Bráhmans, Káyasthas, and wealthy bankers received instruction from a Bráhman *gurumaháśaya.* This *gurumaháśaya,* or *maháśaya,*—as he is usually called in the Burdwan district—belonged to a race of hereditary pedagogues, since his father, grandfather, great-grandfather, and all his ancestors up to the fourteenth generation backwards, were the schoolmasters of the village. There was in the village, however, another pedagogue whose school bore to the other one the same relation which a dissenting chapel in England bears to the parish church. He occupied a far inferior social position: indeed he was not a Bráhman, but a Káyastha, and therefore obtained only a third part of the pupils of the other. Any day you might have seen in the school of the Bráhman pedagogue between sixty and seventy boys, whereas in the other school you seldom saw more than twenty. And yet the Bráhman was by no means a better teacher than the Káyastha. The former, though he had read a part of the *Sankshipta-Sára*—the Sanskrit grammar in vogue in the Vardhamána district—and would repeat a lot of Sanskrit *ślokas* with which his conversation was interlarded, yet made ludicrous mistakes in Bengali orthography; the latter made no pretensions to Sanskrit scholarship, but was universally acknowledged to be an arithmetician of the first water; and he was strong in zamindári accounts, a subject of which the Bráhman *mahásaya* had no knowledge. Though the school of the Káyastha teacher was attended chiefly by the lower castes and the poorer classes, there was amongst them a sprinkling of Bráhman boys, particularly those whose parents wished to give them a mathematical education and an insight into the mysteries of zamindári accounts. Badan preferred the Káyastha to the Bráhman teacher for two reasons:—*first*, because the school of the latter was the more aristocratic of the two, and he wished his son to be educated along with those who were his equals in social position, or at any rate, not very much higher, and *secondly*, because he wanted Govinda to learn zamindári accounts. Accordingly Badan and Govinda proceeded to the house of Ráma Rúpa Sarkára (for that was the name of the Káyastha pedagogue), who held his school in the yard of his house, in the shade of an umbrageous *Kánṭála* tree (jack tree), excepting in the rainy season, when he removed it to the verandah of his cottage.

"Well, Badan, what is the news? what brings you here?" asked Ráma Rúpa seated on a mat before about a dozen pupils variously engaged in writing on paper, or plantain-leaf or palm-leaf.

Badan. "You see, *mahásaya,* this boy of mine; I wish to put him under you, that you may make a man of him."

Ráma. "Well done! Badan! You wish your son taught *lekhá-paḍá,* a thing you don't know yourself! Well, you are right. The poet Chánakya says—*Vidyáratna mahadhanam,* that is to say, learning or education is a great treasure."

Badan. "Yes, sir, that's quite true. A man who cannot read and write is a truly poor man—he is blind. Though I have two eyes, I am really blind, for I cannot read what is written on a bit of paper."

Ráma. "Badan, you had better sit down, and smoke. Modo! go and make tobacco ready."

Badan sat down on the bare ground, Govinda stood near him, and Madhu, one of the advanced pupils of the school, went away to get tobacco and fire for his teacher. In Bengal, and I suppose in other parts of India, pupils, especially in the villages, do, without a grudge, even menial services for their teacher; indeed, they regard it as an honourable distinction to be so employed. Turning to Govinda, the *mahásaya* said, "Well, my little man, so you want to be a *Panḍit.* Come near me." Poor Govinda trembled from head to foot. He had heard from boys of his own age that every schoolmaster was a second Yama or Rhadamanthus, and every school a place where boys were unmercifully flogged. He therefore hesitated to go near Ráma Rúpa; but Badan shoved him forwards to the pedagogue, who patted him on the head and told him to be a good boy, and not to be afraid of his teacher. One of the advanced pupils was then ordered to trace on the ground the first five letters of the Bengali alphabet. Badan took out the *rámkhaḍi* from his boy's clothes, and put it into his hand. Ráma Rúpa took hold of Govinda's hand, with the chalk in it, and led it over all the letters traced on the ground. In the meantime, the advanced pupil, Madhu, brought the hookah reeking with the fragrant weed, and put it into the hands of Ráma Rúpa. As Badan and Ráma Rúpa were of different castes, they could not smoke in the same hookah. The latter therefore gave to the former the earthen cup called *kalki,* which contains the tobacco and the fire, and Badan grasped the lower part of it with both his hands, and smoked away through the opening between the thumb and the forefinger of his right-hand. After he had smoked two or three minutes he returned the *kalki* to the *mahásaya,* who began to puff away with great zest.

As the redoubtable pedagogue of Kánchanpur, now in the act of smoking, is in a state of repose—and tobacco, they say, is a wonderful sedative—we shall make an attempt to photograph his likeness, which is not always practicable, especially when, urged by a tempest of passion—as was frequently the case—his body trembles in every inch with rage, and his cane descends, thump after thump, with electric rapidity, on the backs of his unfortunate pupils. From the form of one of his legs, and the position in which it was put, you might have inferred that he was lame, and the inference would have been confirmed by the sight of a crutch that lay beside him. His lameness, to say the truth, was of no ordinary kind; he could with difficulty go, with the help of his crutch, from one room of his house to another; and, as for going out into the street, he scarcely went out even once in six months. Owing to this bodily defect, he was always called *khoṇḍá mahá-śaya*, that is, the lame schoolmaster, in contra-distinction to the Bráhman pedagogue. His pupils often lent him a helping hand in going from room to room, and sometimes, I am sorry to say, assisted him to a fall, as a sort of retaliation for the caning they so frequently received from him. He was about forty years old, had a dark skin, a spare body, an aquiline nose, and a rather high forehead for a Bengali. He stooped a great deal. In addition to his lameness, he had another bodily defect, which considerably marred his influence, and made him often an object of derision—he spoke through his nose. When narrating the conversation he had with Badan, we found it impossible to represent his nasal intonation in the English language, though it would have been quite easy in Bengali. In uttering the words, "how do you do?" Ráma Rúpa would say—"*hnow dno ynou dno?*" His nasal twang was so strong, that, if he were speaking at night in a dark room, he might be mistaken by children for a ghost—for Bengali ghosts speak strongly through the nose.

But though a hopeless cripple as regards his body, and ghost-like in his speech, Ráma Rúpa had natural talents of no mean order. He was the first mathematician in the village. He had not only Subhankara, the Indian Cocker, at his fingers' ends, but was acquainted with the elements of the Víjagaṇita or Algebra. There was, indeed, another mathematician in the village who looked down upon the pedagogue with perfect contempt—and that is our friend Dhumketu, the astrologer; but there was this difference between the two geniuses, that whereas the astrologer dealt in celestial mathematics, the schoolmaster applied his mathematics to things terrestrial. But Ráma Rúpa was not only mathematical, he was eminently logical. Though he had not read the *Sútras* of Gotama, he was an acute reasoner. Whenever the Christian missionary of Vardhamána came to the village in the course of his itineracy, he did not fail to pay a visit to the lame schoolmaster, who had many a tough argument with him; and the villagers always thought that the missionary was invariably worsted. Indeed, his reputation for logical subtlety was so great that it might be truly said of him that

> He was in logic a great critic,
> Profoundly skill'd in analytic;
> He could distinguish and divide
> A hair 'twixt south and south-west side;
> On either which he would dispute,
> Confute, change hands, and still confute.

Ráma Rúpa was a strict disciplinarian. He had by him constantly, besides his crutch, a thin but longish twig of bamboo, which often resounded, not only on the palms of his pupils' hands, but on their heads and backs; and sometimes also with cruel ingenuity he used to strike their knuckles, their knee-joints, and their ankles. You could hardly pass by the door of the house during school hours without hearing the *shop-a-shop, shop-a-shop* of the bamboo switch. But he had other ways of administering discipline. One famous mode of juvenile punishment was called *náḍu-Gopál,* that is, Gopál (the god Krishna) with a sweetmeat in his hand. This consisted in making a boy sit on the ground with one leg in a kneeling posture: the two arms were then stretched, and a large brick was placed on each. In this posture a boy is expected to remain still for several hours. Should either of the bricks fall from the hand, down comes the bamboo switch on the pate of the delinquent. We shall mention only one other clause in Ráma Rúpa's penal code. The juvenile offender was handcuffed, and his feet were tied by strings to the trunk of the jack tree of which we have spoken. While the boy thus stood handcuffed and chained, the leaves of a stinging plant called *bichhuṭi (Tragia involucrata)* were applied to different parts of his body. Whoever has been stung by a wasp or a hornet can have some idea of the sensation produced by the application of *bichhuṭi* to the skin. The agony is intense: perfectly helpless, unable to run away, unable even to stroke with his hand the part stung, the boy can do nothing but shriek. In justice to the lame schoolmaster of Kánchanpur, I should here remark that the above disciplinary process was not the product of his own fertile brain; it is a time-honoured institution which has been handed down from generation to generation of Bengali village schoolmasters.

A few words on Ráma Rúpa's finances will conclude this chapter. The schooling fee was, on the average, one *anna* (a penny and halfpenny) a month per boy. Supposing he had thirty or thirty-two boys—I don't believe he ever had more—his monthly income would amount to two rupées, or four shillings. Besides this, he had a system of "requisitions." Most of the boys, when they came to the afternoon school—for the school was held first from early in the morning till about eleven o'clock, and again from three o'clock in the afternoon till candlelight—brought from their houses for their teacher either a betel-leaf, or a betel-nut, or a small ball of tobacco. In addition to these daily donations, every boy was expected to give to the *mahásaya* once a month a *sidá,* which consisted of a quantity of unboiled rice, with a suitable accompaniment of vegetables, split pulse, mustard oil, salt, and even clarified butter. All this, no doubt, made a considerable addition to his income of four shillings a month, yet it was quite insufficient to support the pedagogue, his wife and two children; the deficiency was supplied by the produce of about ten *bighás* of land which, as he was unable to cultivate them himself, he held in partnership with a neighbouring husbandman.

Such was the celebrated pedagogue of Kánchanpur, at whose feet Govinda was made to sit for instruction. What progress our hero makes in his studies, and how long he remains in the school, will form the subject of a future chapter; but in the meantime the attention of the reader must be drawn to some other matters.

CHAPTER XIII.

THE MATCH MAKER.

> That night the envoy, entertained
> With honour and all care, remained.
>
> GRIFFITH'S *Rámáyana.*

I THINK I hear my English reader exclaim—"What a fool of a writer this novelist is! An orthodox novel generally ends in a marriage, but this fellow talks of a match maker, and consequently of a wedding, before he has well begun his story." Well, my defence against this grave charge is, that I cannot help it. Málati must now get married, whether I wish it or not. The customs of the country require it. Málati is already more than eleven years old, and people are blaming Badan for not having given her away in marriage. Often has Alanga shed tears at the remarks made by the women of the village, especially at the bathing *ghát*, where women hold conversations on all sorts of subjects. Some of the women have sometimes told her—"Well, Alanga, when is Málati going to get married? She is becoming quite a big girl. Dear me, she is shooting up like a plantain-tree! and you are taking no thought of her marriage!" The fact is, Indian legislators insist on the marriage of a girl before she attains the age of puberty, and as that seldom takes place, in a tropical climate like Bengal, later than in the twelfth year, the maximum age at which a girl can remain unmarried is eleven years. Badan would have long ago given away his daughter in marriage but for the expenses it was sure to entail, and which he was ill able to afford. But matters have now come to a crisis. Whether he has means or not, the girl must be married off, otherwise he would become a proverb and a hissing among his fellow-villagers. As to the ways and means, he must beg or borrow, it being out of the question for so respectable a ráiyat as Badan to have recourse to the other alternative of stealing. I cannot say he was ashamed to beg —a Bengal ráiyat seldom shows such a sense of delicacy—but if he did beg, few people would respond to the call. Recourse must therefore be had to borrowing; and Badan was sure of getting the loan of any reasonable sum from his *mahájan*, Golak Poddár, the money-lender of the village, who charges interest generally at the rate of one hundred per cent. and sometimes one hundred and fifty per cent. per annum, but who takes from his especial favourites —amongst whom Badan had the felicity to be numbered—only seventy-five per cent. It was resolved to borrow, and enquiries were set on foot in search of an eligible young man on whom to bestow the hand of Málati.

One evening, after Badan, Kálamánik, Gayárám, and the cows had come home from the fields, and while Alanga was going about with a lamp in her hand from room to room, and scaring away the ghosts and evil spirits of every description, which might seek shelter for the night in any room which had been unvisited in the evening, even for a minute or two, by any sort of light, a stranger entered the house and stood in the yard. Badan at once recognized the stranger and said—"Hullo! here is the *ghaṭak*. I am glad you have come; I hope you have brought good news. Málati, bring a *ghaṭi* of water for the *ghaṭak* to wash his feet with. Gayárám, go and get the hookah ready." In a moment the water was brought, with which the *ghaṭak* washed his feet. In a minute or two the hookah was brought and he went on puffing at a great rate.

But what *is* a *ghaṭak?* the English reader asks. Though this gentleman bears a name extremely guttural in sound, his occupation is about the pleasantest in the world. To spinsters and bachelors the sound of his name is more musical than Apollo's lute. He is the professional match maker, and therefore an under-servant of Kámadeva, the Indian Cupid. As in India, young men and young women do not themselves choose their partners in life, they have to depend on the good offices of this happy functionary, who, however, bears his commission not from the parties themselves, but from their parents and guardians. We have said that his occupation is one of the pleasantest in the world; and what occupation can be more pleasant than to be daily conversant with amiable bridegrooms, and blooming brides, to tie the knot of holy matrimony, and to be thus instrumental in the promotion of human happiness? This worthy functionary's character is as amiable as his occupation is pleasant. He possesses the highest Christian virtue in perfection, inasmuch as he possesses an unlimited measure of that charity which covers a multitude of sins. He has never been known to find any fault with any young man or young woman of marriageable age. The spinster may be as ugly as one of Shakspeare's witches, and the young man may be as deformed as deformity itself, the *ghaṭak* sees no defect in either. The one, in his eye, or at any rate in his mouth, is as beautiful and gentle as Lákshmi, and the other as handsome and accomplished as Kártikeya. The reader must not suppose that the gentleman now smoking in Badan's house is a *ghaṭak*, in the proper sense of the term. A *ghaṭak*, properly speaking, is a Bráhman of a very high order, and confines his services only to the priestly class. A Bráhman *ghaṭak* is often a man of learning, and invariably a man of persuasive eloquence; and he has the whole of the Indian "Burke's Peerage" and "Baronetage," at his fingers' ends. But every caste has its own *ghaṭaks;* and the worthy individual now before us is a *ghaṭak* of the ugra-kshatriya, or Aguri caste. He had been commissioned by Badan and Alanga to seek out a nice young husband for Málati; he had had, before this time, several interviews with them, and with the parents of the young man of his choice; and he had now come to make the final arrangements. What those arrangements were, and who the happy young man was that was to obtain the hand of Málati, the reader will know from the conversation, a translation of which we give below.

Badan. "Well, *ghaṭak*, what's the news? I hope everything is *páká* (ripe)."

Ghaṭak. "All *páká*, by the blessing of Prajápati. Your daughter Málati must have been born in an auspicious hour to get such a handsome, able-bodied, and accomplished husband as Mádhava Chandra Sen, the son of Keśava Chandra Sen, of Durgánagar, the highest ugra-kshatriya *kulin* in all Ráḍh."

Badan. "You *ghaṭaks* always praise everybody.

But tell me truly whether the young man has any bodily defect."

Ghaṭak. "Ráma! Ráma! do you think I am joking with you? Mádhava is a second Kártikeya, the handsomest young man in all Durgánagar. As for his property, his father, old Keśava, has two *maráis* (granaries of paddy); of his brass vessels there is no reckoning. Besides the lands for which he pays rent, he has ten *bighás* of *lákhráj* (rent-free) land."

Alanga. "What ornaments have they agreed to give to Málati?"

Ghaṭak. "Old Keśava will cover his daughter-in-law's body with ornaments from head to foot. He has ordered one *chaudrahár*, a pair of *mals*, a pair of *painchhás*, one *báuṭi*, a pair of *palákánṭis*, one *tabij*, a pair of *jhumkos* and *pásás*, a pair of *bálás*, and one *nath*. Did you, old lady, get so many ornaments at your wedding?"

Alanga. "Why, when I got married, *ghaṭak*, people were not so fond of ornaments as they are now. Those days were days of simplicity, of thick clothes and coarse rice; but the present days are days of luxury."

Badan. "What is Mádhava's exact age?"

Ghaṭak. "He is nineteen years, ten months, and five days old; I saw his horoscope."

Badan. "I hope his *gotra* (the name of his tribe), is different from ours."

Ghaṭak. "Well done! Do you, Badan, take me for a fool? I have become grey in *ghaṭkáli*, (that is, the profession of a *ghaṭak*), and you teach me my trade!"

Alanga. "We have no objection to the marriage.

Let measures be immediately taken. Málati has evidently put rice in the *háṇḍi* of Máḍhava. It seems to be the tying of Prajápati. Who can prevent the union?"

The *ghaṭak,* delighted with the result of the conversation, took some refreshment, laid himself down on a mat on the verandah of the big room, and, as he had become tired by the day's walk, soon fell asleep.

CHAPTER XIV.

MALATI'S MARRIAGE.

Here Sítá stands, my daughter fair,
The duties of thy life to share;
Take from her father, take thy bride,
Join hand to hand, and bliss betide.
A faithful wife, most blest is she,
And as thy shade will follow thee.

GRIFFITH'S *Rámáyana.*

EARLY next morning the *ghaṭak* rose from his bed before crow-cawing, and started on his journey to Durgánagar, which was about twenty miles distant. The way was long and tedious, but the prospect of a substantial reward considerably lightened the fatigue of the journey. He did not stop in the way, except a minute or two here and there for the purpose of smoking; and the only considerable halt he made was on the banks of the brook Máyá, where he bathed, ate the *muḍi* and treacle which Alanga with thoughtful kindness had put into his bundle, and drank from the stream, the water of which is so wholesome that it is said to possess the rare quality of dissolving even iron shots if they are taken into the stomach. "The lowing herds wind slowly over the lea," kicking up as they went a cloud of dust, and the ploughman was plodding homeward his weary way, when the *ghaṭak* reached Durgánagar. Keśava Sen and his wife rejoiced at the success of the match maker, and looked forward to their son's marriage with great pleasure.

Two days after, Keśava set out for Kánchanpur with a distant relation, who carried with him a pair of *sádis* and a *hándi* of the best sweetmeats manufactured at Durgánagar. Badan received the guests with joy. Keśava was delighted with the beauty and sweet simplicity of Málati, and *vágdán*, or betrothal, was consummated. As the parents of both bride and bridegroom were anxious that the marriage should be soon celebrated, Dhumketu, the astrologer, was requested to fix a day for the purpose. After a world of calculations he fixed upon the 24th of Phálgun, which he represented to be eminently auspicious, as the solar, lunar, planetary, and stellar influences on that day were all benignant. After two days Keśava and his friend returned to Durgánagar.

Two weeks before the wedding, the sound of festivity and the din of preparations were heard both at Kánchanpur and Durgánagar. The relations of Badan, whether near or distant, whether residing in the village or elsewhere, all flocked to his house to mingle their gratulations with his; and those near relations who had come from distant villages, stayed till the solemnities were all over. Preparations were made for feeding a large number of persons, consisting of Badan's own relations and friends, and of those of the bridegroom. The pedal was incessantly active, husking away large quantities of paddy; the hand-mill was always in motion, splitting *kalái*, *arhar*, and other sorts of pulse; advances of money were given to the fishermen of the village for a good supply of the only animal food used by the Hindu peasantry—the fish of Badan's own tank being insufficient for the purpose; and contracts were given to the village milkmen for huge quantities of curds, of which Bengal ráiyats are so fond. Alanga, Sundari, Áduri, and the women of neighbouring houses, busied themselves also with the clothes and ornaments of Málati; while the young women of the village put their heads together to concoct plans for amusing and teasing the bridegroom on the night of the wedding. In every Bengali marriage *haridrá* (turmeric), plays an important part; indeed, without it, there can be no marriage. What the philosophy of using turmeric in marriage is, we do not pretend to fathom; perhaps it is used to improve the complexion, which in Bengal is rather dark. Whatever may be the reason, turmeric is largely used in all Bengali marriages. Accordingly, a large quantity of turmeric was ground, and reduced to powder by Alanga and Sundari; the body of Málati was profusely besmeared with the yellow dye, mixed with mustard oil; and other members of the family, as well as relatives and neighbours, beautified their persons with it. Great was the exultation of the women when the nuptial drug was for the first time applied to the skin of the would-be bride. Shouts of *ulu! ulu! ulu!* rent the air; and those shouts were repeated every forenoon when the operation of besmearing the body with turmeric took place, before bathing. The din of preparation, the sound of festivity, the loud talk and laughing of the women, the turmeric-coloured clothes of every one connected with the family, and the shouts of *ulu! ulu! ulu!*—all showed to the little world of Kánchanpur that there was to be a marriage in Badan's house.

At Durgánagar the sound of festivity was still

greater. Every morning the *chanḍimanḍap* of Keśava's house was crowded with people, old and young, who talked of nothing else but of Mádhava's marriage. About ten o'clock in the morning, the shouts of *ulu! ulu! ulu!* from the *andarmahal* (Zenana) announced to the public of the village that the would-be bridegroom's body was being besmeared with turmeric. A great deal of fun was made, many jokes were cracked by old and young women, as Mádhava's body was anointed with oil and turmeric. Ablutions then followed. During these days, the bridegroom ate what is called, *anúḍhabhojana,* commonly termed *áibaḍabhát,* or bachelor's dinner. Those dinners are given by the near relations of the bridegroom, and are so termed from the circumstance that they are amongst the last dinners the bridegroom eats in the condition of a bachelor. They are usually accompanied with a deal of fun and festivity, made chiefly by young men and young women. When Mádhava sat with his companions in the *chanḍimanḍap,* the *ghaṭak* would come and descant eloquently on the nameless graces of Málati, to the infinite amusement of the party, and institute a droll comparison between the forthcoming marriage, and the union of Mádhava and Málati in the Sanskrit play of that name. Business was, however, mingled with these merry-makings. As Mádhava was Keśava's only son, the father had resolved to spend as much money as he possibly could in celebrating the marriage. Accordingly, a costly dress for the bridegroom had been purchased; the village *málákar* (flower-man) was ordered to prepare as gaudy a crown as he could make—for all Bengali bridegrooms, however poor, put on tinsel crowns at the wedding; equally gaudy shoes, embroidered with silver, had been brought up from Calcutta; and the *chaturdolá* (marriage Pálki) of a wealthy neighbour was borrowed for the conveyance of the bridegroom to the village of the bride; torches were prepared, and a number of *rangmasáls*, "Bengal Lights" as they are called by Anglo-Indians, were manufactured to illuminate the path of the bridegroom. A band of musicians was also engaged, one set of *jagajhampa*, four *ḍhols,* two *kánsis,* two *sánáis,* and one set of *rasanchaukis.* This precious band used every day, several days before the wedding, to give forth harmony not unlike that which, we may suppose, was made at Babel at the Confusion of Tongues.

At last the long-looked-for day, the auspicious twenty-fourth of Phálgun, arrived. Keśava had made all necessary preparations for the marriage-march, and before the crows of the village commenced their cawing, the marriage procession had begun its journey—for the object was to reach Kánchanpur in one day. The procession consisted of the bridegroom, seated in the *chaturdola,* of which I have spoken, carried by four stout bearers, his father, about a dozen relations and friends; the band of musicians, already described; the *guru,* or spiritual director of the family; the family priest, and last, but not least in importance—the family barber. The party, without halting anywhere, made a forced march of nineteen miles, and reached Devagráma, only one mile distant from Kánchanpur, at about three o'clock in the afternoon, where they bathed and cooked a hasty meal, and made preparations for entering the bride's village in great pomp.

But while the hymeneal party are making preparations to take Kánchanpur by storm, the reader must accompany me for a few minutes to the house of the bride, and see for himself what *her* friends are about. Since the dawning of that bright and happy day, there was infinite bustle in Badan's house. The noise of gladness was heard everywhere. Friends of every degree of amity were there; relations even to the "fortieth remove" were there; the sounds of *ulu! ulu! ulu!* were ever and anon heard; there were also the family *guru,* or father-confessor, the family *purohita* or priest, the family barber and his partner in life—the indispensable *nápitni* (she-barber)—besides a heterogeneous mass of men and women, old, young, and middle-aged, who were neither friends nor relations, but simple spectators. All these men and women were sitting in the open yard of the house, now covered below with a *satranja* (coarse carpet), and above by a canvas canopy, both borrowed from the zamindár of the village. But the chief object of attraction was the bride herself. The daughters and the young wives of neighbouring husbandmen had come, with one accord, and busied themselves from early dawn with adorning the person of Málati, and making her look as handsome as they could. They made a mixture of turmeric and curds, and rubbed her body well with it. She was then bathed. The girls and young women then attacked her hair, which they wove into many a fantastic braid. They then put on her person the several ornaments of which I have already spoken. The skill of the barber's wife was also had in requisition. She washed the little feet of Málati, and neatly painted them all round with *alakta* or lac. Last of all, she put on a *sáḍi* of red silk. Thus attired, she waited for the coming of the bridegroom. It was an extraordinary day for poor Málati, but she hardly knew why her parents and friends made such an idol of her. She knew it was the day of her marriage, but what marriage was, what its duties were—of all that she knew nothing.

The sun had sunk behind the mango-tope of Devagráma; the cows had returned from grazing, followed by neat-herds carrying baskets of cow-dung on their heads; the birds had retired to their respective trees for the night, and were squabbling among themselves for their beds; and the shades of evening had descended over all the plain, when the bridegroom's party began their festal procession. Mádhava sat in the *chaturdola;* the torches and *rangmasáls* were lit; the musicians began to play, and the jackals of the neighbouring thickets, frightened by so unusual a noise and so bright a light at such a time, set up an unearthly yell as an accompaniment to the marital music. The party assembled at Badan's house, all on the tip-toe of expectation, heard with delight the sound of the nuptial music. Badan's heart, and especially Alanga's, leaped with joy. As the sound of the music became louder and louder, the pulse of Badan and Alanga beat faster and faster. As for Maláti, she had scarcely any feelings one way or the other, as she understood little of the matter; on the whole, I think she was sadder than usual, as she knew that she would have to leave a beloved father, a dear mother, and a still dearer grandmother, and go to a strange place with a man whom she had never seen. As the procession was approaching the village, men, women, and children ran into the street, exclaiming, "The bridegroom is coming! the bridegroom is coming!" Suddenly the music stopped at the entrance of the village. A party of the villagers had assembled there in great force, who said that they would not allow the procession to pass on till they received the fee of *ḍhelábhángáni* (stoning), that is to say, the bridegroom and his party must purchase by a bribe the abstention of the villagers from throwing stones at them and breaking their vehicles and dashing out their brains. After a great deal of loud talk on both sides, the father of the bridegroom paid five rupees on the spot, after which the procession was allowed to pass on.

Shortly after, another party stopped the procession and demanded some fee for the *gráma,* or village, which was given; and a third party, composed chiefly of boys, demanded fee for the village schoolmaster. The procession at last stood at the door of Badan's house. Badan went out and welcomed them. The hero of the night, Mádhava, sat in the middle of the open yard under the canvas canopy, surrounded by a large assembly of the friends of the bride. Many hookahs went around, as almost everybody smoked. They talked on all sorts of subjects; and the pupils of Ráma Rúpa the pedagogue, who had mustered strong to witness the marriage of their schoolfellow's sister, attempted to puzzle each other with difficult questions in arithmetic, to the great amusement of the wedding party. The family barber, Gangá Nápit, was the busiest man in the whole assembly, for he was attending to the smoking of the guests, filling one *kalki* after another as soon as it was exhausted. And his amiable consort, the *Nápitni,* was of equal service amongst the women guests, who sat, crowded like bales of cotton on the verandah of the big room, not, indeed, in supplying them with tobacco—for Hindu women do not smoke, though some of them chew tobacco-leaf with *pán*-leaf—but in enlivening the conversation and contributing to the gaiety of the scene.

At last the auspicious hour arrived—the hour on which sun, moon, planets, and stars had shed their selectest influences, and in which Mádhava and Málati were to become man and wife, when Badan, with folded hands and a sheet of cloth round his neck, in token of his humility and submission, stood in the midst of the assembly and said, "Sirs, as the *lagna* (propitious moment) has arrived, if it be the command of the assembly I shall no longer delay in beginning the good work, but shall proceed to celebrate the marriage of my daughter with Mádhava Chandra Sen, the son of Keśava Chandra Sen of Durgánagar." Several voices cried out, "We have no objection. Begin the ceremony. And may the blessing of Prajápati descend on the bridegroom and bride." The ceremony of *stri áchára* (or the behaviour of women, which immediately precedes that of marriage properly so called), takes place in the zenana, that is, in the inner courtyards of Hindu houses; but, as poor people like Badan have no inner and outer yards in their houses, it takes place in the only yard they have. The *chhálnátalá* (the place where the ceremony is performed) had been prepared in that corner of the yard which was between the big hut and the pedal-hut. There was a flat wooden stool on the spot; at its four corners stood four young plantain trees, round which threads were passed. Mádhava stood on the stool, and Málati was now brought forward and whirled round the bridegroom and the plantain trees seven times.

During this process, amid the exclamations of *ulu! ulu! ulu!* blows not unfrequently fell on the back of the poor bridegroom, as it is deemed unfair that a man should carry away a girl without suffering some pain. Sundari then performed what is called *baran,* that is, she took a brass plate filled with the products of the earth, and touched with it the forehead of the bridegroom. Nothing more was wanting to complete the union than the tying together of the skirts of each other's clothes, the exchange of garlands of flowers, and the repetition of holy *mantras.*

The marriage over, Badan now addressed himself to the onerous task of providing the whole assembly with refreshments. The *Satranja* on which they had been sitting was now taken up. A little quantity of water was sprinkled on the ground, to allay the dust; a plantain leaf was spread on the ground for each guest; boiled rice, boiled pulse, vegetable curry, fish curry, fish in tamarind, and curds, were distributed. The men ate on without speaking, the silence being now and then broken by loud cries of "Here, more fish!" "more curds on this leaf!" They all washed their hands and mouths in the adjacent tank; each got a *pán,* with the usual spices, to chew; the hookah went round and round, after which the assembly dispersed. The women were then feasted on the verandah of the big hut. The same delicacies were served up; they made less noise than the men, but I have been told that they ate more. After eating, washing their hands and mouths, and chewing *pán,* they all went away to their homes, excepting a few young women who had made up their minds to spend the rest of the night in the *vásarghar.* What that is, the reader will be told in the next chapter.

CHAPTER XV.

THE VÁSARGHAR.

Now farewell, bride, and bridegroom
Blest in thy new-found sire!
May Leto, mother of the brave,
Bring babes at your desire,
And holy Cypris either's breast
With mutual love inspire.

Theokritos.

It is not to be supposed that while the friends of the bridegroom and of the bride were entertained, the bridegroom and bride themselves should fast. But, to tell the truth, though the choicest viands—as choice viands, that is to say, as a Bengal ráiyat can procure—were set before them, they could scarcely eat anything. Intense excitement arising from the scenes enacted during the night had taken away Mádhava's appetite; and as for Málati, she scarcely thought that what she was passing through was a reality. But there was another reason why Mádhava made a poor supper that night. The room was crowded with a number of young women whose only vocation seemed to be to amuse themselves at the expense of the bridegroom. Alanga tried to clear the room of these women, but she failed. Scarcely had Mádhava taken a handful of rice into his mouth, when one of the young women said—"Our friend Kártikeya has a beautiful set of teeth; each one is as small as a hoe, and as white as a hookah pipe," which is usually made of ebony. Another said,—"His eyes are beautiful, exactly like those of a cat." A third admired his nose, which was beautifully flattened at the tip. A fourth came behind and dealt such a blow on his back that it sounded like a ripe palm-fruit falling to the ground from a lofty palmyra tree; on which the women raised a loud guffaw. But the longest dinner or supper has an end, and Mádhava was removed to the *Vásarghar.*

Vásar, or Vásarghar, is the room in which a married couple spend their first night after marriage, or rather the remainder of that night in which the wedding takes place. Bengalis, whether rich or poor, have no honeymoon; but the English reader of this authentic history must admit, after perusing the following account of the *vásar* night, that on that night is concentrated the honey not only of one moon but of twelve moons. Badan's bed-room, which was a compartment of the big hut, and the best room in the house, was converted into *vásarghár*. As Badan was too poor to have a *khát*, that is, a wooden bedstead with tester frames and mosquito curtains—he and all his people always sleeping on mats spread on the floor—he had borrowed from a neighbour for the newly-married couple a *taktáposa*, which may be described as a large but low kitchen table. On the *taktáposa* was spread a quilt, with two or three pillows. At the bidding of the young women, Mádhava sat on the bedstead, and the women sat on the floor on a mat, amongst whom Málati took her place. After a little, a near relation of her mother's took Málati in her arms, and made her sit on the left-hand side of Mádhava. Málati blushed, and covered her face with the skirt of her *sáḍi.* The old women next went to the bridegroom and bride, and blessed them, invoking the gods and praying that they might lead a happy life, that they might become immortal, that they might rejoice at seeing the faces of many children, especially sons, and that their basket and their store might never fail. When this benediction was pronounced, Mádhava and Málati came down from the bedstead, and, touching the ground with their heads, made obeisance to them. Mádhava then resumed his seat on the bedstead, but Málati stayed with the women on the mat on the floor. The reader might suppose that the women would now surely retire, and leave the bridegroom and bride to themselves. Not a bit of it. Alanga came to the door and told Mádhava to go to sleep, and he would have gladly done so if the women had allowed him. One woman said, "Oh mother! what kind of marriage is this? Does any bridegroom sleep on the night of his marriage? Mádhava must sit up the rest of the night with us. The spring has just begun, and what bride or bridegroom ever thinks of sleep? Come, friends, let us all be gay." Turning to the bridegroom, the same woman said, "Well, brother, you have got a handsome and gentle wife; I hope you will treat her well."

Mádhava. "What man ever ill-treats his wife?"

First Woman. "What man ill-treats his own wife! You must be a ninny not to know that. Are there not hundreds of cases in Kánchanpur? Here is Kádi, for instance, who is beaten almost every night by her husband."

Mádhava. "It is very wicked to beat one's

wife. In my opinion no man ought, under any circumstances, to beat his wife."

First Woman. "The bridegroom seems to be a nice man. O, *lo!* Málati, your forehead is good. You have got such a nice husband."

Second Woman. "You seem, sister, to be in love with the bridegroom. You had better go and sit on his left hand, and we shall all cry, *ulu! ulu! ulu!* The bridegroom's words have pleased you. Now his words are honey-like, but afterwards they will turn into poison. It is the same with every bridegroom. All men are bad. They all ill-treat their wives."

Mádhava. "You seem to be speaking from personal experience."

Second Woman. "Well done, friend! You seem to be a bit of a wit. There is some juice in you. You are not the dry stick I took you for. At first I took you for a cow; but it seems there is some stuff in you. *Sábásh!* (well done!) *Sábásh!* May you only live long!"

When these words were uttered, the other women showed some displeasure at the sarcasm, and expressed the hope that there would be nothing disagreeable on that joyful night. The woman who had spoken, however, protested that she was not at all angry, and that what she had said was all in fun.

One of the party asked Mádhava whether he could tell stories for the amusement of all; on his saying that he would greatly prefer being a listener to being a narrator, one of the young women told a story which provoked no end of laughter. When the story was drawing to a close, Mádhava unfortunately fell asleep, on which the reciter of the story, a young woman, gaily went up to the *taktáposa* and pulled his ear, which produced roars of laughter. On hearing the cry of a cuckoo from a neighbouring tree, one of the party suggested that Mádhava should regale the company with music. Mádhava did not deny that he could sing, but said that woman's voice was a great deal sweeter than man's; he hoped, therefore, that one of the young ladies would sing. Most of the women there present could not sing at all, as it is reckoned disreputable in Bengali women, even of the peasant class, to sing; but there was one woman in the company who could sing, and she sang a love song, containing allusions to a parrot imprisoned in a cage, and longing to be free, and to soar away into the regions of delight. The voice was so sweet that it was immensely applauded. Mádhava at last yielded to the wishes of the ladies, and favoured them with a song. The song was scarcely at an end, when Alanga suddenly opened the door of the room, and said, "Son, Mádhava! the crows are cawing, it is morning, the sun will be up shortly. You had better get up and perform your morning ablutions. Where is Málati, dear?" Málati was lying on the mat in deep sleep. The women said they would not allow Mádhava to get up from bed till they got their fee of *Sayyátoláni*, that is, for putting up the bed. After a great deal of laughter the sum of two rupées was given to the women, who put up the quilt and the pillows and went to their homes. The money they got they invested in sweetmeats. Thus ended the pleasures of the *vásarghar*, or *phulsayyá* (flower-bed), as it is more generally called in the Vardhamána district, from the circumstance of the bed being adorned with flowers. Two days after the married couple started for Durgánagar.

CHAPTER XVI.

THE VILLAGE GHOST.

I've heard my reverend grannie say,
In lanely glens ye like to stray;
Or where auld ruin'd castles gray,
　　Nod to the moon,
Ye fright the nightly wand'rers 'way
　　Wi' eldritch croon.

Burns.

"WHY were you looking so intently on that young *Vairági* (mendicant), who came to ask alms this morning?" said Gayárám to his wife Áduri, one night on retiring into his room, and bolting the door.

Áduri. "What *Vairági?* I look at another man's face!"

Gayárám. "*What Vairági?* as if you know nothing of the matter! You seem to have dropped from the clouds!"

Áduri. "In the name of *Guru* (spiritual director), I have never gazed on any man's face except on your's. Do not accuse me falsely."

Gayárám. "Accuse you falsely, you cunning jackal! Have I not seen it with these two eyes? The *Vairági* was standing in the middle of the yard; you came from the store-room with a handful of rice, and put it into his pumpkin; and, in the act of putting it, you looked into his face, and he looked at yours, and you gave an arch smile. I was in the cow-house, and saw it all. Dare you deny this?"

Áduri. "In the name of Gopináth (a name of

Krishna), it is all false. It is true I put a handful of rice into the young *Vairági's* bag, but I deny that I looked at him and smiled."

Gayárám. "You *did* look; you *did* smile. Don't say No. I saw it all from the cow-house."

Áduri. "You are a very suspicious husband; in other respects, you are good. You always suspect that I look into other people's faces, and that I speak to men; whereas, I never do any such thing. How many times since marriage have you suspected me! But *Paramesvara* (God), knows that I am innocent."

Gayárám. "I am not accusing you of any positive crime. But you have a bad heart, and you always look at the faces of young men. Why don't you confess that you smiled at the young *Vairági* this morning?"

Áduri. "I did not smile. You are speaking a lie."

On this Gayárám's anger was roused, and he slapped his wife on the face. Áduri screamed, fell down on the floor, and screamed again as if she was in danger of her life. Alanga, who was in the adjoining hut—the same on the verandah of which was the pedal—rushed out, and, going to the door of Gayárám's hut, enquired what the matter was. On being told that nothing was the matter, only that *chhoto bou* (the younger wife) screamed simply because she was rebuked for her naughtiness, she went back into her room, advising her son to treat Áduri gently, and not to beat her. Áduri, lying flat on the ground, muttered to herself, "O Vidhátá, what an amount of misery hast thou written on my forehead! Happy should I be if I die! The air would then enter into my bones."

Gayárám. "Now confess that you smiled on the *Vairági*, and promise that you will not do it again; then I'll forgive you."

Áduri. "In the name of *Guru*, I did not do it. Don't think evil of me, O lord of my life."

Gayárám. "Dare you again deny it, when I have told you that I have seen it with mine own eyes."

Áduri. "But suppose I did look and did smile on the *Vairági?* What of that? Have I committed any crime?"

Gayárám, with his Hindoo ideas of female delicacy, was so shocked at this outrageous answer that he got up from his bed, went to the corner where Áduri lay, and dealt on her back two or three vigorous fisticuffs. Áduri screamed again: but Alanga was asleep and did not hear her. There was no more conversation; Gayárám slept on his bed, which was simply a mat spread on the floor; and Áduri, sobbing and groaning for a long time, at last fell asleep in the place where she was lying. Gayárám woke up early in the morning, took no notice of his wife, who was then fast asleep, and went to the cows.

Áduri got out of her room at the usual time, and engaged herself with Alanga and Sundari, in the ordinary househould duties; Badan and Kálamánik went to the fields, whither Gayárám had already gone, and Govinda repaired to the *páṭhsálá* of Ráma Rúpa Mahásaya, along with other boys of the neighbourhood. Sundari bathed first, as she was now the chief cook of the family, having no baby to nurse, and Alanga being too old and infirm to undertake the work. The gentlemen of the house returned home about the middle of the day for their dinner, and Govinda returned from the *páṭhśálá*, his face and hands being besmeared with ink, clear proof that he had begun to write his letters in right earnest. The men took their meal first and went again to the fields; and Govinda to the afternoon school. The women then ate their dinner and, as usual, scoured the plates and dishes at the *gháṭ* of the tank with mud, ashes, and straw. Alanga then sat to her *charká*, and Sundari and Áduri brought drinking water from the *himaságara*, each in an earthen *kalsi* gracefully placed on the left side of the waist, with the left arm going round its neck to support it.

It was about five o'clock in the afternoon, when Sundari and Áduri, sitting beside Alanga, were carding cotton for her, that an extraordinary scene occurred. Suddenly Áduri burst out into a loud laughter and fell down on the ground. On being raised up, she laughed still more, and began to jump about the verandah. Having never seen Áduri laugh so immoderately, Alanga and Sundari were quite confounded and ascribed her strange behaviour to the influence of *bátás* or "air"—that is, to demoniacal agency. The news of Áduri's possession ran like wildfire through the village, and reached Badan and his brothers who were in the fields. They immediately came to their house, which they found filled with a large crowd, and where they saw a sight which they had never before witnessed. The reader has been already told that it is reckoned a great sin in a Hindu (at least a Bengali Hindu woman) even to see the face of the elder brother of her husband—at any rate her eyes ought never to meet those of his. Accordingly Áduri, since her marriage, had never looked into the face of either Badan or Kálamánik: when they were in the house she went about completely veiled. The same Áduri had now become quite a changed being. She had taken off her *sáḍi* from the head and the upper part of her body, and was therefore naked from the waist, upwards. In this state she came before Badan and Kálamánik, and laughed and danced and jumped about. They both became convinced that an evil spirit had taken possession of her. But there are two sorts of possession, in Bengal at least;—one by a witch and the other by a ghost: and the question was—Was Áduri under the influence of a witch or of a ghost? And it was important that the question should be speedily answered, as the two sorts of possession required two entirely different systems of treatment, and the doctor that expelled a witch was unable to cope with a ghost. At the suggestion of an old woman who happened then to be in the house, the matter was satisfactorily settled. She suggested that a piece of turmeric should be burnt and brought near Áduri's nostrils; if she quietly bore the fume and smell it would then be concluded that she was under the influence of a witch; but if she could not endure it, then it was plain that she was possessed, or "eaten," as the expression is in Bengali, by a ghost. Accordingly Gayárám and three other stout men caught hold of Áduri—for she seemed to have become superhumanly strong—and a piece of turmeric was burnt below her nostrils, with the smell of which Áduri was no better pleased

> Than Asmodëus with the fishy fume
> That drove him, though enamour'd, from the spouse
> Of Tobit's son, and with a vengeance sent
> From Media post to Egypt, there fast bound.

The moment the fume of the turmeric entered Áduri's nostrils, she gave an unearthly shriek, and tried to get off from the four strong men who were holding her. There was no doubt that it was a case of demoniacal possession, or rather ghost-possession. There lived at Devagrám, a village only a mile distant from Kánchanpur, an exorcist called *Bhutaḍiyá* (demon-expeller), or more commonly *ojhá*, whose fame was in all the neighbouring villages. This person was speedily sent for. As it will take some time before the mighty physician whose jurisdiction extends to the world of invisible spirits arrives, let me improve the interval by giving to the reader a brief account of the different classes of Bengali ghosts, their habits and modes of appearance, or strictly speaking, of Bengali-Hindu ghosts, for of Muhammadan ghosts, usually called *Mámdos*, who are regarded as infinitely more mischievous than Hindu ghosts, I do not at present enquire.

Of Bengali ghosts, that is, the spirits of Bengali men and Bengali women, there is a great variety; but there are five classes which generally make their appearance, if not in cities and towns—for they seem altogether to have left the seats of enlightenment and civilisation—at least in the villages of Bengal. The first and most honourable class of ghosts are those which pass by the name of *Brahmadaityas*, or the spirits of departed Bráhmans. They generally take up their abode in the branches of the *gayá-asvatha (Ficus cordifolia)*, the most sacred species of the *Ficus religiosa*, and also in the branches of the holy *sriphal (Ægle Marmelos)*. Unlike other ghosts, they do not eat all sorts of food, but only those which are considered religiously clean. They never appear, like other ghosts, to frighten men, such an object being beneath their dignity. They are for the most part inoffensive, never doing harm to benighted travellers, nor entering into the bodies of living men or women; but should their dignity be contemned, or their *sanctum sanctorum* be invaded or desecrated, their rage knows no bounds, and the neck of the offender is ruthlessly wrung and broken —a species of vengeance to which they are somewhat partial. Hence a Hindu will hardly ever climb up the *Ficus cordifolia* except in dire necessity; and if Bráhmans must often climb the *Ægle Marmelos* for obtaining the sacred trefoil so largely used in Bráhmanical worship, they do it only after offering prayers to the gods in general, and to the *Brahma-daitya* in particular who may have taken up his abode in the tree to be climbed.

Another class of ghosts, and they are by far the most numerous class, are simply called *bhútas*, that is, spirits. They are the spirits of departed Kshatriyas, Vaisyas, and Sudras. They are tall as palmyra trees, generally thin, and very black. They usually live on trees of every description, excepting those, of course, on which Bráhmanical ghosts have taken up their abode. At night, especially at midnight—the hour and power of darkness—they go about in the villages and fields, frightening night-walkers and belated travellers. They prefer dirty places to clean, and have never been seen in the precincts of the temples of the gods. They are always stark naked. They are rather fond of women, whom they usually possess. They eat rice and all sorts of human food, but their favourite dish is fish. Their partiality for fish is so well known, that a large bribe is necessary to induce a Bengali peasant to go at night from one place to another with some quantity of fish in his hand. If he has the foolhardiness to go, especially to the outskirts of a village and to the fields, he is sure to be attacked by a ghost or ghosts anxious to devour the fish. If two ghosts attack him, the peasant has reason to be thankful, for in that case the two ghosts are sure to quarrel with each other, and the peasant to escape scot free. The best way to defend one's self from the attack of a *bhúta*, is to repeat the names of the gods and goddesses, especially of Káli, Durgá, and Siva, the last one being named *bhútanath*, or, the lord of ghosts. Another mode of preventing the attack of a ghost is to carry with you a stick or rod of iron, a metal of which spirits are, somehow or other, greatly afraid. Hence Hindu peasants, who require in some seasons of the year to go out to the fields at night, carry with them rods of iron. But neither the repetition of the names of the gods and goddesses, nor an iron rod, will prevent a ghost from frightening a man from a distance; they are safeguards only against a ghost touching his person. All ghosts, owing to the peculiar conformation of their mouth, speak through the nose.

The *bhútas* are all male ghosts; but there are two classes of female ghosts, called *petnis* and *sánkhchihnis*. Of the *petnis* not much is known, except that they are terribly dirty—the stench of their bodies when near producing violent nausea in human beings; that they are very lascivious, trying to waylay benighted passengers for the gratification of their lusts; and that intercourse with them is sure to end in the destruction of both the body and of the soul. *Sánkhchihnis*, or *Sankhachurnis*, so called, in the opinion of some demonologists, because they put on clothes as white as *sankha* (conch-shell), and, in that of others, because they are fond of breaking conch-shells to pieces, are female ghosts, not so filthy as *petnis*, but equally dangerous. They usually stand at the dead of night at the foot of trees, and look like sheets of cloth as white as any fuller can make them.

Another class of ghosts are the *skandhakáṭás*, so called from the circumstance that their heads have been cut off from above their shoulders. These headless ghosts are probably the most terrible of the whole set, as they have never been known to spare any human being with whom they have come in contact. They generally dwell in low moist lands, outside a village, in bogs and fens, and go about in the dark, rolling on the ground, with their huge arms stretched out. Certain death awaits the belated peasant who falls within the folds of those gigantic arms. It is time, however, to put an end to this ghostly dissertation, as I perceive from the flutter amongst the inmates of Badan's house that the ghost doctor is at the door.

Before the arrival of the *ojhá* (ghost-doctor), Áduri had been carried *vi et armis* into Badan's sleeping-room, where she was jumping, dancing, stamping on the floor, making herself almost naked, now shrieking, now muttering unintelligible sounds. As soon as the *ojhá* entered the room, she sent forth an unearthly yell, and went to a corner. The exorcist, who was an able-bodied, middle-aged, rough-looking peasant, sat on a wooden plank on the floor, and began to blow with his mouth, and to utter some *mantras*, of which we give the following specimen :—

Dhulá sattam,
Madhu pattam,
Ládhulá karam sár;
Ási hájár koti bandam,
Teis hájár lár.
Je pathe yáya amuk chhede de kes,
Dain, yogini, pret, bhut,
Báo, bátás, deva, dut,
Káháro náiko nabaleo.
Kár ájná?
Kánader Kámákhya hádijhi chandir ájná:
Siggir lág, lág, lág.

Rising from his seat and approaching Áduri, the doctor said—"Who are you? Where do you live?"

Áduri, with a strong nasal accent, said—"What have you to do with me or my place of abode?"

Ojhá. "But you must tell me who you are, or you will feel the consequence."

Áduri. "Do your worst. I won't tell you who I am. I defy you to injure me."

Ojhá. "By Mahádeva! if you do not reply to my questions, I'll pound your bones in a mortar."

Áduri. "I won't reply to your questions."

On this the *ojhá* began to mutter the *mantras*, to blow with his mouth with all his might; and then belaboured poor Áduri with a bamboo twig which was in his hand. Áduri shrieked with agony, and then said, with the invariable nasal twang, that she was ready to answer all his questions.

Ojhá. "Who are you?"

Áduri. "I am a *bhúta*, a subject of Mahádeva."

Ojhá. "Where do you live?"

Áduri. "I formerly lived in the big mango-tree on the south-west corner of the tank *himásagara*; but some time ago I changed my residence, and have taken up my abode on the *tál* (palmyra) tree in the corner of Badan's house."

Ojhá. "Before you became *bhúta,* whose body did you animate in this world?"

Áduri. "That is a question which I am forbidden to answer. It is a secret of the spirit-world."

Ojhá. "But why have you come into the body of *chhoṭo bou?*

Áduri. "Because she is vain of her beauty, and because she looks into the faces of men and smiles."

Ojhá. "You must leave her immediately."

Áduri. "You cannot force me to leave her."

Ojhá. "I *can't,* you say? Just wait."

So saying, he again began unmercifully to flog Áduri, who flew about like lightning from one end of the room to the other, her eyes staring wildly, her hair dishevelled, her clothes falling off her body, the *ohjá* closely following. Thump succeeded thump. Groans, shrieks, and unearthly nasal sounds filled the room, and everyone present was horror-struck. After a little Áduri took breath and said, or rather the ghost in her, that she would go away in the course of an hour. The *ojhá* insisted on instant departure; and flagellation commenced afresh. At last the *ojhá* took out of his bag the root of a certain herb, wrapped it up in a *pán* leaf, and forced it into the mouth of Áduri, who chewed and swallowed it. She remained perfectly still for a few minutes. The *ojhá* again said: "Are you going immediately to leave *chhoṭo bou?*"

Áduri. "Yes."

Ojhá. "What sign will you give of your departure? How shall we know that you have left her?"

Áduri. "When I go away I shall carry with my teeth a curry-stone from this room to the end of the verandah."

Ojhá. "Very good."

The *ojhá* ordered the curry-stone of the family to be brought. It was about ten pounds in weight. Áduri caught it between her teeth and proceeded towards the door, the threshold of which she had scarcely stepped over when she fell down and fainted. Alanga, Sundari, and Málati—for the last had returned from her father-in-law's house—took her up insensible and in lock-jaw. A pair of *yánti* (nut-crackers made of iron) was pushed between her teeth, a little water was poured down her throat, and she revived. On becoming conscious she pulled the veil down her face, and, looking at Sundari, said in a whisper, "Why am I here, sister? Why are so many people assembled here?" The ghost-doctor, at whose supernatural skill everyone wondered, was rewarded with one rupée and an old *dhuti*, and the crowd dispersed. That night, and many following nights, Gayárám would not sleep in the same room with his wife; and he got reconciled to her only after she had been purified by a religious ceremony performed by the family priest.

CHAPTER XVII.

GOVINDA AT SCHOOL.

> And then the whining schoolboy, with his satchel,
> And shining morning-face, creeping like snail
> Unwillingly to school.
>
> *As You Like It.*

We must now return to our hero, and notice what progress he was making in reading and writing under that redoubtable pedagogue, Ráma Rúpa Sarkár, of Kánchanpur. We saw him on the first day trace his letters with chalk on the ground; he remained at it for about six months, after which he exchanged the ground for palmyra-leaves, and chalk for the reed and ink. I say the *reed*, for the natives of Bengal, whether Rájá or ráiyat, do not use goose-quill, or swan-quill, or steel pens; their *kalama* (*καλαμος*), is made of the reed *khágḍá* (*Saccharum spontaneum*), only the learned professors of Sanskrit *ṭols* or colleges prefer to it the more common bamboo. As for the writing material, slates were unknown, till they were introduced into the country by the English, and are used only in schools organised on the English model. The leaves of the fan-palm are preferable to slates for beginners, for three reasons:—in the *first* place, the palm-leaf costs nothing, especially in the villages; *secondly*, it is more lasting, as it never breaks, and seldom tears; *thirdly*, it is lighter than a slate, and therefore can be more easily carried by children. Provided with a bundle of about twenty pieces of the palmyra-leaf under his left arm, the reed-pen resting on the upper hollow of his right ear, an earthen ink-pot in his left hand, and his right hand free, our hero used every morning and afternoon to go to the *páṭhśálá*, with other boys of the neighbourhood. He always returned home with his hands, face, and *dhuti* bespattered with ink; for whenever he wrote on the palm-leaf a wrong letter or an ill-formed one, he immediately used to brush it off with his hand, or his wrist. But Alanga and Sundari were rather pleased with the sight than otherwise, for the abundance of ink on his body and clothes only showed how diligent their darling was in his studies.

In the old-fashioned, orthodox village *páṭhśálás*, which are even now found all over the country, a boy only writes for some years, and does a little arithmetic, but seldom reads a book, the two subjects to which the greatest attention is paid being caligraphy and arithmetic. Early in the morning, when Govinda went to school, he spent some hours in writing the fifty letters of the Bengali alphabet, the compound letters which are so puzzling to foreigners, the numerals from one to a hundred, and the like. Before the forenoon school was dismissed he recited, in a chorus with other boys, those compound letters and the numerals. In the afternoon school he again wrote those very things, and in the evening, before being dismissed, recited in a sing-song manner, along with other boys, the whole of the Multiplication Table up to twenty times twenty, a table with which Bengali boys are more familiar than any other boys in the world. Next to the writing of the alphabet followed the writing of proper names, especially of persons; the names of all the boys in the school, and those of the major part of the inhabitants of the village successively, appeared on the stage of the palm-leaf.

The study of arithmetic went on *pari passu* with caligraphy and orthography. First came a lot of arithmetical tables, which were all committed to memory; addition, both simple and compound, followed; next, subtraction, both simple and compound; then the boy at once passed on—for Bengali arithmetic has not the formal processes of multiplication and division—to what in European arithmetic is called Proportion, or the Rule of Three, but which in Bengali goes by the various names *serkashá, mankashá, kánchánámáshá, sudkashá* (interest), *káthá-káli, bighákáli* (mensuration), according to the subjects to which the doctrine of Proportion is applied. The reader must not suppose that Govinda went through this course of arithmetic; his school course was cut short, as we shall see by-and-by, after he had mastered compound subtraction. As slates are not used in the village schools, and black-boards are as unknown in the *páṭhśálás* as Babbage's Calculating Machine, and as palm-leaves are ill adapted for containing long rows of figures, all arithmetical operations are carried on, at least for some years in a boy's school life, on the mud floor of the school-house.

The lowest class of a Bengali *páṭhśálá*, of the primitive orthodox fashion, is the chalk or *floor class;* in this class Govinda remained about six months. The next class is the *palm-leaf class,* in which our hero studied for about three years. In the beginning of his fourth year he was promoted to the *plantain-leaf class.* Higher than the plantain-leaf class is the *paper class,* in which boys write on paper instead of on plantain-leaves; but Govinda's education did not come up so high. His education ended in the plantain-leaf class, of which some detailed account may not be unacceptable to the reader. Govinda now threw away his palm-leaves, and took to the plantain, of the leaves of which he had an abundant supply in his own house; but if the supply was now and then exhausted in consequence of the celebration of a feast, on which occasion plantain-leaves do, as we have seen, the duty of plates, he had only to beg or borrow, or to steal them from neighbouring houses or gardens. Govinda now gave up the writing of merely personal names, and took to epistolary composition. This same study of epistolary composition, or correspondence, is a most important branch of Bengali education, and is pursued for years in the village *páṭhśálás.* Essay-writing is unknown in the primitive schools of Bengal, simply because it is not necessary to the purposes of life. Whatever is required in practical life is assiduously studied; and it must be acknowledged that the writing of letters is of essential importance to persons engaged in business. Nor is Bengali letter-writing an easy task. There are hundreds of set forms in which men are to be addressed according to their station in life, and to the relations in which they stand to the writer. The form in which the writer of a letter should address his father is different from that in which he should address his uncle, and the paternal uncle different from that in which he should address his maternal uncle; and the same is true of all the degrees of consanguinity and relationship; so that the set forms of epistolary address are practically infinite. On this dark and unfathomable ocean of epistolary composition our hero was now launched.

By the way, our English schools and colleges in Bengal might take a hint in this respect from the village *páṭhśálá*. Our educated young men, our B.A.'s and M.A.'s in general, can hardly write a common letter in every-day English. They will write you a long Essay on the Feudal System in Europe, or a critique on "Macbeth," or an analysis of "The Flower and the Leaf;" but they will murder the Queen's English in writing a common business letter. There must be something vicious, something essentially wrong, in such a system of education. Of the two systems, the system of the village *páṭhśálá*, which aims at the practical and the useful, is infinitely more sensible. By all means have the ornamental part of education, but do not sacrifice utility to ornament. An M.A. and Fellow of the Calcutta University, when joining his appointment at a Mofussil Station, thus notified his arrival to his official superior: "Sir, I beg to inform you that I have arrived here yesterday." *O tempora! O mores!* Can nothing be done to remedy this disgraceful state of things?

It may be easily believed that our hero was often subjected to that system of disciplinary correction of which Ráma Rúpa was so warm an advocate. A peasant's son, young, vigorous, and in rude health, Govinda hated the restraints of a school, and often played the truant. Instead of going to school he often repaired to the high embankment of some distant tank, or to some mango tope or tamarind grove, and there played with boys tending cattle. Ráma Rúpa, however, adopted vigorous measures for the seizing of truants. He had formed a sort of detective police, consisting of four able-bodied *sardárpoḍos*, or senior pupils, who were sent out whenever a truant had to be caught. Whenever Govinda was absent from school, these detectives went to his house, and asked his mother or grandmother where he was. If told that he had gone to school as usual, they sought for him in the outskirts of the village, and especially his favourite haunts, and invariably captured him. If he showed resistance, his legs would be caught hold of by two of the lads, and his arms by the other two. Thus suspended between four stout bearers, Govinda, half dead with fright, was often brought to the *páṭhśálá*, and there well thrashed by the pedagogue. This detective police was useful to the village schoolmaster in other ways. Whenever there was a feast in his house—and feasts are ever and anon occurring in Hindu houses, however poor—and he stood in need of plantain-leaves, to serve as plates for his guests, he had only to order his detectives to procure them; and they forthwith entered some garden and stole plantain-leaves for their teacher, who, asking no question for conscience sake, gladly received them with thanks.

Govinda was successively going through these varied processes of mental quickening, healthy discipline, and excellent moral training, when his school career was suddenly brought to a close by an accident, a description of which must be reserved for a future chapter.

CHAPTER XVIII.

THE SATÍ.

> O sight of misery!
> You cannot hear her cries—their sound
> In that wild dissonance is drown'd;
> But in her face you see
> The supplication and the agony;
> See in her swelling throat the desperate strength
> That with vain effort struggles yet for life;
> Her arms contracted now in fruitless strife,
> Now wildly at full length
> Towards the crowd in vain for pity spread;
> They force her on, they bind her to the dead.
>
> *Curse of Kehama.*

It was somewhere about this time, when Govinda was between seven and eight years of age, that he witnessed one of those horrible scenes which, in former times, were daily enacted on the plains, and especially on the banks of the sacred Bhágirathi, but which, thanks to the enlightened humanity of the British Government, have now been altogether suppressed. Every one at Kánchanpur had taken his midday meal—for the hour was about three o'clock in the afternoon—and Govinda was on his way to the *páthsálá,* with his bundle of palm-leaves and mud ink-pot, when his ears were regaled with a peculiar beat of the drum which he had never heard before. As the sound proceeded from near the house of his father's family priest, Rámdhan Misra, Govinda, instead of going to school, turned towards that lane, especially as he saw numbers of men, women, and children were running in that direction. Rámdhan Misra's father had died that morning, and the peculiar beat of the drum, to which we have alluded, announced to the inhabitants of the village that his wife, or rather widow, had resolved to burn herself on the same funeral pile with her husband. Govinda entered the house with difficulty, as it was filled with a large crowd. In the middle of the court-yard of the house he saw Rámdhan's mother sitting surrounded by a great many women. Far from weeping on account of the death of her husband, she was every now and then laughing, and seemed to be the gayest of the gay. She looked clean and bathed; the nails of her fingers and toes had been pared off by a female barber, and the sides of her feet, as well as the tips of her toes, had been painted red with the *alakta;* she was dressed in a suit of new clothes, or rather in a new *sáṭí;* she was dazzling in ornaments in all parts of her body; her forehead was painted red with vermilion; her lips were red with the paint of catechu and lime in the *pán* which she was chewing; and she waved in her hand a small twig of the mango tree with leaves; altogether, she looked not as a widow mourning for her deceased partner, but "prepared as a bride adorned for her husband." The dead body of her husband had been already carried to the place of cremation, and she was about to follow thither. As she walked through the streets—for the burning place was in the outskirts of the village—she said to the hundreds of men and women who had flocked to see her, that that was the day of her marriage, the happiest day of her life; and she raised the well-known marriage shout, *ulu! ulu! ulu!* There was not a single person in the village, male or female, who did not look upon her with the utmost reverence. They called her *satí*, or the Chaste One, by way of eminence, as her conjugal fidelity was such that she was following her husband into the invisible world. They compared her to Sávitri—the ideal of a Hindu wife, and praised her for her extraordinary piety, her conjugal faithfulness, and her heroic fortitude. As the procession went on, exclamations of *ulu! ulu! ulu! Hari bol! Hari bol! Hari bol!* rent the air; and the deafening *tom-toms* kept time with those sounds. At last the procession reached the side of the tank, where the pile had been prepared, on which the body of the deceased had been already laid. The pile was between seven and eight feet long, about four broad, and three high. There was a goodly array of faggots and flax; a pot filled with clarified butter was also there.

The *sati* now took off the ornaments from her body, and distributed them amongst her friends and relations, who were standing around her; and she threw among the crowd handfuls of fried paddy (*khadi*), and shells (*kaḍi*), which she had with her. Great was the scramble among the crowd for the fried paddy and the shells, for it was believed that they had the singular property of miraculously healing all sorts of diseases. Mothers not unfrequently tied one or two of these shells round the necks of their children as a charm against all disease. Govinda was fortunate enough to get one of these shells, which he carefully secured in a corner of his *dhuti*. She next went through the ceremony of *pradakshin*, that is, she went seven times round the pile on which the body of her deceased husband had been laid, scattering about her all the time fried paddy and shells.

Circumambulation over, she went up to the pile with unfaltering steps, and laid herself down beside the body of her deceased husband. The living and the dead were now tied together by strong ropes, and faggots were heaped upon them. A death-like stillness followed. Rámdhan, the son of the living and the dead, now approached the pile with a lighted faggot in his hand, to discharge the last offices of filial affection prescribed in the holy books. With averted eyes he applied the faggot to the mouth of his deceased father, and to the pile. The pile blazed up in a moment, and the women and other relations of the deceased set up a loud scream. As the flame reached the *satí's* body, she shrieked; but the drums were beat in full chorus, to drown the cries of the unhappy woman. More faggots were applied, and quantities of *ghi*, or clarified butter, were poured upon them to aid the combustion.

But lo! the *satí* has disengaged herself from the ropes by which she had been tied. She sits up. She stretches out her hands imploringly. She screams. She attempts to escape. The intoxication of superstition had hitherto kept her up, but she now gives way to nature. But in vain. The drums are now beat at their loudest; deafening shouts of *Hari bol! Hari bol!* pierce the skies; and by means of two bamboos, which were kept in readiness, the *satí* is prevented from getting down. It is all over with her. She has fallen a victim to grim superstition. More faggots and *ghi* were had in requisition till the bodies were quite consumed. What Govinda felt on witnessing this shocking scene I know not, for he has left no record of his thoughts; but it is not too much to assert that there was not a single man or woman in all Kánchanpur who felt that there was anything wrong in that dreadful act of self-murder; on the contrary, all regarded it as an act of the highest piety, and looked upon the unfortunate victim of Bráhmanical superstition as an especial favourite of Heaven.

This was the last time when the *satí* rite was performed at Kánchanpur, for in a few months after this event, Lord William Bentinck, one of the most beneficent of rulers that ever wielded the destinies of an empire, had the moral courage to enact, on 4th December, 1829, that law which for ever put a stop to that murderous practice.

CHAPTER XIX.

EVENINGS AT HOME.

I could a tale unfold, whose lightest word
Would harrow up thy soul; freeze thy young blood;
Make thy two eyes, like stars, start from their spheres;
Thy knotted and combined locks to part,
And each particular hair to stand on end,
Like quills upon the fretful porcupine.
Hamlet.

I FORGET whether I told the English reader—for the Bengali reader does not require to be told it—that in the village of Kánchanpur there was no such thing as a tavern. There was, indeed, a grog shop in the outskirts of the village, where spirits distilled from rice were sold, but it was resorted to only by the lowest people, like *háḍis* and *ḍoms*, people much lower in social status than the agricultural class to which Badan belonged. Besides, in the grog shop no company could be had; people went there merely for drink, and after getting what they wanted, they returned to their homes. Badan and any member of his family would no more think of drinking spirits or wine than of committing murder—the former habit being reckoned almost as heinous a crime as the latter. Badan, Kálamánik, and Gayárám, therefore, generally spent their evenings at home; only now and then they visited their friends. In the summer months, beginning in February and ending about the middle of June, after returning from their day's work in the field, and after they had washed their feet and hands, they spread a mat in the court-yard, sat upon it cross-legged, smoked, and talked on the events of the day. Alanga often sat near them, not on the mat, but on the ground at a little distance, and joined in the conversation. The subjects of conversation were often the state of the weather; bullocks; the progress made in ploughing, or harrowing, or sowing, or irrigating; the zamindár's rent; and the *mahájan's* (money-lender's) interest. In all these matters old Alanga took as keen an interest as Badan himself. Sometimes a neighbour dropped in, to whom was administered the never-failing hospitality of the hookah.

Govinda was invariably present at these evening parties. At sun-down, he returned from the *páṭhśálá;* put away in a corner of the verandah of the big hut his bundle of palmyra-leaves, his reed-pen, and earthen pot of ink; washed his hands, feet, and mouth, at the tank; ate in the kitchen his *dál* and *bhát*, dealt to him either by his mother or his grandmother—for, as a little boy, he could not wait so late as eight or nine o'clock, when the men and the women (excepting Alanga, who, as a widow, had only one meal), usually had their supper: and sat on the mat in the yard beside his father and uncles. Sitting there he was made to recite the Multiplication Table, and other lessons which he had learnt at school. Badan, though not initiated into the mysteries of reading and writing, often put arithmetical questions to his son and heir. The following are specimens of the questions he put:

"If for one pice you get ten plantains, how many plantains would you get for four pice?"

"If for one pice you get ten plantains, what would be the price of fifty plantains?"

The first time Badan proposed such questions, Govinda in his simplicity, asked,

"Which sort of plantains, *Bábá?* (*Bábá* being invariably used in Bengali for papa.) Is it the *martamána*, or the *kántáli* kind?"

Badan, giving a smile significant of superior wisdom, sagely replied,

"It does not matter, Govin, what sort of plantain it is, the calculation is all the same."

Over a question, Govinda would sometimes spend a quarter of an hour, and Badan, fearing that the little mathematician had fallen asleep, would ask,

"Are you sleeping, Govin?" when Govinda would immediately answer,

"No, Bábá, I am not sleeping; I am calculating it in my mind."

But Badan had the good sense not to torture him with a large number of questions; after one or two questions, he allowed him to do whatever he chose. And what Govinda chose every night to do, was to go to a neighbouring hut, which was occupied by an old woman famous for story-telling.

Sambhu's mother—so the old woman was called —was about fifty years of age, a widow, who supported herself by spinning thread and selling it to weavers. She had a son of the name of Sambhu, who, being about ten years old, made himself useful and earned a little money by tending the cows of a neighbour. Sambhu's mother was acknowledged to be the best story-teller in her part of the village, and was therefore looked upon with admiring awe by all the children. As soon as the lamps were lit, children dropped in into her hut, sometimes singly, sometimes in groups of two or three, to listen to the marvellous upakathás (stories) of Sambhu's mother. It was this party of children that Govinda joined every night after extricating himself from the arithmetical cross-examination of his father and uncles. The old woman sat in her hut before a dim lamp, the oil of which was supplied to her every evening by one or other of her infantile audience. She was not, however, idle while reciting stories, she incessantly turned the *charká* which went round merrily to the tune of *ghnan, ghnan, ghnan.* When describing a pathetic or an awful scene she would drop the handle of the wheel from her right hand, and the carded cotton from her left, and make gestures suitable to the narrative.

Sambhu's mother's stories were usually on three subjects—kings and queens, ghosts, and the travels of four friends. Every king of Sambhu's mother had two queens, one of whom, called *Suo,* was always good; and the other, called *Duo,* was always bad; and the story always ended in the punishment of the bad queen and the prosperity of the good one. "Four Friends in Travel" was the stock-theme of another class of stories; and though their adventures were different in different stories, the four friends were always the same, viz., *ráj-putra* (king's son), *pátrer-putra* (minister's son), *koṭoáler-putra* (son of the prefect of the police), and *sadágarer-putra* (merchant's son). But the most popular of all her stories were those about ghosts, in reciting which she exerted her utmost powers of description. When describing the approach of a ghost, she would lower her voice into a whisper, and when the ghost spoke she always spoke through the nose. On such occasions the young listeners always got frightened; they drew towards each other and towards Sambhu's mother; they felt a shiver through the system, and their hair stood on end. When the last story of the night was a ghost-story, the children were afraid to go to their homes singly; they formed themselves into a group, from which each one dropped off as he came to the door of his house, the boldest of the company being the last to reach home. Though Govinda was the story-teller's next-door neighbour, he never could go home alone after hearing a ghost-story; his comrades always accompanied him not only to the door, but to the inside of his house. These ghost-stories, volumes of which are heard by every Bengali boy, produce two effects on his mind —they strengthen his idea of the supernatural, and make him timid and cowardly.

CHAPTER XX.

THE HINDU WIDOW.

> Sche weepeth, weyleth, cryeth piteously;
> To slen hirself sche wayteth pryvyly.
>
> *The Knighte's Tale.*

It was the month of August. The elephants of the quarters were dipping their gigantic trunks in the universal ocean, and scattering the limpid element in the face of the heavens. The rain was descending in torrents, each drop of which was so thick and heavy, that the people of Kánchanpur compared it to the pestle of a pedal; and the oldest inhabitant of the village declared that he had never seen since his birth such copious showers. The embankments of the mighty Ajaya broke, the banks of the Máyá overflowed, the country for miles was under water, and Kánchanpur looked like an island in the ocean. All husbandry was of course put an end to; the cows were pent up in their folds; and the peasants either smoked in idleness or spun packthread in their rude reels, except those adventurous spirits who went out with hand-nets to catch fish in the surrounding waters. When, after a few days, the waters had subsided, and the balks of the paddy fields were just visible, Badan, Kálamánik, and Gayáram went to see those fields on which grew the *Áus* paddy, which before the late heavy rains was almost ready for the sickle. Each of the three brothers had the peasant's *pánchan* or bamboo stick in his hand, without which they never went to the fields. As Gayárám was walking upon a balk between two paddy fields, a *keuṭiya* serpent, a species of cobra di capella, jet black in complexion, about three cubits in length, reared its hooded head above the waters, stood almost bolt upright for a second, and darted like lightning towards him. It was not unlike those snakes in the forests of Calabria, of which Virgil speaks in his "Georgics," a passage from which we give in Dryden's translation:—

In fair Calabria's woods a snake is bred,
With curling crest and an advancing head:
Waving he rolls, and makes a winding track;
His belly spotted, burnished is his back.
While springs are broken, while the southern air
And dropping heavens the moistened earth repair,
He lives on standing lakes and trembling bogs,
And fills his maw with fish, or with loquacious frogs.

Such was the snake which made a dash against Gayárám. There was no time to escape. In the twinkling of an eye the serpent darted its fangs near his ankle-joint, turned again, and gave a second bite. Kálamánik, who was at a short distance, rushed forward, and with one blow of his heavy bamboo, put an end to the malignant career of the venomous reptile. But it was too late. The poison of the *keuṭiya* is quicker in its effects than that of almost any other species of serpent. Gayárám dropped down. Badan, who had now come up to the spot, tied his *gámchhá* (bathing towel) above the part bitten, and with the assistance of Kálamánik carried him home. The women set up a loud lamentation. The neighbours, and the inhabitants of the village in general, came in crowds, and were struck with horror. Many were the prayers silently offered to the goddess Manasá Devi, the goddess of snakes, for Gayárám's recovery. Some proposed one drug, some another; at last it was decided that the famous *mál* (serpent-catcher) of Chandraháṭi, a village two miles distant, who was a well-known curer of serpent-bite, should be sent for. The only thing that Badan did in the meantime, was to bind the leg tightly above the ankle, and to wash the wound with milk. But the poison was evidently working into the system. Gayárám now shrieked in agony, and now was falling into a stupor, and they tried their best to keep him awake. As Gayárám was very young, very gentle in his disposition, and never did any injury to any one, the sympathy of the whole village was excited on his behalf. Many old women proposed many nostrums, some of which were tried, but without effect.

The *mál* of Chandraháṭi at last arrived, and immediately began operations. He rubbed down the body of Gayárám, as if trying to bring down the poison which had coursed up; blew over it with his mouth, and muttered many *mantras*, one of which was as follows:—

Háya more ki holo!
Ghaṭáite bish molo!
Nái bish, bishárir ájná.

But the *ojhá* did not resort to mere charms and incantations. He made the patient swallow several roots of plants reduced to powder, and a substance which looked very like *nousádar* (ammonia), though he refused to mention its name. The whole night the *mál* tried his utmost, now calling upon the gods, chiefly Mahádeva; now rubbing down the body; now blowing with his mouth; now administering drugs. But in vain. Before dawn, Gayárám was a lifeless corpse.

This dreadful event filled with unutterable sorrow the members of the humble family whose fortunes form the subject of this book. Badan felt as if his right hand had been cut off, for though Gayárám was the youngest of the three, he had wisdom beyond his years, and often gave salutary advice in times of difficulty. Kálamánik, though less demonstrative than Badan, and somewhat stern and unengaging in his outward demeanour, had within his rough exterior the sterling gold of a truly generous and sympathetic nature; and his inward agony of mind at the premature and terribly sudden loss of an affectionate brother, which was all the more intense that it found no outlet, visibly told on his health. Alanga's grief was infinite. As the deceased was her youngest son, she had perhaps greater affection for him than for the other two. Day and night she wept over her son prematurely cut off. She began and ended the day with lamentations, her mournful dirge being often prolonged to the silent and solemn hour of midnight. For a long time she did not touch the *charká*, but spent the afternoon in loud lamentations, which might have been heard from distant huts, and in which she dwelt on every feature of the person and every trait of the character of her favourite son. It was Rachel weeping for her child, and refusing to be comforted because he was not. The recollection of the sort of death which Gayárám had met with added to the poignancy of Alanga's grief. It was an unnatural death. Death by serpent-bite, by lightning, by fire, by a fall, and other sorts of accidental and sudden end, are regarded as visitations from the gods for sin. And Alanga could not understand why *they*, of all people in the village, should be visited with such a dreadful calamity. She said to herself: "Don't we fear and worship the gods? Don't we respect Bráhmans? Don't we give alms according to our means? Don't we practise the usual religious ceremonies? Why then should the gods be angry with us? What sin have we committed that we should be visited with so heavy a calamity? O Vidhátá! was this in thy mind?"

Áduri's sorrow was, however, the gloomiest, though perhaps less disinterested than Alanga's. It was the blackness of dark despair. Her married life was now at an end. Though young, she must remain a widow all her life. Association with a husband is regarded as the *summum bonum* of womanly existence. Is life worth anything now that happiness has become impossible? What made her saddest was the horrible prospect of perpetual widowhood. Her sun had gone down while it was noon. Hope, that comes to all, never visited her. The rest of her life—if life it could be called—was to be one continued midnight, without the remotest prospect of a dawn. It is impossible not to sympathise with a Hindu widow. It is not that she is persecuted and tormented by her relations and friends—that is a fiction of foreign writers, of people unacquainted with Hindu life in its actual manifestations—but the peculiar wretchedness of her condition lies in this, that the fountain of her heart, with its affections and desires, is for ever dried up. She becomes a soulless thing, and her life a blank. Áduri did not, like Alanga, fill the house and the neighbourhood with her cries, nor did she expatiate in her lamentations on every good quality of her amiable husband. Such a thing would have been deemed indecent in a widow. Her grief was a silent grief. She sobbed day and night. She broke her ornaments, whether of conch-shell, or sealing-wax, or silver; she broke the iron ring on her wrist, the symbol of wifehood; she no longer braided her hair; she gave up daubing the top of her forehead with vermilion, which distinguishes a Hindu wife from a Hindu widow; she gave up putting on *sáṭis* with coloured borders. Her share of the pleasures of life had been exhausted; her part on the theatre of life had been played out: henceforth, though in the world, she was not to be of the world.

English people have, somehow or other, got the idea that a Hindu widow receives harsh and cruel treatment from the relations of her husband. This is not true. There are no doubt exceptional cases, but, as a general rule, Hindu widows are not only not ill treated, but they meet with a vast deal of sympathy. Old widows in a Bengali Hindu family are often the guides and counsellors of those who style themselves the lords of creation. We had the happiness of being acquainted with a venerable old Hindu widow who was not only the mistress of her own house, consisting of a considerable number of middle-aged men and women, but she was often the referee of important disputes in the village of which she was an inhabitant, and her decisions were received with the highest respect. Nor is this an exceptional case. Old widows, provided they have intelligence and good character, assert, on account of their experience in life, their superiority over men younger than they. As to the privations of widows, a little too much is made of them. Besides the one supreme privation of having the fountain of their affections sealed up, the others, of which foreign writers make so much, are not worth speaking about. The most considerable of these minor privations is that only one meal is permitted them in twenty-four hours. But this restraint will cease to be regarded as a privation when it is considered that a widow's meal is usually larger in quantity and heavier in weight than that of a married woman; that the meal is taken in the afternoon not many hours before sleep; that most widows are sleek and stout; and that many of the strong and able-bodied peasants of the North Western Provinces, and the Hindu Sepoys in the Bengal army, take only one meal in twenty-four hours. Let not the reader suppose that we are extenuating the misery of Áduri. Her case was truly pitiable. Though not anticipating unkind treatment from the rest of the family, she felt that she was socially dead; at any rate, that she was ALONE in the world.

This calamitous event in Badan's little household altogether changed the colour and complexion of our hero's destiny. It is idle to conjecture what he might have become if his education had been carried on; he might perhaps have become a *moharir* (clerk), a *gomastá* (agent), or a *naib* (manager) to a zamindár. But the untimely death of Gayárám put an end to all those hopes. Govinda could not be conveniently allowed to continue his studies. Gayárám had charge of the cows and of the bullocks. Now that he is gone to the other world, who is to attend on them? Badan and Kálamánik were required for cultivation; and the women—excepting little girls—of Badan's class of peasants do not usually tend cows in the field. The resolution was at once taken that Govinda should no longer go to the *páṭhśálá*. Thus closed our hero's career at school, where he had learned to add, to subtract, and to sign his name. But there is another education quite different from that which is given in schools; how Govinda profited by it will be seen in subsequent chapters.

CHAPTER XXI.

ODDS AND ENDS.

> There is a tear for all that die,
> A mourner o'er the humblest grave.
>
> *Byron.*

AFTER the terribly sudden death of Gayárám, the family in whose fortunes we are interested became unclean for a month; for what is called mourning amongst Europeans, is called *ásoucha* (uncleanness) amongst Hindus, not unlike the custom of the Jews of old. Upon people whose life is a continual scene of privation, *ásoucha* does not press heavily: still it entailed some hardship on the little family. Fish, which is an essential accompaniment of Bengali diet, being eaten along with rice both at mid-day and at night, was not touched by any member of the family during the thirty days of uncleanness. To Alanga alone this was no privation, as she had ceased to be piscivorous since the commencement of her widowhood. Free social intercourse with friends was not cultivated, as a person who is unclean cannot touch another without defiling him. The hair on Badan's chin and forehead—parts which are always shaven, unless a Hindu, like the Jewish Nazarite, dedicates it to some god—was suffered to grow; and mustard oil, with which a Bengali, whether Rájá or ráiyat, anoints his body before bathing, and which makes his face to shine, was discontinued. The greatest austerities are naturally practised by the nearest relations of a deceased person—by his eldest son and his widow; but as Gayárám had no children, they were practised by Áduri alone. She put on the same piece of *sáṭi*—without a coloured border—day and night for a whole month; and after bathing every day, she kept on her person the *sáṭi* dripping wet, till it dried of itself. She did not join the family meal, and did not eat what had been cooked by others; she cooked for herself: nor was she allowed to eat what the others ate—she had to be satisfied with one meal a day of simple *átap* rice, boiled with a little milk or clarified butter. In this manner, Áduri and the rest spent the whole of the unclean month. On the thirtieth day took place the purification. The male members of the family were shaved by the family barber, and the female barber pared the nails of the fingers and toes of the women. They then bathed in a tank, put on new clothes, performed certain religious ceremonies called *sráddha*, with the assistance of the family priest—and thus became clean, and restored to the society and communion of their fellow-men.

We have more than once, in the course of this narrative, spoken of Badan's family *guru*, or spiritual director, family priest, and family barber of both sexes; and the English reader may ask how could a poor man like Badan, a mere cultivator of the soil, afford to keep such expensive articles as a father-confessor, a priest, and a barber. But whether they are expensive or not, those three gentlemen are essentially necessary to every Hindu family. There cannot be a Hindu family which has not its *guru*, its *purohita*, its *nápita;* and the reason is that there cannot be a Hindu family without its religion, religion being interwoven with social manners and customs.

Nor are these officers expensive. Gangá Nápita, the barber, once a fortnight shaved the forehead and chin of Badan, Kálamánik, and afterwards of our hero; and his worthy partner in life, whose name we never heard, as she was always called *Napitni*, or more familiarly *Napteni*, once a month pared the nails of the women. And what did the couple receive for these fortnightly and monthly services? Why, not more than half a *man* (maund) of paddy about the time of harvest, the price of which in the days of which we are speaking could not have been more than four annas, or sixpence, besides some occasional presents at a marriage, on purification after the death of a member of the family, at the birth of a child, and the like. The *purohita* (priest) of the family, Rámdhan Misra, the same whose mother became *satí*, who officiated at births, marriages, deaths, and all religious celebrations, hardly received anything except the offerings (consisting of rice, plantains, and the like) made to the gods on those occasions, and occasional presents of the products of the earth in their seasons, like brinjal, potatoes, pulse, sugar-cane. Though most Águris are of the *Sákta* sect, Badan was a Vaishnava, and had therefore a *gosvámi* for his *guru*, or spiritual guide, whose name was Vrındávana Gosvámi, of the village of Áográm, many miles distant from Kánchanpur. He visited the family once a year in the course of his ecclesiastical visitation, the object of which was not so much the imparting of ghostly instruction as the fleecing his flock as much as he possibly could. Indeed, he did not give instruction at all. The only thing he ever did to any disciple during that disciple's lifetime was to whisper once into his ear one or two unmeaning sounds like *kling krishna*, or *ring dhung*, or *dhung phaṭ*, which unmeaning sounds are called *vija-mantras*, or *seed-prayers*, and which the disciple had to repeat, either mentally or in a whisper, every day of his life at least one hundred-and-eight times. When the gosvámi inflicted Badan with his annual visit, he had to give him an eight-anna piece (a shilling), except on occasions of initiation into the *seed-prayers*, when the spiritual guide expected perquisites. The English reader may think that the *guru* is the bishop, and the *purohita* is his curate; such is, however, not the case. The two persons are quite independent of, and may be unknown to, each other, their functions being entirely different. The *guru* is something like a Father Confessor, and the *purohita* like a Chaplain. The intelligent reader will thus perceive that a Bengali ráiyat like Badan is not too poor to entertain the services of a Father Confessor, a domestic chaplain, and a family surgeon —for Gangá Nápita wielded both the razor and the lancet—since the total annual cost for keeping those three dignitaries did not come up to more than six shillings.

It may be asked again by the simple English reader, if the remuneration of the spiritual guide, the priest and the barber, be so little, how do they maintain themselves and their families? In the first place, these three personages render services to a great many people, and every little makes a muckle. The barber of Badan was the barber of hundreds of other people in the village, since every Hindu requires the services of the craft, and no Hindu shaves himself; Badan's priest was the priest of a great many other families, some of whom were rich, and gave him a great deal; while Badan's spiritual guide had disciples, not only at Kánchanpur, but in hundreds of other villages scattered all over the country, from all of whom he received his yearly stipend. In the second place, the spiritual priest and barber do not depend for their livelihood on the income of their trade or profession: each has some acres of land, which he cultivates by employing labourers.

In the villages of Bengal, nearly all classes of people, excepting the peasantry, get their clothes washed by members of the *dhobá* caste, who have been washermen from generation to generation. In Badan's house the women did the washing, which took place once a month. On such occasions, the clothes, put in *hánḍis* containing water, cow's urine, and ashes—especially the ashes of burnt plantain trees, which have a powerful alkaline property—were subjected to the process of boiling, and then taken out to the tank near the house and beaten upon a plank or a big stone, and subsequently washed in water and put in the sun. Exceptionally fine clothes, like those worn on high days and holidays, were given to the professional washerman. I should, however, remark that every member of Badan's family washed in water his or her *dhuti* or *sáṭi* every day at the time of bathing, as it is reckoned unclean, from a ceremonial point of view, to put on during the day the same piece of cloth in which a person has slept at night. Hence a Hindu, though poor, must have two pieces of cloth—one to bathe in (bathing naked being unknown in the country), and another to put on while the first one is drying in the sun; and if a peasant be the poorest of the poor he has his *gámchhá*, or bathing-towel, which he wraps round his waist whilst his *dhuti* is drying. Considering that Bengali Hindu peasants bathe every day throughout the year, and every day wash their clothes in water, we have no hesitation in saying that they are about the cleanest peasantry in the world.

CHAPTER XXII.

PASTORAL SCENES.

A various group the herds and flocks compose:
Rural confusion! On the grassy bank
Some ruminating lie; while others stand
Half in the flood, and, often bending, sip
The circling surface. In the middle droops
The strong laborious ox, of honest front,
Which, incomposed, he shakes; and from his sides
The troublous insects lashes with his tail,
Returning still.

Thomson's Seasons.

OUR hero has bidden adieu to the school of Ráma Rúpa, and enrolled himself a student in the great school of Dame Nature. He has done with primers, with palmyra and plantain-leaves—at least so far as writing on them is concerned; while the music of the multiplication table he has exchanged for the harmony of warblers of the grove. We have seen what Govinda did every day when he attended the *páṭhśálá;* let us now see what he did every day after he had been installed neat-herd of the family.

Govinda rose early every morning before crow-cawing, went to the straw-loft, took down some bundles of paddy straw, and, with the assistance of his uncle Kálamánik, began chopping them with a large sickle called *bonṭi.* With the chopped straw, mixed with water and some pieces of mustard oil-cakes, he filled those *nánds* or earthen tubs, which were half sunk in the ground on the yard near the stack of straw. Having made ready their food, he brought out of the cow-house all the cows and bullocks, and tied them to their respective tubs. While the cows were munching their breakfast, he went into the cow-house, made a heap of the dung in a corner of the yard, and threw the refuse into the dunghill behind the kitchen. He next swept the cow-house and made it as clean as he could, strewing the wet places with ashes. After some time the cows were milked; but as Govinda was not yet equal to the operation, he contented himself for some time with merely catching hold of the calves by their ears, while Kálamánik, sitting on his toes in a kneeling posture, and resting the milk-can between his knee-joints, went on milking, at a great rate, to the delightful tune of *chan-cho, chan-cho, chan-cho.* The next thing he did was that he went out, with a large quantity of the milk and a half *seer* measure, to a Bráhman family in the neighbourhood who had contracted with Badan for a daily supply. On returning home he made preparations for going out to the fields with the cows. These preparations consisted in putting a quantity of tobacco in an earthen cup—for our hero, though only twelve years old, had already taken to smoking—in pouring a little quantity of mustard oil into a *chongá* (bamboo phial) to anoint his body with before bathing, and in tying some fried rice in his *gámchhá.* The preparations over, he loosened the cows, and took them out to graze beside a large tank, where was an *asvatha* tree, in the shade of which were sitting four lads who had evidently come on the same errand as Govinda. On seeing him one of the lads said, "Hullo, Gove, what is the matter? We thought you were not coming to-day."

Govinda. "I am a little late to-day. I was delayed in the house of the Bhaṭṭacháryas, where I stopped a long time before they took milk. The *ginni* (mistress) had gone to bathe, and there was nobody in the house to take milk."

First Lad. "How much milk does Mangli give now? I thought she was about to cease giving milk."

Govinda. "She will do so soon; but in the meantime she gives one *seer* of milk both morning and evening."

Second Lad. "She is a Lakshmi cow. Do you know, Gove, that your father bought Mangli from my father?"

Govinda. "Yes? It is curious I never heard of that. How much did my father pay for her?"

Second Lad. "He paid only ten *ṭákás.*"

I may state here that the word rupeyá, or as it is commonly written rupée or rupi, is unknown to the peasantry of Bengal, at least to Bengali Hindu peasants; the word they invariably use is ṭáká.

Govinda. "That is very cheap; for she is a good cow."

Second Lad. "Of course, it is very cheap. My father gave her away almost for nothing, as he was in arrears with the zamindár."

Third Lad. "Look! look! there is a *hanumán* (baboon) coming towards us with something like a gunny-bag in its hands. What can it be?"

Govinda. "It is a gunny-bag of *baḍi.* The rascal has stolen it from the roof of some house."

Third Lad. "Very likely. Look! the *hanumán* has gone up the tree. I hope the fellow will not pelt our heads."

Govinda. "If he did you should be thankful, as *Hanumán* was Ráma's beloved servant and devoted disciple. Your head would be sanctified."

Third Lad. "Sábásh! Sábásh! (Well done!) By going to *páṭhsála* two or three years, Gove has become a Pandit. May you live for ever, Gove!"

Govinda. "What have I done to call forth such sarcasm? I don't pretend to be wiser than you all."

Fourth Lad. "Look! another *hanumán* is coming with a baby monkey suspended on her chest."

Second Lad. "Gove! see your Mangli is going into Padma Pál's sugar-cane field. If he sees it he will drive the ghost out of you by abusing you."

Govinda. (*Bawling aloud and directing his voice towards the cow Mangli about to enter the sugar-cane plantation.*) "Heh! heh! heh! Mangli! Don't go there, you *syálá* (wife's brother, used as a term of abuse) of a cow."

Second Lad. "Mangli does not care for your words; she is now fairly in."

Govinda now ran towards the sugar-cane plantation, and brought back the cow, not without getting some abuse from Padma Pál, the owner of the plantation, who happened to be there at the time.

After this the five boys began in fun to throw clods of earth at the baboons on the tree. One of these baboons was what is called a *godá,* that is to say, a baboon of unusually large size, and fierce in proportion. The *godá,* being provoked to wrath, started up, reared its long tail in the form of a circle, leapt from branch to branch, and filled the air with sounds of *Oop, oop, oop;* it again sat on a branch, showed its teeth at the lads in a fierce manner, and gave out from its deep chest the harsh cry, *khakor,*

khakor, khakor: at last being completely foiled by the missiles of the juvenile assailants, it came down from the tree and galloped away to a distant one, the female baboon following with her cub.

After the baboons had gone away, Govinda and his associates ate the parched rice which each one had brought for himself, and then sauntered among the thickets and climbed up trees for fruits. They ate a lot of wild fruit called *bainchi*—the shrub on which it grows abounding in the place, and an acid fruit called *Karanchá*; but the fruit which they liked best, and which they found growing on a large tree in the vicinity, was the *phalsá (Grewia asiatica).* They all climbed up this tree, and, sitting on its branches like so many baboons, ate its little pleasant fruit. They then went to look after their cows and to bring them together, as they had dispersed in different directions. This done, they anointed their bodies with mustard oil, which each one had brought for himself in a bamboo phial. Bathing then followed. The tank was full of aquatic plants of a hundred species, of which the *raktakambal (Nelumbium speciosum)* or red lotos, was the most magnificent-looking. Our cow-herd boys tore up large quantities of various sorts of water-lilies, the pods of some of which and the stalks of others are edible. After this feast of fruits was over, and after they had again put on their *dhutis*, which had been extended on the grass for sunning, Govinda said—"Well friends, I am going home to eat *bhát*; please take care of my cows during my absence; I shall be late in coming, as I shall have to go to the eastern meadow with *bhát* for my father and uncle, but Sambhu will come before me, and relieve you all three." So

Govinda and Sambhu, his neighbour, the son of the story-telling woman of whom we have spoken, went away. Govinda ate his *bhát* at home, took his father and uncle's dinner to the fields on the east side of the village, and returned to his place at the foot of the *asvatha* tree, where he found Sambhu sitting alone, as the other three had gone home for their dinner. After some time those three returned, and the party spent the afternoon in very much the same manner as the forenoon—now going after their cows to prevent them from injuring the crops, now climbing up trees and playing pranks on their branches, now singing songs about cows and women, and now playing at *háḍuguḍu.* But the great object of their solicitude in the afternoon was the gathering of a basketful of cow-dung, on the failure of which they would be sharply rebuked by their parents, guardians or masters.

The sun has now set, though a few of his departing rays are still visible on the leafy top of distant palmyras. It is twilight—in Bengali very appropriately called *godhúli,* or *cow's dust*—the cows must be taken home. Each neat-herd boy, with a basket of cow-dung on his head, and a bamboo stick in his right hand, is behind his herd of cows, ever and anon shouting aloud, either bidding the obedient kine to walk faster, or calling back any cow which has strayed from the right path. They proceed by threes, or fours, or sixes, in a row, according to the breadth of the road, which is not always a constant quantity; they kick up a great deal of dust, as the roads are never watered except by heaven; they block up sometimes the whole road—the women, with *kalsis* of water on their waist, standing on both sides to make room for them. In this fashion Govinda takes his cows home; ties them to their respective stalls in the cow-house; fills their tubs with chopped straw, water, and cakes of mustard oil; milks some of them, with the assistance of Kálamánik; makes a good fire, or rather smoke, of cow-dung cakes to drive away mosquitoes and fleas; and then shuts up the cow-house for the night—and with it we also shut up this chapter.

CHAPTER XXIII.

GOVINDA'S FRIENDS.

> **The friends thou hast, and their adoption tried,**
> **Grapple them to thy soul with hoops of steel**
>
> *Hamlet.*

THE system of caste prevents the different classes of Hindus from full social intercourse with one another. Águris will not eat and intermarry with any that do not belong to that caste; and the same is true of the thirty-six castes into which the whole Hindu community in Bengal is said to be divided; but, short of eating, drinking, and intermarrying, there is a good deal of intercourse and kindly feeling between members of different castes. An Águri may have a *goálá* (milkman), or a *sadgopa* (agricultural caste), or a man of any other caste, as his most intimate friend, although they may not enjoy each other's company at dinner—a thing somewhat unintelligible to the dinner-loving Anglo-Saxon, who, we suspect, can hardly conceive of friendship, except through the stomach. Amongst the different classes of the peasantry and artisans of Bengal, there is a vast deal of friendly intercourse; and it is by no means an uncommon thing for lads of different castes to vow eternal friendship with one another. The friendships of which we are now speaking are not unlike those we read of among the ancient Hellenes, as in the mythical story of Damon and Pythias, the half-legendary tale of Harmodios and Aristogeiton;

and some instances of which are charmingly told us in the *Dialogues* of the "Attic Bee." But it is impossible to avoid the suspicion, especially from the lively descriptions of Plato, that, generally speaking, there was something morally rotten in those outwardly graceful friendships, and that a Hellenic *erastés* was not always a virtuous friend. The friendships of the peasant youth of Bengal, however, are generally virtuous and disinterested. One peasant boy vows eternal friendship with another peasant boy, or with a boy of the artisan class, and the fact is not only known to the parents and relatives of both—and the same was doubtless true, in most cases, of the Hellenic *erastai*—but the formation of the sacred tie is ratified and strengthened by exchanges of presents. Two friends, of the sort of which we are speaking, do not mention each other's names; the one calls the other, whether in private or in public, simply *friend*. Youthful friendship amongst the Grecians seems to have been excessively jealous—an *erastés* guarding the youth he loved almost with the same jealousy with which a man guards his wife. Friendship amongst the youthful peasants of Bengal is different. Indeed, a Bengali peasant lad has generally three friends, all of them close and intimate; and there does not seem to be the slightest jealousy manifested by them. The three friends have three different names. A boy generally has a *sángát*, a *bandhu*, and a *mitá*—all meaning the same thing, namely, friend. But when one peasant boy says to another peasant boy "You are my *sángát*," he can never become his *bandhu* or *mitá;* the *sángát* remains *sángát* all his life: and the same is true of the *bandhu* and the *mitá*. Nor do these words indicate different degrees of intimacy, as a boy is equally intimate with all three. A *mitá* is usually one's namesake, but this is by no means invariably the case. Our hero, who was a sociable spirit, contracted in early life friendship with three lads of about the same age with himself, a short account of each of whom, as they will sometimes appear on the scene in the course of this narrative, it is desirable to give here.

The *sángát* of Govinda was Nanda, the son of Kuvera Karmakár, the blacksmith of the village. Kuvera was a tall thin man, strong built, and muscular; with a rather high forehead; with eyebrows joined together over the root of the nose, which was aquiline in shape; his bright black eyes were sunk deep in their sockets; and his lower lip was ever and anon put upon the upper one—a sure sign of determination of character. He was probably the hardest worked man in the village. As he was the only blacksmith at Kánchanpur his hands were full of work. All day from early dawn to a late hour in the night, the forge was ablaze; and every now and then large pieces of iron, like broken fragments of the "sheeted lightning" used to be put on the anvil and hammered and stretched to the requisite size. The *kámársálá* (smithy) was always crowded with people come on business. One has come to get his ploughshare mended, another his *kaṭári* (bill-hook), a third his *káste* (sickle), a fourth his *kuḍul* (axe), a fifth his *kodáli* (hoe); a woman has come to get her *bonṭi* (a sort of sickle used in the kitchen) toothed; a *páṭhśálá* boy has come to get his rude penknife sharpened by the addition to the blade of a little steel which he has brought with him; while a lot of peasant boys are sitting there for fishing hooks which Kuvera has promised to make for them. Kuvera was assisted in the smithy by his son Nanda, who was the very picture of his father, and who bade fair to become one of the best blacksmiths in the whole district, almost equal to Visvakarmá—the Hephaestos of the Hindus. This lad, about sixteen years old, was our hero's *sángát;* and Govinda saw him in the smithy almost every evening after discharging his pastoral duties in the cow-house.

Govinda's *bandhu* was Kapila, the son of Ságara Mistri, a carpenter. Having never been to Calcutta, and being employed only in village carpentry, Ságara had never made chairs or tables, since those articles of furniture are not used by either the Hindu gentry or peasantry, except a few of the former, who have formed Anglicised tastes. But he could make excellent sleeping *kháṭs* (wooden bedsteads), richly carved at the head, boxes of all sizes and of various sorts of wood, neat *pinḍás* (flat stools) of jack-wood, stools of every description, doors and window-frames, and *pálkis* (palanquins), better than those made at Vardhamána, and almost equalling in fineness those manufactured at Kapáliṭolá, in Calcutta. But that in which he chiefly excelled was the making of earthen images of the Hindu gods, which, though constructed in Calcutta by potters, were made at Kánchanpur by carpenters. His skill was every year called forth, especially at the time of the Durgá Pújá, the image of which goddess he made almost to perfection, according to village ideas of perfection in mud sculpture. All the inhabitants of the village used to be in raptures with the image of Durgá and her group which Ságara made for the zamindár of Kánchanpur. The women declared that the images were so life-like that speech and locomotion were only wanting to make them living gods and goddesses, while the painted canopy above the images they extolled as a piece of perfect painting. But Ságara exercised other functions than those of a carpenter, a mud modeller, and a painter: he made, or rather the women in his house made, and sold *chiḍá*. I don't know how the case stands in other parts of Bengal, but in the district of Vardhamána, at any rate in the village of Kánchanpur, *chiḍá* was always made and sold by carpenters, though I confess I see little connection between carpentry and *chiḍá*-making. But what is *chiḍá?* the English reader will ask. It is rice soaked in water, and then taken out and flattened by means of the pedal or the rice-husker. This when dried by exposure is called *chiḍá*, largely eaten by the peasantry with curds and treacle, or fried dry, in which state it is recommended by Bengali physicians to convalescent patients as a light diet. Kapila, the *bandhu* of Govinda, inherited the many-sided genius of his father, and could with equal facility make a jack-wood *pinḍá*, paint Durgá, and flatten rice.

Govinda's *mitá* was Madan, the son of Kási Datta, one of the *mudis* or grocers of the village. I have called Kási a grocer, though he dealt in scarcely any articles sold by European and American grocers. Webster, in his Dictionary, says, that a grocer is one who deals in "tea, sugar, spices, coffee, liquors, fruits, &c." Kási *mudi* had no fruits in his shop, though some of the Calcutta *mudis* sell plantains and cocoa-nuts; he sold no liquors, and, if he had sold them, he would have been excommunicated, and would have lost his caste; of coffee, neither he nor his village-men had ever heard the name; spices of some kinds he certainly had; sugar he perhaps had, but chiefly, I suspect, in the shape of molasses; and, though he had heard the name of *tchá,* or tea, he had none in his shop, as no one in the village, not even the rich zamindár himself, drank it. What did he sell then? He sold rice, paddy, pulse of various sorts, salt, mustard oil, cocoa-nut oil, ginger, turmeric, tobacco, pepper-corns, coriander seed, cummin seed, *tejpát* (*Laurus cassia*), betel nut, betel leaf, cardamums (of both sorts, the bigger, and the smaller, usually called Gujráṭhi), nutmegs, treacle, &c., &c. Govinda's *mitá* Madan, the retail merchant to be, assisted his father in selling articles in the shop, and in going out in the evenings to the houses of customers, for payment of bills. Govinda fixed upon this lad as his *mitá,* as, though he was called Madan by every body in the village, his zodiacal or astronomical name—and every Hindu has his astronomical name determined by the position of the sun in the zodiac, at the time of his birth—was Govinda.

Such were the three friends of our hero—his *sángát,* his *bandhu,* and his *mitá*—with whom he was very intimate, and to whom he communicated his secrets, his joys, his griefs, and who in their turn reposed in him the like confidence. But, besides these three bosom friends, there were three other lads who, though neither *sángát, bandhu,* nor *mitá,* were his companions and associates, and to whom, therefore, the term "friend," in a loose and general sense, may not improperly be applied.

One of these was Chatura, the son of Gangá

Nápit, the family barber of Badan. He had lately begun to ply his razor on the foreheads and chins of people; and though he was not yet very skilful in what is reckoned the most difficult branch of the craft, viz., the paring of nails, yet it was generally admitted that he was no unworthy scion of a noble barber's house. In addition to shaving, Chatura, like his father, had taken to surgery, for in the villages of Bengal the barber discharges the duties of a chirurgeon; and I have been told by persons competent to form an opinion on this difficult subject that the skill shown by Chatura, young and inexperienced as he was, in lancing boils, drawing teeth, cutting corns, extracting thorns from the soles of peasants' feet, and setting dislocated bones, was so great that there was scarcely any doubt that in time he would vastly excel his father in reputation as a surgeon. Under the auspices of his father he was also getting initiated into the mysteries of births, marriages, and deaths, in all of which the barber, like the priest, plays so prominent a part. Chatura was quick-witted like his race, who are said to be as shrewd amongst men as the jackal is amongst quadrupeds, and the crow amongst bipeds possessing feathers; and those who knew him best declared that his intellect, though he had not had the benefit of *páṭhsálá* training, was as keen as the edge of the razor he wielded.

Another of our hero's companions was Rasamaya, the son of a *modaka* or confectioner. I do not know that any other nation in the world consumes so many sweetmeats as the higher and middle classes of the people of Bengal. In other countries sweets and comfits are for the most part eaten by children; in

Bengal they are eaten as much by grown men and women as by children. In some feasts all the courses consist of sweetmeats from beginning to end. Is this the reason why the Bengalis have not left off their state of pupilage as a nation? But whether this is the case or not, the fact is undoubted that Bengalis consume an immense quantity of sweetmeats. Hence confectioners are as plentiful in the land as crows. Kánchanpur was famous for one sort of sweetmeats which were not so well made in any other village of Bengal. As Vardhamána is celebrated for its *olá*, Chandernagore for its *rasagollá*, Mánkar for its *kadmá*, Dhaniyákháli for its *khaichur*, Sántipur for its *moá*, Birbhum for its *morobbá*, Vishnupur for its *matichur*, Ambiká for its *suatolá-monḍa*, so Kánchanpur was famous for its *khájá*, which may truly be said to be the rájá (king) of sweetmeats. Vardhamána certainly gets the credit of this monarch of sweetmeats, as well as of *olá*; but those who are well acquainted with the matter know that the best manufacturers of *khájá* in Vardhamána are all natives of Kánchanpur; and of these Rasamaya's father was the most distinguished. Badan, as a husbandman, was not in circumstances to buy sweetmeats for his son or for his wife—the only sweetmeat consumed by the peasantry being, besides treacle in its raw unmanufactured state, *muḍki*—that is, parched paddy (with the husk taken off) dipped in treacle—and in high days and holidays *páṭáli*; but thanks to Govinda's friendship with Rasamaya, he was not unfrequently presented with sweetmeats used by the higher classes, and especially with *khájá*, the rájá of confectionery.

The last companion of Govinda we shall mention is Bokárám, the son of a weaver—indeed, the son of that identical weaver to whom Alanga had given threads of her own spinning for weaving a *dhuti* for our hero, when he ceased for the first time to revel in his infantile state of Adamic nudity. Lancashire weavers are, we believe, very sharp—some say a little too sharp—in their dealings; but we know not how it is that the Bengal weaver has, from time out of mind, been noted for his stupidity. In point of mental acuteness, he is the very antipodes of the barber. Bokárám did no discredit to his caste, as he possessed no ordinary degree of stupidity. His friends used to say that Providence had meant to make him an ass, but through inadvertence made him into a man. But though his head was a block, he had a good heart, and was ready to help his friends to the utmost of his power. Govinda never asked his advice in any matter, as he had no great respect for his understanding, but valued him greatly for the transparent sincerity and perfect guilelessness of his character.

Our hero may, I think, be congratulated on the choice he made of his friends and associates, as each of them was noted for some one good quality in a high degree of development:—Nanda for great energy and physical activity, Kapila for his æsthetic taste and artistic skill, Madan for prudence, Chatura for shrewdness, Rasamaya for cheerfulness, and Bokárám for sincerity.

CHAPTER XXIV.

GREAT SENSATION IN THE VILLAGE.

O horror! horror! horror! tongue nor heart
Cannot conceive, nor name thee!

Macbeth.

One summer noon the people of Kánchanpur were in tremendous excitement. About the fifth or sixth *danḍa* of that morning, the second daughter of Padma Lochan Pál—the same who had a sugar-cane field into which one of Govinda's cows had strayed—a girl of about six years of age, came out of her house to the street and began to play with other girls. It is usual with little boys and girls who go out to play, to come home about nine o'clock to eat some *muḍi* and *muḍki*, or to drink some milk. Yádumani (for that was the name of the girl) had hitherto always come at that hour to her mother to eat something; but that day she did not come at the usual time. Her mother became somewhat anxious. She said to her eldest daughter—"Where is Yádumani, that she has not yet come to eat *khábár* (food)?" The girl replied that she had seen her sister go out about an hour or two before, and that perhaps she was playing with some girls in the street. The mother went to the outer door of the house facing the street, and called out—"Yádumani! *O lo* Yádu! come and eat your *khábár*." But no Yádumani answered. She asked some of the passers-by whether they had seen the girl; they replied in the negative. Padma Pál, who was in the *chandimandap* (an outhouse for sitting), on hearing the voice of his wife, went to the outer door, and said—" Why are you so anxious about Yádumani? She is gone somewhere to play—perhaps to the smithy or to the Bráhman's house—and will be here presently. You had better go in." The wife obeyed, but somehow or other she had in her mind a foreboding of some evil to come. With a heavy heart she went into the house, and resumed her operations in the kitchen. But she had hardly any mind to cook. Her body was in the kitchen, but her mind was away in all parts of the village in search of her daughter. I was going to say the village clock struck twelve—not remembering that villages in Bengal have not clocks as in England—well, two *praharas* of the day were nearly over, that is, it was near noon, and Yádumani had not yet come for her *khábár*. The anxious mother had left the kitchen a dozen times and asked everyone that passed by whether he had seen her daughter. An hour more elapsed and it was nearly the time of *bhát khábár* (eating rice), and yet no news of the missing girl. It was then that Padma Pál himself was alarmed. As for his poor wife, her eyes were filled with tears, her heart was beating like a pedal, and she was half dead with fright. She could not contain any longer. She burst out crying "O my Yádumani! my darling! my treasure! Why have you not come to eat your *khábár?* Where are you, my darling?" All the men, women, and children of the adjoining houses ran to Padma Pál's house to inquire what the matter was. The news that Padma Pál's second daughter was missing ran through the village like the blaze of a hedge of the reed *sar* set on fire. Though it was the dinner hour, all the people of the village—men, women, and children—came out of their houses to search for the girl. The sympathy of the whole village was excited—and Bengalis are a very sympathizing people, let foreigners say what they please. Every street was searched, every house, every bush and thicket, every mango tope, every tamarind grove, every plantain garden, in the outskirts of the village. All the bathing *gháṭs* of all the tanks of the village were examined, and two or three little pools in the neighbourhood of Padma Pál's house were dragged through with drag-nets, and though large quantities of fish were caught, the body of Yádumani was not found. The grief of all the people was indescribable. Most of them that day went without their dinner, for they were all diligent in the search. Parties went off in different directions to make fresh search. The fishermen of the village—and there was a good lot of them, as the Bengalis are an essentially piscivorous race—brought out all their largest drag-nets, and offered to drag all the tanks; but the name of those tanks was legion, and dragging them all was not the work of a day: indeed, some of them, as the reader knows, could not be dragged through. Every nook and corner of the village was searched, but in vain. The lamentations of the people were loud. As for the poor mother, she rent the air with terrific screams, fell down on the ground, and rolled in the dust writhing with agony, just as a kid, whose neck has been half cut by an unskilful sacrificer, writhes in pain on the altar of some image of the Moloch-like goddess Káli. The sun was just setting behind the lofty tamarind trees of the village, and yet no clue to the fate of the missing girl had been found. The whole village was filled with horror. But murder will "out."

Govinda Sámanta, our hero, had been the whole day with his cows, which were grazing on an uncultivated patch of land in the outskirts of the village, excepting the short time when he had come home for his meal; and it was at that time that he had heard of the mysterious disappearance of the second daughter of Padma Pál, or as Govinda and his companions called him, Podo Pál. Not far from the place where Govinda's cows were grazing, his father and uncle were working in the fields; for the reader must remember that the few acres of land which Badan cultivated did not lie in one side of the village, but were in various places. At sunset Govinda was bringing his cows home. They came in a line, climbed up the high embankment of the tank Krishnaságara, went down the slope on the other side, going very near the water's edge, as cows are accustomed to do. One of the cows, wishing to drink water, went to the edge, and put her fore-legs fairly into the water, but in a moment she started back and ran up the embankment. Another cow, which was behind, came up to the same spot, and was stooping to drink, when she too started back, apparently with fright, and ran up the embankment. Govinda, who noticed both, naturally thought that the cows must have seen something unusual, otherwise they would not have turned away from the water without drinking. Going to the spot, what should he see but a human corpse floating at some yards' distance from the shore, half-covered by the aquatic plants. As his father and uncle were coming behind he shouted to them, and in a moment they joined him. They inferred from the size of the corpse, and from the profusion of hair on its head, that it was the body of a little girl, and they had no doubt in their minds that it was the corpse of Yádumani, whom they had often seen. The news was soon spread, and the whole village came to the tank. But how was the body to be brought to land? The reader will recollect that the Krishnaságara was regarded with mysterious awe, and that scarcely any person dipped his feet in any other part of the tank than at the bathing *gháṭs*, which were sadly out of repair. Amongst the hundreds of spectators crowding the slope of the embankment down to the water's edge, none offered to undertake the task. At last, Kálamánik, the boldest man in the village, went down into the water, swam up to the corpse, and dragged it ashore. The crowd shrieked with horror; there was no mistaking it—it was the veritable Yádumani, but without life, without clothes, without her silver ornaments. The poor child had been evidently murdered for the sake of the jewels on her person.

The question now was, not as it would have been in other countries—who was the murderer?—but whether the body should be burnt that very night or not. The pressing necessity of an immediate solution of the question will be apparent to every one who remembers that Hindus consider it a great calamity and a great sin if the body of a deceased person is not burnt within twenty-four hours after his death. The invariable practice is to perform the rite of cremation immediately after the spirit has left its clayey tenement. But in the present case it was contrary to law to burn the body without the knowledge and sanction of the police. It was therefore deemed advisable to ask the advice of the zamindár of the village. The landlord, as an orthodox Hindu, was for immediate cremation; but to guard against unpleasant consequences he sent for the police-constable of the village, called *phánḍidár*, and ordered him (for he was the zamindár's humble and obedient servant) not to send a report of the affair to the *thánά* (police-station) of Mantresvar, which was the head police-station of Parganá Sáhábád, in which Kánchanpur was situated. On receiving a *douceur* the *phánḍidár* agreed to hush up the matter.. The corpse was then that very night taken from the Krishnaságara to another tank, where the remains of all the deceased persons of that part of the village were usually burnt, and the rite of cremation was duly performed.

Next morning the whole village were on the alert to discover, if possible, the perpetrator of that atrocious deed. One old woman came forward and said that she had seen, the day before, at about eleven o'clock, Yádumani going along with Bejá Bágdi and his sister towards Krishnaságara. Scores of people immediately ran to the hut of Bejá Bágdi, caught hold of him and of his sister, and dragged them to the Cutcherry of the zamindár. On the way the culprits were half killed with slaps, blows, cuffs, and kicks of the angry multitude. The zamindár ordered them to be tortured till they confessed the crime. The bamboo torture soon compelled them to make a clean breast of the affair. They said that they had enticed away the girl from the street, where she was playing, with the promise of giving her some fine mangoes, that they had taken all her ornaments, which were only of silver, killed her, and hid the corpse among the flags of the Krishnaságara. I need scarcely say, that at this confession, the crowd, almost maddened with rage, poured such a hailstorm of blows, kicks, and cuffs, upon the culprits, that they were almost within an inch of their lives. But the question was—what was to be done to them? They could not be handed over to the police, for that would have put both Padma Pál and the zamindár into a scrape, for having burnt the corpse without the knowledge and permission of the police. The zamindár resolved to expel the murderers from the village, warning them, that if they returned to the village, they would be handed over to the police, and hanged. There and then the miscreants were expelled from the village, accompanied with a whirlwind of abuse, and a hailstorm of brickbats and old shoes. Thanks to the easy virtue of the village constable, the higher police authorities never got a scent of this affair.

CHAPTER XXV.

THE VILLAGE MARKET.

Some, burthened with their homely ware,
Journey to village hát or fair.

H. H. Wilson.

Háṭs, that is markets, whether held weekly or twice in the week, are a very useful institution; they not only supply with the necessaries of life the inhabitants of those little *hamlets* in which there are no shops, but also promote social intercourse between people of different villages. The *háṭ* of Kánchanpur, as the reader knows already, was held on Tuesdays and Saturdays on a plain in the south-west corner of the village. It was not a large one compared with the monstrous *háṭs* held in other parts of the country, especially in Eastern Bengal, still it was a pretty good one, being attended by between two and three hundred people. There were no sheds of any kind erected in it, so that if a shower came on, the *háṭ* would be dispersed—the only protection against rain being a few trees on the spot, especially that gigantic banyan tree of which we have already spoken. On market days almost every family in the village sent one of its members to the *háṭ* to buy whatever was needed. Kálamánik and Govinda both regularly went to *háṭ,* but with different objects. Kálamánik went to sell, whereas our hero went to buy. It was customary with Badan to hoard up in the *marái* (granary) a quantity of paddy sufficient to supply all the members of the family with food from one harvest to another; and if there happened to be a surplus, it was converted into rice and sold in the village *háṭ*, especially when rice became dear; and sometimes Kálamánik bought rice in distant *háṭs* and sold it at an advantage in the *háṭ* of his own village. It was not much that he had to sell, usually two sacks of rice on the back of a bullock. Govinda went to buy for the family a few necessary articles which, though procurable in the village shops, were sold at lower prices in the *háṭ*. The two weekly markets were not called the market of Tuesday and the market of Saturday; they were almost always named according to the number of days which elapsed between one market day and another. Thus the market of Tuesday was called the *market of three*, because three clear days intervened between that day and the following Saturday; and the market of Saturday was called the *market of two*, because there are only two days intervening between that day and the following Tuesday. Usually more things are sold in a *market of three* than in a *market of two*, as people lay in more provisions on the former occasion than on the latter.

Let my reader accompany Govinda to a *háṭ of three.* Scarcely have you come to the outskirts of the village when your ears are regaled with the buzz, as it were, of many millions of bees, wafted through the surrounding groves of mango, and the long avenues of the *asvatha* and the tamarind. The buzz increases in loudness as you proceed, and it becomes quite deafening when you are fairly on the scene of action. For a good, varied, and rich noise commend us to a village *háṭ*. The noise of a mob on Trafalgar Square, or on the boulevards of Paris, is nothing to it. A London or a Paris mob may have in it a larger number of people than most *háṭs* in Bengal, but all who make up that mob do not speak at the same time; whereas in a village *háṭ* every one, without exception, whether he be a buyer or a seller, is, at the same moment of time, speaking in an assembly of some hundreds at the top of his voice.

The first thing you notice as you enter the *háṭ* is a large number of red-looking bran-new *háṇḍis* (cooking-pots) and earthen vessels of all sorts and shapes, both on your right and on your left: those have been brought from a neighbouring village, and are sure to have a good sale, as there is not a single potter at Kánchanpur. The sellers of goods have formed themselves into five long rows or streets, most of whom are squatting on the bare ground, a few on gunny bags spread upon the earth, and fewer still on low wooden stools; while the articles for sale are put out, according to their nature, either on the ground, or in gunny bags, or in baskets. One row you see entirely filled with greens and vegetables, the names of which it were endless to mention; for of greens the people of Bengal eat an infinite variety, excepting only those which are either poisonous or noxious in any other way: and as to other vegetables their name is legion. Greens and vegetables, indeed, require to be numerous, as Bengalis are thorough vegetarians; the only animal food they use being milk, clarified butter, and fish. Amongst the vegetables exposed for sale you notice some curious ones. A woman here has in her basket bright-red radishes, each about three feet long; a man there has pumpkins and gourds of monstrous size; a third has that wonderfully rich and nutritious fruit, though somewhat disagreeable to the taste, called *kánṭál* or jack fruit, each of which weighs forty pounds avoirdupois. But what in the name of wonder is that curious looking fruit, resembling a huge boa-constrictor, and measuring about two yards in length? It is the *chichingá,* or snake-gourd, the *Trichosanthes anguina* of botanists. One of these snake-gourds is amply sufficient to furnish a large family with breakfast and dinner when made into curry and eaten along with boiled rice. A stranger looking at the long array of greens and vegetables might mistake that part of the *háṭ* for an agricultural show, if he did not know that they constituted the chief food of the people.

The second row consists of grocers and confectioners, and infinitely varied are the articles exposed for sale in that range. You have a hundred sorts of spices, spices for cooking, for *pán,* and for other purposes; of sweetmeats you have every variety, from the humble *muḍki* and *páṭáli* to the delicate *khájá*—the king of the tribe. This row is frequented chiefly by the village boys—and both the pedagogues of the village give their boys half-school on market-days—who with one pice (somewhat less than a halfpenny) in each one's waist—I cannot say *pocket,* for a genuine village Bengali boy having no pocket, keeps little sums of money wrapped in the folds of his *dhuti* around the waist—are standing before the confectioners, and debating in their minds what sweetmeat they should select. Nor is the debate an idle one; for with a halfpenny a boy may get a large quantity of *muḍki* or *phuṭkalái,* a good number of *kadmás,* or a considerable bit of *páṭáli.*

A third row consists chiefly of clothes exposed for sale by those who have woven them—inelegant and coarse, but stout and lasting, and therefore good for husbandmen and the working classes. A fourth row displays country-made cutlery—plough-shares, hoes, sickles, bill-hooks, *bonṭis,* axes, knives, *káṭaris,* &c., &c., all the implements of husbandry, village carpentry, masonry, and cookery. A fifth row consists of articles manufactured from leather, like shoes, or rather slippers—for the majority of Bengalis use only slippers and not shoes, boots being of course out of the question—thongs, toys, and other nondescript things; while apart from all the rows, under the magnificent banyan tree already spoken of, are on one side, paddy and rice sellers with their bullocks, and on the other a lot of fisherwomen, selling an infinite variety of fish, from the Liliputian *punṭi* to the Brobdignagian *boál* and *rohita.*

Who is that up-country man with a red turban on his head, and a large basket in his hand, accompanied by a man who looks like a clerk? It is the zamindár's servant, who has come to take *tolá* (rent), for the landlord of the village, from every trader in the market. The piece of ground on which the *háṭ* is held, belongs to the zamindár of the village, for which ground no one pays him rent; the landlord, therefore, reimburses himself by taking, on each market day, from every trader a small quantity of the goods in which he deals. Should the commodities be valuable, like cloth or jewels, a few pice are paid as an equivalent for the articles. I need hardly say that, by adopting this method of remunerating himself, the zamindár gets a hundred times more than he would have obtained if he had charged a fair rent for the ground; and yet there can be no doubt that the traders themselves prefer the zamindár's method, to paying a monthly sum. Who is that Mahomedan-looking man, with a long beard, a skull-cap on his head, and a bâton in his hand, followed by a coolie with a basket? He is the *phánḍidár* (police constable), of the village. He has also come for his *tolá;* and, though the traders do not give him as much as they give to the zamindár, yet they give him something, as they are afraid of incurring his displeasure. Half-a-dozen boys are also going the round of the stalls, to raise *tolá* for the Bráhman *gurumahásaya* (schoolmaster), of the village; but the poor pedagogue, though he gets a little from some of the traders, gets a great deal less than the police constable. But there is a fourth *tolá*-raiser, going about from stall to stall with a basket in his hand. He is a Bráhman, exacting a tax for the village *bároáripujá* (joint-stock idol worship), which is held annually at Kánchanpur, attended with much pomp and many exhibitions, and for the expenses of which each seller of goods is bound to give something on each market day.

The *háṭ* began at about one o'clock in the afternoon. It is now four o'clock, and business is at its height. Both buyers and sellers are speaking their loudest, and the noise is deafening. The scene is a perfect Babel. It is not only the confusion of tongues, but the confusion of tongues worse confounded. But, lo! who is that European gentleman who has just entered the *háṭ,* and is standing in the shade of that big *vaṭa* tree to which I have so often alluded, with a Bábu-looking person beside him, and a coolie with a bag under his arm? At the sight of the *Sáheb* a number of people leave off bargaining and rush towards him. The Bábu opens a book which he has with him, and begins to read. Govinda and scores of other people listen attentively. It is something about God, about sin and salvation, about a Saviour for the children of men. Govinda distinctly heard the name *Jesu Khrishṭa.* The fact is, the Rev. Friedrich Kleinknecht, a German clergyman connected with the Church Missionary Society, was out itinerating in the district of Vardhamána, and had, in the course of his evangelistic peregrinations, reached Kánchanpur that very afternoon, and was now taking advantage of the *háṭ* to preach the Gospel to the people. From the way in which the people salute the reverend gentleman, and the nature of the questions they put him, it seems that he is no stranger to them. The truth is, Mr. Kleinknecht's station is Kánáináṭśálá, on the suburbs of the town of Vardhamána, only seven miles distant from Kánchanpur; he had therefore been often in the village and preached at the *háṭ* as well as at Sivatalá, as the middle part of the village, where there were two temples, was called, and had sometimes visited some of the influential inhabitants in their houses. As Mr. Kleinknecht was very affable in his manners, and had no hauteur or arrogance in his demeanour towards the children of the soil—as he was exceedingly simple in his habits, like most Germans—as he never lost temper in his discussions with Hindus, though it was sorely tried by the irrelevant arguments and incoherent reasonings of his opponents—as he sometimes gave medicines to the poor people of the village if sick at the time of his annual visit—

and as he spoke the Bengali language almost like a Bengali (and Germans, as a rule, speak Bengali better than Englishmen), excepting now and then confounding his b's with his p's—he was universally liked by the inhabitants of Kánchanpur; indeed, little boys used to go up to him, and, catching his coat-tails, used to say—"Padre Sáheb, *salám.*"

Such was the missionary who now stood under the gigantic *vaṭa* tree in the market-place of Kánchanpur. After his catechist had read a chapter of one of the Gospels—and I have been told that it was the eleventh chapter of the Gospel of St. Matthew—and had briefly expounded it to the crowd, which was receiving accession of listeners every minute, Mr. Kleinknecht addressed the people, taking for his text—"Come unto me all ye that labour and are heavy laden, and I will give you rest." The reverend gentleman drew such a vivid picture of the sorrows and sufferings of humanity, and manifested such glowing sympathy for the labouring poor, that the audience (the majority of whom were of that class) seemed to be greatly affected. While the preacher was going on with his subject with great earnestness and fluency, one here and another there exclaimed—"All that the Padre Sáheb is saying is quite true!" When, however, he touched on the last clause of the text and spoke of the eternal rest as the gift of the Saviour, he did not seem to carry along with him the sympathy of his audience. At the conclusion of the address a discussion followed, in which some Bráhmans and Káyasthas took part, but the arguments of which it is here unnecessary to detail. At the close of the discussion, Christian tracts written in the Bengali language were distributed gratuitously among the people, who showed such eagerness to obtain them that they trod upon one another's toes, and nearly threw the missionary and his catechist off their legs. In the *melée* our hero got hold of a tract entitled the *Satya Ásraya* ("The True Refuge") which he took home and used occasionally to read. As the sun had already set, the *háṭ* broke up, and buyers and sellers wended their way homewards—some to Kánchanpur, and others to neighbouring villages.

CHAPTER XXVI.

LADIES' PARLIAMENT.

> But chief do India's simple daughters,
> Assemble in these hallowed waters,
> With vase of classic model laden,
> Like Grecian girl or Tuscan maiden,
> Collecting thus their urns to fill
> From gushing fount, or trickling rill.
>
> *H. H. Wilson.*

THOUGH Bengali women in the villages visit one another in their houses for friendly conversation, nowhere do so many women meet together and talk on so many different subjects—village politics not excluded—as at the bathing *gháṭs* of those tanks to which they resort for their daily ablutions. I have already told the reader that Kánchanpur has a great many large and beautiful tanks, but all of them were not popular for bathing purposes. The two tanks in the village which were resorted to by the largest number of bathers were the *Himságara* in the south, and the *Ráya's* tank in the north of the village. As Badan lived in the northern division of the village, the members of his family all bathed every day in the *Ráya's* tank, so called from the zamindár, who belonged to the Ráya family. It had two bathing *gháṭs*, one for men, and the other for women, and they are so situated with respect to each other, that the men who bathe in the one *gháṭ* cannot see the women who bathe in the other. Both have flights of steps built of masonry, going pretty far into the tank, which is very deep. These steps are enclosed by walls of masonry, which, however, do not rise above the surface of the water. At the head of the steps is a large floor, also of masonry, where the people, after coming out of the water, wipe their bodies, their hair, and sometimes change their wet clothes for dry ones, though the general custom is to go home, however distant, in wet clothes. On two sides of the floor are two *tulasi* plants, raised above the floor by masonry work.

If the reader wishes to listen to a conversation carried on by a number of women, let him accompany me about the middle of the day, say between eleven and twelve o'clock, to the women's *ghát* of the *Ráya's* tank. It is, however an expedition attended with some peril, for if we are seen standing near the *ghát*, and listening to the conversation going on, we are sure to be called all sorts of names, and abused as Bengali women only can abuse. We must therefore get to the *ghát* some one or two hours before, and conceal ourselves among the thick foliage of a sacred *sriphal* tree (*Ægle Marmelos*) which stands just a little beyond the floor.

It is eleven o'clock. The women are dropping in one by one. Most of them are bringing with them brass *kalasis* (water-vases), and a few have earthen ones, in which they intend taking home drinking water, and which they all put down on the floor described above. Their faces are all looking glossy, for they have been well rubbed with oil. Women of all ages, of all ranks, of all castes except the very lowest, are there. There is a venerable-looking old woman of seventy, all her hair white as flax. She has no *kalasi*, as she is too feeble to carry one filled with water. There are matrons thirty and forty years old, women of twenty, and blooming girls of sweet sixteen—in England they call it "sweet seventeen"; in Bengal the sixteenth year of a Hindu young lady is thought to be the sweetest and most charming. Some of them, you observe, are very handsome in their features, and their complexion is like the whiteness of milk mixed with the redness of the *alakta* (*lac*), a colour which most Bengalis prefer to the snowy whiteness of the European. The quantity of jewels, most of them of pure gold, with which the persons of many of them are loaded, shows that they belong to the aristocracy of the village. Most of the women, shortly after their arrival at the *gháṭ*, sit down on the steps of the water's edge, rub their teeth with a black dentifrice, called *misi*, which each woman has brought with her wrapped in a bit of paper, gargle their mouths for a full quarter of an hour, and begin scouring their feet with their *gámchhá* (bathing towels). They then go down the steps —with their clothes on, of course—and stand in the water up to the chin. In this position the rubbing of the body commences, the object of which is to take off the oil with which every part of the body has been anointed. Then, the rubbing over, they dip their heads in water I know not how many dozens of times, and remain standing there up to their chin for a long time, for they seem to enjoy bathing very much. Various parties are, of course, engaged in various operations. Some have already bathed, have filled their *kalasis* with water, and are going away, others have just come, others are rinsing their teeth, others are sitting on the steps and rubbing their feet, others are standing chin-deep in water, and a few others, especially Bráhmani women, are engaged in reciting prayers. During all these operations lively conversation is going on, and there is no lack of either talkers or listeners, for at any moment between eleven and one o'clock you are sure to find at the *gháṭ* at least twenty women.

A woman who is rubbing her feet sees another woman preparing to go, and says to her,

"Sister, why are you going away so soon? You have not to cook; why are you then going so soon?"

"Sister, I shall have to cook to-day. The elder *bou* is not well to-day: she was taken ill last night."

"But you have not to cook much. You have no feast in your house?"

"No; no feast, certainly. But my sister has come from Devagráma with her son. And the fisherman has given us a large *rohita*, which must be cooked."

"Oh! you have guests in your house. And what are you going to cook?"

"I am going to cook *dál* of *máshkalái*, one *tarkári*, *baḍi* fried, fish fried, fish with peppercorns, fish with tamarind, and another dish, of which my sister's son is very fond, namely, *ámḍá* with poppy-seed."

"The everlasting *baḍi* and poppy-seed. You banias are very fond of these two things. We Bráhmans do not like either of them."

"The reason why you Bráhmans do not like *baḍis* is that you do not know how to make them well. If you once taste our *baḍi* you will not forget it for seven months. You would wish to eat it every day. As for poppy-seed, what excellent curry it makes."

"Why, sister, you are so eloquent in the praise of *baḍis,* that my mouth is almost watering. If I were not a Bráhmani woman I would have tasted your *baḍi.*"

"Never mind, though you are a Bráhman, once taste my *baḍi. Baḍi* will not destroy your caste."

So saying, the banker woman went away with the *kalasi* on her waist.

Another woman who was in water up to her chin, addressing another woman sitting on the steps, says; "When did you get that ornament, *Sai?*"

"Which do you mean, *Sai?* This *jhumko,* you mean, I got it only two days ago. *Sidhe* goldsmith has made it. You like it?"

"Oh, that's exceedingly well made. There is no end to your ornaments. You are covered with jewels from head to foot. You are lucky in getting a husband who makes it the chief business of his life to please you."

"I hope, *Sai,* you have also got a good husband. They also say he loves you very much."

"My husband loves me very much! *Há! Vidhátá!* Jackals and dogs weep and howl at my misery."

"Why? what great misery are you suffering? You are not in want of clothes, of food, or of any of the necessaries of life; and he loves you very much, they all say."

"He gives me clothes, certainly, but they are not half so nice as yours. Food also he gives me, but everyone eats food, even dogs. And as for his loving me, what is the use of *dry love?* But what can I say? All this misery has been written on my forehead. There is no escaping it except by death. I shall be happy when I die."

"Oh, *sai,* why are you so sad about nothing? Ornaments are no sign of a husband's love. A man may load his wife's person with ornaments, and yet may not love her. I have heard many rich people of Calcutta are of this sort. Their wives are adorned in every limb, and have jewels the very names of which I never heard; and yet those rich Bábus seldom sleep at night at home. They sleep at Máchhuá Bázár. But your husband is very good; after candlelight he never goes out of doors; he is very gentle; he never beats you, nor rebukes you. What do you want more? It is true, he has not given you many ornaments. But is it his wish not to give you? He would, if he could, give you a houseful of ornaments; but Mother Lakshmi has not smiled upon him. Don't grumble, *sai;* you should be thankful that you have got such a dear lord of your soul."

"Oh Bagalá! You seem to be in love with my husband! I wish Prajápati had given me your husband, and mine to you."

"Oh, *sai!* What kind of language is that? It is improper language. Whatever husband fate has given you, with him you must be content. It is a great sin to be discontented in such a case."

"You have become a great Paṇḍit, Bagalá! You speak in that manner, only because you know how to read and to write. Forgive me, *sai,* if I have offended you. I am an ignorant woman, like other women."

"I am no Paṇḍit, *sai*. It is true my husband has taught me to read and to write, but I am as ignorant as you in many things, only I have read a few books from which I have learnt that conjugal happiness does not consist in the abundance of ornaments, but in the union of hearts."

"You are right, Bagalá." I'll try and console myself with what you have just now told me."

Just at this time Sundari, Badan's wife, came to the *ghát* with an earthen kalasi at her waist. As most of the women at that time bathing were of higher castes and of superior social standing, she instinctively went to one of the side steps and descended into the water. An elderly woman noticing her said—"I hear, Málati's mother, that your son Govinda is going to get married to Dhanamani, Padma Pál's eldest daughter. Is that rumour true?"

"Yes, there has been some talk on the subject, but nothing has as yet been settled."

"It would be a good match. Dhanamani is a very nice girl. She is gentle like the goddess Lakshmi herself."

"Don't praise her too much, lest the gods take her away from the world. If Prajápati has tied the knot, the marriage will take place; if not, not."

"You need not be anxious about it. Padma Pál seems to have a great liking for your son. I am sure the marriage will take place."

"So let it be, by the blessing of you all."

After Sundari had uttered the above words there was observed some excitement amongst the women bathing; several voices at once cried out—"Look there! Hemángini, the zamindár's daughter, is coming here." All looked towards the way leading to the *ghát* from the village, when there was seen a very beautiful girl of about sixteen years of age coming up to the bathing place. Her head was uncovered; her body covered in every part with ornaments; she was somewhat stout, and as she walked slowly, like a young elephant, as the old Sanskrit poets would have said, the silver anklets of her feet made a tinkling noise. She had been married some years since to a young zamindár of another part of the district, and was now on a visit to her parents. All eyes were directed towards her. She had no *kalasi* at her waist, was attended by two maid-servants, and looked as proud as, to compare small things with great, Pharaoh's daughter might have looked when she went to make her ablution in the Nile. An old woman, who seemed, from a massive gold chain round her neck, to belong to a respectable and wealthy family, broke the silence by asking—"What man was that sitting in the portico of your house with your father? I saw them both as I was coming to the tank."

"That is the Dárogá of Mantresvara."

"Dárogá! Why, what has he come here for? I have not heard of any *dacoity* or murder in the village."

"No murder! Have you forgotten the case of Yádumani, Padma Pál's second daughter?"

"But that is an old affair. It was all settled long ago."

"It was not settled—it was only hushed up. Bu it seems it has come to light now."

"And what has your father said to the Dárogá."

"I am sure I don't know what he has said to him; but I believe he has given the Dárogá hush-money?"

Some of the women then launched upon a long argument on the merits of the case, some defending the practice of giving hush-money, and others condemning it. Such is a sample of the sort of conversation which takes place in the parliament of Bengali women. Other topics of conversation are:—the cruelties of husbands, the quarrels of two wives of the same man, the atrocious conduct of step-mothers, the beauty of the women of the village, and the like. After a world of talk of the above description the women one by one left the *ghát*, almost all of them in clothes dripping wet, and with *kalasis* filled with water on their waist. As no eye is now upon us, let us, gentle reader, come down from the tree and take to our heels, lest some late bathers discover us and beat us with broomsticks for having committed so ungallant an act as to overhear the conversation of ladies.

CHAPTER XXVII.

THE NECTAR-MOUTHED MOTHER-IN-LAW.

Hir mouth was sweete as bragat or meth,
Or hoord of apples, layd in hay or heth.
The Milleres Tale.

Boswell tells us that Dr. Johnson, who was a great admirer of the novels of Richardson, gave the following reply to Thomas Erskine, who had remarked that that novelist was tedious. "Why, sir, if you were to read Richardson for the story, your impatience would be so much fretted, that you would hang yourself; but you must read him for the sentiment, and consider the story as only giving occasion to the sentiment." I should be very sorry, indeed, gentle reader, and should never forgive myself, if my clumsy management of the story of Govinda's life should lead you to make an end of your existence. I would therefore humbly beseech you, on my knees, to try me a little longer before putting the halter round your neck. But if, after reading some ten or twelve chapters more, you do not find the story increasing in interest, you will be at perfect liberty either to put a rope, or to tie a *kalasi* round your neck, just according to your liking for an airy or a watery death; only in that case you will not lay the blame at my door, for it would then be proved that I had not the faculty to please, and therefore am not responsible for what I have not: I have thought it proper to premise thus much, at the commencement of a new volume, in order to wash my hands clean in this matter.

It would, however, be doing simple justice to myself, were I briefly to state the reasons why the story has not as yet become interesting. In the first place, the reader will please remember that nothing very striking *does*, in point of fact, ever occur in the history of a boy in his *teens*, and especially of a Bengali peasant boy. I could have, if I had pleased, concentrated into this biography the collected striking incidents in the lives of a thousand Bengali peasants; but in that case I should have been writing the life of a *possible*, or at best of a *probable*, ráiyat, whereas my object in this book is to write the history of an *actual* ráiyat—a ráiyat that may be found at any hour of any day in any district of Bengal. If, therefore, there be any dearth of interest in the annals of the boyhood of Govinda, the defect is not mine, but that of NATURE, whom I follow. In the second place, the reader is to bear in mind that the primary object of this book is to draw a picture of the "social and domestic life of the rural population and working classes of Bengal," and that the story, to use the words of Johnson, "only gives occasion" to the drawing of that picture. At the same time I should be sorry if anybody thought that I had no story to tell. I could not, in all conscience, say with the Knife-grinder, "Story? God bless you, I have none to tell, sir!" I have a story to tell, as the reader will see, if he will have only the patience to wait a bit.

We have not met Málati since her marriage,

which took place some years ago, excepting once for a single second in her father's house, when Áduri had an attack of hysteria: I shall therefore give the reader some account of what she had been doing all this time. The reader will recollect that two days after Málati's marriage she went away with her husband to his house at Durgánagar, where she was received with great kindness by her father-in-law, mother-in-law, and other relations of her husband. There was great rejoicing in Keśava Sen's house; relations and friends were every day feasted, and the newly married couple often went out to dinner in the houses of Mádhava's relatives. The small village of Durgánagar, about thirty miles east of Kánchanpur, was close upon the river Bhágirathi, the Hooghly of English maps, being not far from the large village Dakshinpalli, the seat of a wealthy zamindár family on the one hand, and from Nilḍángá, an indigo factory, on the other. The inhabitants for the most part were engaged in agricultural pursuits, being chiefly of the Sadgopa and Águri castes, though there were a few Bráhman families and the usual complement of the other castes. It formed part of the zamindári of the wealthy Bandyopádhyáyas, or Bánḍuyes, as they were commonly called, of Dakshinpalli. There was nothing remarkable about the little village of Durgánagar; there were the usual mango groves, the eternal paddy fields, the thick clumps of bamboos, the lofty *asvatha* and *vaṭa* trees of all Bengal villages. Two trees, however, were more common here than in Badan's village, namely, the date-palm and the jack-tree, the former yielding a large quantity of sugar, and the latter giving the poor people a richly nutritious fruit, though somewhat disagreeable to the taste. But in this village there was one sort of cultivation which was unknown at Kánchanpur, and that was indigo. The blue dye was manufactured at the indigo factory of Nilḍángá, under the superintendence of a European planter, of whom the reader will hear more afterwards. Such was the village where the lot of Málati was cast, and where she remained only one week on her first visit, and then returned to her father's house.

The English reader, accustomed to the sweets of the honeymoon, will think it strange that Málati should leave the company of her husband only a few days after her marriage. But then it is to be borne in mind that she was but a girl of eleven, and as such was unqualified to discharge the duties of the married state. Hence it is customary with a Bengali girl, after stopping only a few days in her father-in-law's house—for we can hardly call it her own house—to return to her father's, where she remains at least one year, and sometimes two or three years, according to circumstances, though occasionally she pays flying visits to her husband. The poor girl, however, always looks upon those visits as great trials; nor can it be wondered at, that a girl of so tender an age should prefer her father's thatch to that of one who is a perfect stranger, albeit her wedded lord. Besides, she enjoys greater liberties at her father's house than she possibly can at her father-in-law's. She is *bou* (bride) at the latter place, and must therefore go about covered with a veil, whereas, in the former place, where she was born, she puts on no veil, not only in the house, not even in the streets. Málati, however, after her marriage, while she remained in her father's house, was not allowed, as formerly, to go out to the fields, either with the cows or with her father's dinner, as she was now considered to be another man's property. But she did a great deal of work in the house; and Alanga, who was a first-rate housekeeper in her small way, initiated her into the mysteries of cooking, of husking paddy, of making *muḍi*, of frying *khadi*, of washing clothes, of manufacturing cow-dung cakes, and the like.

When the first year of her marriage was over, an envoy arrived from Durgánagar bearing a verbal message to the effect that the father and mother of Mádhava were anxious that Málati should go to their house for good. Alanga and Sundari were very unwilling that she should be sent so soon, and Badan, who shared the same feeling, dismissed the messenger with the reply that he would send her in a short time. But that short time became very long. At last a second messenger, a woman, arrived from Durgánagar, with a *ḍuli* (a litter) and two bearers, for carrying Málati. Badan saw that there was nothing for it but to send her. The village astrologer was accordingly consulted for an auspicious day, and due preparations were made for her departure. The day fixed by the astrologer soon came; the *ḍuli* was at the door; Málati put on her best clothes and all her ornaments. Alanga, Sundari, and Áduri set up a loud cry, as if somebody had died in the house; and Málati cried the loudest. The scene was quite affecting. It was a Bochim. But go she must. Two stout bearers lifted the *ḍuli* on their shoulders with Málati in it, the women of Durgánagar standing beside it. Málati rent the air with her cries

—"O father! O mother! O mother! O father! where are they taking me?" The streets through which the latter passed resounded with the same cries; and men, women, and children ran into the street, and said one to another—"There, look, the daughter of Badan Sámanta is going to her father-in-law's house!" Nor did Málati's cries cease when the litter had passed the village and gone into the paddy fields. Her cries, it is true, became less and less loud, but she wept and sobbed, and sighed and groaned. She refused to eat anything when at noon the bearers halted in the outskirts of a village for chewing some *muḍi*, and swallowing country spirits, which, thanks to the considerate and Christian kindness of the British Government, are now available in almost every village, though in the rude and uncivilised days of our forefathers they could hardly be had anywhere, either for love or for money. Thus fasting, sighing, and groaning, Málati reached Durgánagar and the house of her husband's father. Mádhava's father and mother received her with demonstrations of joy, though Mádhava himself did not speak a word to her at the time, as it is reckoned indecent and disreputable for a young husband to speak to his young wife in the presence of even the dearest of relatives.

It may be easily supposed from the state of mind in which Málati reached her husband's house, that she took a long time to get reconciled to her new abode. The fact is, that for a month or two, she used every night, when alone with her husband in his room, to sob and weep for being away from her parents; and it was only on account of the affection and tenderness shown by Mádhava, that she gradually got reconciled to her present condition in life.

A few words concerning Keśava, his family and his occupation, will not be deemed unseasonable here. He was a somewhat respectable husbandman, or rather farmer, as he had ten *bighás* of rent-free land, which one of his ancestors obtained from the Mahomedan Government, for having been the *manḍal* or headman of the village; and he had besides other twenty *bigáhs*, for which he paid rent to the zamindár. Thus he was in better circumstances than Badan, who had not a rood of rent-free land. Keśava, however, was very infirm in health, partly through old age, and partly through an old fever, which every now and then troubled him; he was, therefore, compelled to hire labourers for tilling fields, as Mádhava alone—and he was but a lad—was not able to do all the work. This was a large drawback, and neutralized, in a large measure, the advantage of possessing rent-free land.

As to his family, he had a wife, his only son, Mádhava, and a daughter, who had married early, but had soon after lost her husband, and was therefore living in her father's house. The daughter's name was Kádambini (a cluster of clouds); and, though, true to her name, her complexion was dark, she was an exceedingly well-behaved and affectionate girl. She loved her parents and brother dearly; she was very useful in the house, and was liked by everybody in the neighbourhood, for her gentle and amiable disposition.

The mistress of the house, Keśava's wife, and Mádhava's mother, demands a somewhat longer notice. She was a thin stick of a woman, her head was nearly bald—a rather unusual phenomenon amongst Bengali women, who generally rejoice in magnificent heads of hair; she was squint-eyed and snub-nosed. Her *morale* was in unison with her *physique.* She was by no means an indolent woman; on the contrary, she bustled about all day, and did heaps of work. But she had a most insufferable temper.

> Her only fault (and that is faults enough)
> Is—that she is intolerably curst,
> And shrewd, and forward; so beyond all measure,
> That, were my state far worser than it is,
> I would not wed her for a mine of gold.

She used periodically to quarrel with all the women living in that part of the village where she lived, to rebuke Mádhava sharply for little or nothing, often to bandy words with her husband in the presence of people; and as to curtain lectures, they were so frequent and so vinegar-like in their savour that Mrs. Caudle might well have sat at her feet. Nearly half the month she went without her dinner, at least in the day; for after quarrelling with her husband over-night, she would refuse in anger to eat her rice the following day, though I am not positive as to the fact whether she took her dinner at night when no one noticed it. Some people of the village used to call her *ráyabághini,* or the termagant; and a tigress she certainly was. But the boys of the village insisted on calling her, among themselves, *khenki,* as, like a certain animal of the canine species which it is indecorous to name, she used always to snarl, and eternally make *khenk, khenk, khenk.* Why the name Sudhámukhi (literally the nectar-mouthed) should have been given her at *annaprásana,* is more than I can tell; it must have been suggested in bitter irony by some astrologer who had found out that the malignant influences of sun, moon, stars, and planets had been shed upon the inauspicious hour of her birth.

This nectar-mouthed lady was a source of great trial to poor Málati. For some time she seemed to be very kind to her, but the infirmities of her temper soon discovered themselves and made Málati quite wretched. Whatever she did seemed to displease her mother-in-law. She does not sweep the floor well; her cow-dung cakes are badly made; the curries which she cooks are execrable; she is very ill-bred; she walks more like a boy than a girl; her voice is scarcely audible—it is like the hissing of a serpent: she has a nasty, sneering, sarcastic smile on her lips whenever anything is said to her. Such were the criticisms pronounced by Sudhámukhi on Málati. The young wife's situation would have been truly deplorable if she had not had a sweet sister-in-law in the person of Kádambini. In her Málati found a wise counsellor, a true comforter, and a sympathising friend. It was thought time would mend matters. Not a bit of it. Keśava had a return of his old fever, which ended his earthly career. This circumstance made Sudhámukhi worse than ever. Constitutionally ill-natured, she became more ill-natured on the death of her husband, and the blighting of all hopes of womanhood. She became a greater *khenki* than ever, indeed, a perfect tigress, as the villagers called her. But Málati bore on like a martyr with the aid of her never-failing consoler, her husband's sister. Mádhava, though, like all good sons—and Hindus, as Bishop Heber remarked long ago, have greater filial piety than most nations—he highly respected his mother, the infirmities of her temper notwithstanding, yet he deeply sympathised with his wife, whom he loved tenderly. But there was no helping it; and what could not be cured must be endured. He would as soon think of committing murder as of separating from his mother. The thing was impossible. What would the people of the village say? What would the *ugra-kshatriyas* of the whole of the district of Vardhamána say? Would they not say, "Look there at Mádhava, that unworthy son! He is truly a *kuputra* (bad son). He has separated himself from his mother, who is to him more than God, at the bidding of his wife. He has preferred his wife to that goddess who gave him birth. Atrocious! Shocking!" Such a process of reasoning, which is congenial to the Hindu mind, induced Mádhava to give up all ideas of ever separating from his mother; and he tried his best to persuade his wife to put up with circumstances over which he had no control.

CHAPTER XXVIII.

EVENTS AT DURGANAGAR.

And with that word she struck me on the head.

Taming of the Shrew.

"WHAT is the matter, dearest? Why are you weeping?" asked Mádhava, as one night on entering his bed-room and shutting the door, he found his wife sitting by the bedside and weeping. As Málati did not speak but went on sobbing and weeping, Mádhava again said—"Do tell me dearest, what is troubling you. Do speak, O my life! and break your mind to me. Am I not the lord of your life? In your present state, it is not good for you to cry; some evil thing may happen. Do speak and tell me what it is."

"O lord of my life!" gasped out Málati, her utterance half choked with sighs, "I have no wish to live. My life has become a burden to me. I shall be happy if I die now. The winds will enter into my bones when I die, and I shall have rest. O gods! take me! take me!" and she went on sobbing and weeping more vehemently than ever. Mádhava sat near her, stroked her on the head and shoulders, raised her head, which was resting on her knees, kissed her and said—"Do tell me every thing, dearest; don't be afraid of telling me the worst. You must not weep in your present state; they say it is a bad omen."

"I wish the gods had not brought me into this state. I am weary of mine own life, how then shall I take delight in my child? O gods! take me."

"But why are you not telling me the cause of your distress? Do tell me, O thou garland of my neck!"

"What shall I tell you, my head? My bones are being fried! Mother-in-law slapped me on the cheeks to-day in the afternoon when you were out in the fields."

"Mother slapped you on the face! Is that possible? O Vidhátá! what hast thou written on my forehead? Am I fated to bear all this misery? Why did she beat you?"

"Why? You know to-day is *ekádasi* (the eleventh day of the moon, when every widow is required to fast), and as mother-in-law does not eat rice to-day, I had to boil some milk for her. Well, in the act of boiling milk, I had to go to the store-room for something, and before I could come back the milk had boiled up and overflowed the can. Mother-in-law, who was in the yard, saw this, and rebuked me sharply, giving me all sorts of *gálágáli* (abuse). I only said, "Mother-in-law! why do you abuse me? I did not willingly do it." On this she became furious, came up to me into the kitchen and struck me on the face, saying, "You have learned, wicked girl, to give an answer? Do you not know that your mother-in-law is a goddess to you?"

"O, what misery! what more misery is written on my forehead? But, really, it is a great shame that mother should beat you. I must speak to her."

"But what will speaking do? Do you think she will change her nature on account of your speaking to her? She will no more leave off her bad temper, than the charcoal will leave off its black colour by being washed. It is incurable. It is in her bones."

"What do you propose, then?"

"I propose? You will never do what I tell you. If I were you, I would have sent her away from the house, and provided for her in some other house."

"Fie! fie! Don't bring that word into your mouth. Shall I send away from my house that mother who has brought me into the world, and who is to be obeyed more than the gods? Shall I prefer my wife to my mother? O, wicked thought! A man may forsake his wife without sin; but for a man to forsake his mother, is the greatest of all sins."

"But how is it that *Sáheb loks* (Europeans), whenever they get married, live apart from their parents? I heard that fact from some Bráhmani women the other day, when I was bathing in the tank; they said they had heard it from somebody who was employed in the indigo factory. I think that is a good custom. It prevents quarrels between young wives and their mothers-in-law."

"O fate! what misery! The custom of *Sáheb loks!* What have we to do with their custom? I have become a *Sáheb,* I suppose, and you have become a *Bibi* (European lady)! Have you become mad? Who put this idea into your head?"

"But there are some people of our own caste who have separated from their mothers. There is that Chhidám Pál of the southern division of the village. He does not starve his mother; he supports her, but has given her a separate hut to live in, apart from him and his wife. Why can't you do the same?"

"And pray what glory has that wretched rascal Chhidám Pál got by separating himself from his mother? Does not everybody in the village abuse him? Don't they say he is a *kuputra*—an unworthy son? The thing is impossible. Don't again speak of separating from mother—it is a great sin even to speak of it. A son who separates himself from his mother in order to live with his wife, does not deserve to live; and when he dies the *durva* grass will sprout in his bones, and his soul will go to hell. No, no; separation is impossible. I will speak to mother; and you must just try and get on with her. It is neither your doing nor mother's doing; it is written on the forehead. We cannot escape the decree of fate."

The last argument of Mádhava was irresistible; it was written on the forehead, and there was nothing for it but to submit to that writing. Málati yielded in despair. What else could she do, poor thing? Next day Mádhava took an early opportunity to speak to his mother on the subject, gently telling her that it did not look well to beat *bou*, especially as she was in a peculiar state. The nectar-mouthed lady broke out in a deluge of ambrosia and said:—"And so that wicked girl has been telling you everything? Did I not tell you that you should not marry in that wicked village of Kánchanpur, and into the wicked family of the Sámantas? That fool, your father, concluded the match against my consent. Does *bou* want you to drive me away from the house? And you, unworthy son, you slave of your wife, you that are kicked by your wife every night, you come to rebuke your mother! Forehead-burnt girl! daughter of perdition! a woman in form but a Rákshasi in mind! A broomstick on her face! And you, O unworthy son, have come, at the bidding of your wife, who has bought and sold you, to rebuke your mother who bore you for ten long months, and suffered intolerable agony on your account! Let that daughter of perdition return to her father's house. I will get for you a better and a more thankful wife. Beat her with a broomstick, and send her away."

From this inundation of nectar and whirlwind of ambrosia Mádhava saw no safety except in flight. Without opening his mouth he left the house and went to the fields to breathe the free air of heaven. Kádambini, who heard the whole conversation from the kitchen, tried her best to comfort Málati, dwelling on the duty of submission and on the irreversible decrees of fate. But Sudhámukhi, after venting her rage in the thunderstorm of abuse described above, was not pacified. For a long time she kept muttering something between her teeth, cracked the knuckles of her fingers on the ground, walked to and fro in excitement, banged the doors with great force, dashed brass pots to the ground, and seemed to be beside herself. But Málati and Kádambini were not at all surprised, as they were accustomed to such displays. During the remainder of the day she did not exchange a single word with Málati, and looked sullenly even on her own daughter, who, she thought, took the daughter-in-law's part. The following day her brow was less frowning, and matters went on pretty much as before.

Meanwhile in due time Málati presented Mádhava with a fine little boy. As Mádhava had become a staunch Vaishnava, he did not allow his wife to be confined for a month, as is customary with the bulk of the Hindu population, but adopted the system of what is called *Harir-luṭ*, or Hari's, that is, Krishna's *plunder.* According to this system of Vaishnava midwifery a woman, when delivered of a child, gets up from bed either the same day or the next day, in case the occurrence takes place at night, bathes, gives *Harir-luṭ*, and then engages in domestic work as if nothing had happened. This system is pronounced dangerous by the *Kavirájes* or physicians, but it is alleged by the Vaishnavas that it is dangerous only to the unbelieving. A woman who has faith in Hari is protected by that god from all danger, if she only gives *Harir-luṭ*. The news spread through Durgánagar that *Harir-luṭ* was to take place in Mádhava's house. At the appointed time, which is generally in the evening, scores of boys were assembled in the open yard of Mádhava's house. He took a basket of sweetmeats and threw them by handfuls among the juvenile crowd. The boys shouted out *Hari bol! Hari bol!* scrambled for the sweetmeats, ate them, and made a loud noise. This is the whole of the ceremony. Strange to say, Málati did not suffer from this summary treatment.

In due time the child was named Yádava, the son of Mádhava, who was the son of Keśava—the Hindus delighting in euphonious names.

CHAPTER XXIX.

ALL ABOUT PADDY.

> But Nature's chiefest bounties fall
> To thy productive fields, Bengal.
>
> *H. H. Wilson.*

THE English reader need not fear that we are about to discuss the grievances of Paddy and the expediency or otherwise of "Home Rule" in Ireland—the paddy of which we speak here is a much more manageable subject. In Ireland Paddy makes riots, in Bengal ráiyats make paddy; and in this lies the difference between the paddy of green Bengal and Paddy of the Emerald Isle. But punning apart, whence really have we got the outlandish term paddy? It is certain it is not Bengali, nor Hindi, nor Urdu, nor Sanskrit, nor Persian, nor Arabic, nor Támal; nor does it belong to any of the other languages or dialects spoken in India. We believe there is not a single Bengali ráiyat who has ever heard the word in question; and he invariably calls it *dhán* from the Sanskrit *dhánya*. Paddy is said to be a Malayan word; and Mr. Crawfurd, in his dictionary of that language, puts it as *padi*. The Portuguese in all probability imported it from the islands into the Indian continent. But "what's in a name?" We have to do with the object which it designates; and as in this authentic history of a Bengal peasant we have a great deal to do with paddy, we deem it proper at this stage of our narrative to tell the reader all about it.

The important fact that paddy grows in India was known in ancient times to other nations. Some of the Greek writers, like Theophrastus, call it *ὄρυζον*, and the Roman Pliny says that "in India rice (*oryza*) is the most favourite of all." The English word *rice* evidently comes from the Latin *oryza*, through the French, and the Latin name from the Greek; but I am not sure whether attention has been drawn to the fact that the Greek word was in all probability borrowed from the Támal *arisi*, and that the Sanskrit has no word for rice similar to the Greek in sound. May we not be justified in drawing from this fact the inference that rice used to be grown in India before its conquest by the Aryans? But, as the Bengali proverb has it, "What has the petty trader in ginger to do with the news of ships?" Leaving philology therefore to learned men, let me speak of paddy as it grows on the plains of Bengal.

Viewed from the stand-point of the seasons in which it is sown and reaped, paddy may be said to be of three kinds—*áus*, *áman*, and *boro*. The *áus*, or more correctly, *ásu* (from the Sanskrit *áśuvríhi*, that is, quick-growing) is sown about the end of March or the beginning of April, and is cut in August, or at the latest in September. This rice is somewhat coarse, and is eaten not by the higher and middle classes, but only by the peasantry, of whose food, however, it forms but a small part, as the crop is limited in its quantity. It grows only on high lands, which are not inundated during the rains. The *áman*, or the winter crop (so called, perhaps, from the Sanskrit *hemanta*, winter), is the most important of the three.

It is sown about the middle of May or the beginning of June, and reaped in November or December. This is by far the most important crop, and furnishes people of all classes with food throughout the year. The *boro dhán* is paddy grown in low swamps or marshy grounds. It is sown about January or February, and cut in April or May. At Kánchanpur, and in the district of Vardhamána generally, there is not much *boro dhán*, as the lands are, for the most part, high and dry.

Though there are three sorts of paddy, so far as the seasons of cultivation are concerned, there is an almost infinite variety of the *áman* itself. A learned countryman of ours, the late Rájá Rádhákánta Deva Bahádur, published some years ago a paper in the Transactions of the Agricultural and Horticultural Society of India, in which he gives a list containing no less than one hundred and nineteen varieties of paddy cultivated in the twenty-four Parganas alone; and it is said that in the island of Ceylon there are one hundred and sixty varieties. Every district in Bengal does not produce the same kinds of rice—the inhabitants of one district paying more attention to the cultivation of some particular varieties than to that of others. *Bálám* rice, for instance, is the staple produce of Bákharganja (Backergunge), and the finer sorts of rice are chiefly cultivated in the districts of Dinajpur and Rangapur. Round about Kánchanpur, and in the district of Vardhamána generally, the following varieties are usually cultivated: (1) Noná; (2) Bangoṭá; (3) Káliá; (4) Benáphuli; (5) Rámsáli; (6) Chini-sarkara; (7) Surjya-mukhi; (8) Dádkhámi; (9) Álam-Bádsáhi; and (10) Rándhuni-Págal; and the last one (Rándhuni-Págal, that is, cook-maddening) is so fine and fragrant that, while boiling it, the cook becomes mad with joy.

There is nothing peculiar in the process of cultivating paddy. The ground is ploughed and harrowed, and then the seed is sown by the hand. In the course of a few days the seed germinates and sprouts. Before the setting in of the rains, about the middle of June, great attention is paid to irrigation, the cares of which cease only when beneficent heaven sends down rain in copious showers. But the Bengal husbandman is not without anxiety. If there be a drought, the paddy is parched up; if there be too much rain, the plant is drowned and rots. If the rains set in before the plant is well up and rooted firmly, the crop suffers. The great thing for paddy is to get a fair start of the rainy season. As the rains pour in heavily, the paddy stalks rise rapidly. In the swampy districts of Bákharganja and Jasahar (Jessore) the paddy stalk rises sometimes to the height of ten or twelve feet; though in the high lands of Vardhamána and Birbhum it seldom attains a greater height than six or eight feet. At the end of the rains the paddy stalks droop down, and in that posture they lie during the dewy month of November, till in December they yield to the sickle of the reaper.

When the *dhán* is separated from its husk by the homely pedal, it is called *chául,* or rice. But rice of every variety is of two sorts, *siddha* and *átapa*—parboiled and sun-dried. If paddy is at first parboiled and then dried and husked, it is called *siddha;* but if paddy, without being parboiled, is only dried in the sun, and then husked, it is called *átapa.* Ninety-nine Bengalis in a hundred eat *siddha* rice in preference to *átapa* for two reasons: *firstly*, it is cheaper, and *secondly*, it is less heating. The *átapa* rice is offered to the gods, and is eaten by rigid Bráhmanas and by Europeans living in India. Gods and Bráhmanas eat it, because, not being parboiled, it is deemed ceremonially purer than the other sort; and Anglo-Indians eat it because it has a whiter and cleaner look, and contains more nutriment. Such, in a few words, are the mysteries of paddy.

CHAPTER XXX.

THE NAVÁNNA.

> How often have I blest the coming day,
> When toil remitting lent its turn to play,
> And all the village train from labour free,
> Led up their sports beneath the spreading tree,
> While many a pastime circled in the shade,
> The young contending as the old surveyed;
> And many a gambol frolick'd o'er the ground,
> And sleights of hand and feats of strength went round.
>
> *The Deserted Village.*

IT was on a bright, sunny morn of the pleasant month of November—so different from the "chill November" and its "surly blast" of which the Scottish poet speaks—that the joyous festival of the Navánna, or the *new rice,* took place. This festival, in which the first-fruits of the paddy-field are offered to the gods before they are used by human beings, must not be confounded with the general harvest, which does not take place till a month after. The paddy that is now cut is from early sowings, intended purposely for this festival. While the bulk of the paddy is still standing erect on the field loaded with golden grain, but not yet quite ripe for the sickle, the Navánna *dhán* is cut and husked and made ready for the festival. It is a merry day all over Bengal, especially with the peasantry. Govinda is not to go out to-day with the cows; neither his father nor his uncle is to work. All agricultural operations are suspended for twenty-four hours throughout the country. Early in the morning the peasants are lounging about in their houses and in the streets, talking and laughing and smoking a great deal. They bathe earlier than usual, for the astrologers have declared that after one *prahara* and half (that is, about half-past ten o'clock in the morning) is the most auspicious moment for offering and eating the *new rice*, and no one may eat that rice unbathed. Alanga and Sundari and Áduri have made all the necessary preparations. There is in that basket in the corner of the big room a large quantity of the new rice, untasted yet by man or beast; that large *hándi* is filled with milk; in another basket are contained all the fruits and esculent roots of the season, cut into small pieces. Rám Dhan Chakravartti, the family priest, has just come into the house, as the propitious hour is drawing near. In a large vessel he mixes the new rice (unboiled) with the milk and the fruit and the edible roots, repeats a lot of Sanskrit prayers, blows the conch-shell with his mouth—which means, I suppose, a proclamation to the gods to the effect that the feast is ready, and that they should come and partake of it—and offers the agreeable viands to the invisible deities, who have doubtless come in crowds. The five elements, the great progenitors of mankind, the *Munis* and *Rishis* of the golden age, and Badan's own forefathers, next come in for their share. But there are other guests to be attended to before Badan and his family can partake of the new rice. The cows and bullocks are presented with the rice, which but for their friendly co-operation man could hardly hope to obtain. The other beasts of the field, like the jackal, sacred to the god Mahádeva, and even the birds of the air, must not go without their portion. Govinda is told by the priest to put a plateful of the *navánna* in a neighbouring thicket for the former, and another on the top of a wall for the latter. A small quantity is thrown into the tank near the house for the fishes, and another small quantity is put near a hole in the corner of a wall for rats, mice, ants, and all creatures that creep on the ground. When the gods of every description—celestial, terrestrial, and infernal—and living creatures of every species, have been thus feasted, Badan, Kálamánik, and Govinda squat on the floor, and partake with thankful hearts of the bounty of Providence; and woman, the Creator's last and best workmanship, comes in finally for her share. The religious part of the festival is now over.

We are more concerned, however, with what follows. That day the dinner is required to be unusually grand, and Alanga had made preparations on a magnificent scale. Animal food being prohibited to the class of Hindus to which Badan belonged, and wines being out of the question, the reader may easily imagine in what the magnificence of the dinner consists. There was in the first place, boiled rice, without which no Bengali can exist; in the second place, *dál,* or boiled pulse; in the third place, two or three kinds of greens fried in mustard oil; in the fourth place, about half a dozen sorts of vegetables like the potato, brinjal, *paṭal, uchhe, pániphal,* and others, fried in the same fragrant oil; in the fifth place, a hodge-podge, called *tarkári,* of three or four sorts of vegetables; in the sixth place, fish fried in the eternal mustard oil; in the seventh place, fish cooked in tamarind; and in the eighth or last place, *paramánna,* that is, rice *par excellence,* a pudding made up of rice, milk, and sugar or molasses. Such are the delicacies which serve to make up a first-rate dinner for a Bengal ráiyat; and though the English sybarite may laugh at the concoction till his sides burst, it must be acknowledged by every right-thinking person that the materials of the ráiyat's dinner, though perhaps less nutritive, are more innocuous than the highly-seasoned dishes and intoxicating beverage of the Luculluses of Europe. Let us leave the ladies in the kitchen, and attend to the gentlemen in the streets and the outskirts of the village.

In a spacious lawn, between two mango groves, are seen men and boys, about one hundred in number, engaged in amusing themselves. Our hero, his father and uncle, joined this merry group. Most of them were husbandmen, though of different castes; and the artizan class was well represented. All Govinda's friends were there—Nanda the blacksmith, Kapila the carpenter, Rasamaya the confectioner, Madan the grocer, Chatura the barber, and Bokárám the weaver. They all seem to be enjoying themselves, as ever and anon are heard gleesome shouts, clapping of hands, and merry peals of laughter. One party is playing at *ḍánḍaguli,* the cricket of Bengal. The *ḍanḍa* is a thick stick of the babool wood, about two feet long; and the *guli,* made of the same wood, but thicker, measures about five inches: the former serves the purpose of a bat, and the latter of a ball. Govinda joined this party, as his *sángát,* his *bandhu,* and his *mitá* were in it. He soon distinguished himself in the sport, sending the *guli* to a greater distance than the rest, and hitting it always on its return. Badan, who, on account of his advanced age, did not join the party, and who sat under an adjacent tree smoking along with other old husbandmen, could not conceal the joy he felt in the display of his son's vigour and activity. *Boom! boom! boom!* the *guli* went whizzing through the air. Lo! the forehead of a stalwart lad is struck. The old men sitting under the tree rush to his assistance; the blow has cut through the skin, and brought out blood. The lad is taken away by his relatives; and the play goes on merrily as before.

On a spot not far distant is a party playing at *háḍu-guḍu,* sometimes called *háḍu-ḍuḍu* in other districts. Why the play is so called I do not know, except it be from the circumstance that the lads engaged in that play keep muttering in a low voice the sounds, *háḍuguḍu, háḍuguḍu.* The game is a sort of battle between two juvenile armies. A line is drawn, on the opposite sides of which are ranged the hostile combatants. They have no weapons of any sort—no needle-gun, no chassepot, nor Henri-Martini, nor sword, nor spear, nor sabre, not even a stick—are they not Bengali heroes? The sport begins with a man of the one army crossing the boundary line and invading the ground of the other. If the man, while on the ground of the enemy, succeed in touching one of the enemy, and in escaping to his own side of the line without being caught, the man who is so touched is said in the language of the play to *die,* or to be disabled, and must therefore be removed from the scene. But then this feat is to be accomplished in one breath—the continuity of the breath being ascertained by the player making a sound. Should he lose his breath before returning to his own camp he too is said to *die,* that is, disabled from further playing. The death or disablement of the last combatant on either side concludes the sport.

Under yonder tree a wrestling match is going on. Not mere boys, but men in the prime of manhood are seen there. Our friend Kálamánik is distinguishing himself there. Look how he and another large-built man—no unworthy foe—are catching hold of each other's arms in the middle of the stadium, wrestling with all their might, each trying to bring his opponent to the ground. They are now struggling with all their strength; victory seems to be hanging in the balance; now Kálamánik, and now the other man seems to fall to the ground. At last a loud hurrah is heard. Kálamánik has left his opponent sprawling on the earth.

In these and other ways do the peasantry amuse themselves in the heat of the day, and in the cool of the afternoon, under umbrageous trees, on a common or by the side of a tank, on the day of the festival of the new rice. As it was drawing towards evening, the assembly dispersed, and went home to their dinner, which their mothers, wives, and sisters had prepared for them.

CHAPTER XXXI.

THE HARVEST.

There too he form'd the likeness of a field
Crowded with corn, in which the reapers toil'd
Each with a sharp-toothed sickle in his hand.
Along the furrow here, the harvest fell
In frequent handfuls ; there they bound the sheaves.
Three binders of the sheaves their sultry task
All plied industrious, and behind them boys
Attended, filling with the corn their arms,
And offering still their bundles to be bound.
Amid them, staff in hand, the master stood
Enjoying mute the order of the field ;
While, shaded by an oak apart, his train
Prepared the banquet, a well-thriven ox
New slain, and the attendant maidens mix'd
Large supper, for the hinds, of whitest wheat.

The Iliad.

About a month after the Navánna, or the new rice. came the harvest, a time of joy to the peasantry, As it is of great importance to cut all the paddy at once, Badan obtained the help of his friends, and of those whose fields lay near his own, on condition that he would render to them the like assistance. Of these associates, the foremost was Padma Lochan Pál, who, ever since the murder of his second daughter, Yádumani, whose dead body was first discovered by Govinda, and brought up from the water by Kálamánik, had been greatly drawn towards Badan and his family. On the appointed day, they all repaired to the field with sickles, bullocks, ropes, &c., and commenced operations. The reapers were three in number—Badan, Kálamánik, and Padma. Squatting on the ground on their heels, they incessantly plied the "sharp-toothed sickle" to the cluster of paddy held by the left hand. The paddy stalks were tied into sheaves by the assistants; the sheaves were made into loads, put on pack-saddles, and carried home on the backs of bullocks. Kálamánik, on account of his prodigious strength, was the most successful of all the three reapers. With his huge hand he caught hold each time of a large quantity of the paddy stalks; pressed his lips together, putting them fairly inside the mouth; and cut the corn away with great force. *Mash! mash! mash!* the paddy fell rapidly before the sickle; and this music was greatly enlivened by the sounds of *umph! umph!* which ever and anon issued from Kálamánik's wide nostrils as from two subterranean caves. As soon as the pack-saddles were ready, they were put on the bullocks; and it was Govinda's business to see them safely landed at home, where other husbandmen were waiting to stack them. Many a trudge Govinda had on these harvest days, with the loaded bullocks, from the paddy-field to the house, and from the house back to the paddy-field. He had, however, more leisure than the others, for his work began only when the paddy-loads were ready. During the interval he smoked and chatted merrily with the little boys and girls who had come for the gleanings; for it is a rule amongst Bengali Hindu husbandmen, as it was amongst the Jews of old, not to take up any little paddy stalk that falls from the pack-saddles either in the fields or on the roadside, but allow it to be gleaned by boys and girls who usually exchange the gleanings of the day in the grocer's shop for parboiled peas fried in oil—a delicacy which makes its appearance in village shops at the harvest. There was one bright little girl there with whom Govinda talked oftener than with the rest; and she was the eldest daughter of Padma Lochan Pál, Dhanamani by name, the elder sister, though herself only eleven years old, of the lamented Yádumani. He gave her quantities of the *muḍi* and *muḍki* tied in his *gámchhá*, and handfuls of which he was every now and then putting into his mouth; and he often filled her little gleaning-basket—and it is not reckoned dishonourable for children of prosperous husbandmen to glean—with paddy-stalks from the bundles. The reapers, sheaf-binders, and other assistants, took their noon-day meal, which had been brought by Govinda, under a tree, not far from the field; and though no ox was killed and no bread of the "whitest flour" baked, as in the days of Homer, there was as much joy in the hearts of these vegetable-eating and water-drinking peasants of Bengal as in those of the beef-eating and wine-bibbing swains of old Hellas. On such occasions Dhanamani sat beside her father and partook of the dinner, and went home when Govinda returned next with the laden bullocks.

After gathering in the harvest, and arranging it in the open yard of his house in stacks, Badan, agreeably to previous arrangement, helped his neighbours in cutting their paddy. This being done, the process of threshing commenced. No flails or threshing machines of any sort are known to the peasantry of the Vardhamána district. They place on the ground a simple plank on an inclined plane; the thresher stands at the head of the plane, takes a sheaf of paddy by both his hands, and strikes it against the plank with all his force. Thump succeeds thump, till all the corn is beaten out of the paddy stalk. Should some grains of paddy, after the operation, remain on the stalk, the whole of the straw is laid out on the yard, and some oxen tied in a line to a post are made to tread it; and on such occasions, contrary to the Mosaic rule, the oxen are invariably muzzled, to prevent them from munching straw. The straw thus trodden upon is tied in wisps, and is called *loṭ*—so named from the circumstance that the straw has been tumbled about. This *loṭ* is sold dearer than the ordinary straw, and is used for thatching huts. The paddy is then stored up in the granary, and the straw stacked.

The harvest is followed by a festival, greatly enjoyed by the peasantry, and called *piṭá sankránti*, or the feast of cakes. It is so called from *piṭá*, cake, and *sankránti*, the last day of a month, as it always takes place at the end of the month *Pausha*, which comprises half of December and half of January. The festival lasts three days. Early in the morning of the first day of the feast, Alanga, Sundari, and Áduri bathed, and boiled different kinds of pulse-like grain, *kalái*, *barbaṭi* (*Embelia basaal*), *mug* (*Phaseolus aureus*), which they formed into a sort of thick paste. They next extracted the kernel of the cocoa-nut, mixed it with treacle, and fried it. They then took out a large quantity of rice, which had been previously pounded, made it into a paste, and formed it into innumerable small cups, which they filled with either various kinds of the prepared pulse, or the prepared kernel of the cocoa-nut, or cream, and covered them up. These rice balls were then put in a *hánḍi* of boiling water; and in a few minutes the *piṭá* was fit to be eaten. These cakes are usually eaten with treacle. A larger sort of cakes is usually prepared, called *askes*, which are of two kinds, the *dry* and the *wet*; the former being eaten along with treacle, and the latter soaked in milk. A thinner species, called *saruchaklis*, is very much esteemed. Alanga made heaps of these rice-cakes; and they were greedily devoured by the members of the little household. On one of the festival days Alanga made a *piṭá* of a monstrous size in the shape of a cat, which was offered to *Shashṭhi*, the protectress of children. These rude and somewhat unwholesome cakes may not suit the taste of refined palates, but they are vastly enjoyed by the peasantry, who get no harm by them. The feast of cakes is attended with games and sports similar to those which take place during the festival of the new rice. I had almost forgotten to mention that, in the evening of the first day of the feast, the peasant boys of Kánchanpur sang in chorus some doggrel verses addressed to the harvest month, describing its unnumbered blessings, and praying for its annual return.

CHAPTER XXXII.

MATTERS HYMENEAL.

Thus ben theay weddid with solempnite;
And atte feste sittith he and sche,
With othir worthy folk upon the deys.
Al ful of joy and blis is the paleys,
And ful of instruments, and of vitaile,
The most deintevous of al Ytaile.

The Marchaundes Tale.

THE reader has already come to know from the women at the bathing *ghát* of Kánchanpur that there has been for some time past some talk about our hero getting married to the daughter of Padma Pál, and he may therefore not unnaturally have come to the conclusion that we purposely put Dhanamani in the way of Govinda at the harvest-field, in order to make up something like a courtship between the two. We solemnly declare that we had no such purpose. The fact is, neither the boy nor the girl knew anything of the affair. They had not the remotest idea that their parents were contemplating their union for life. Indeed, if Govinda had known it, he neither would have been seen in company of the girl, nor would he have spoken to her; and if Dhanamani had known it, she would have always kept herself at a respectable distance from Govinda—such is the reserve maintained by Bengalis in matrimonial matters. This may appear odd to the English reader, but it is the simple fact. Not only is there no courtship in

Bengal, but if a boy and a girl, whom Prajápati and their parents had determined to unite together, were to be found walking together or speaking to each other, their conduct would be universally deemed unbecoming and indecent. Whether Govinda's interest in the girl was not something warmer than simple friendship I will not take upon me to determine; but I have no hesitation in saying that Dhanamani was unconscious of any tender feelings towards Govinda. The truth is, they were both ignorant of the wishes of their parents regarding themselves.

Alanga, now that she had become an old woman, was anxious to see her grandson married before she left the world; and Sundari, like every Bengali woman, thought it the highest happiness of her life to have a daughter-in-law beside her, and to dandle a grandchild on her knees. Nor was Badan unconcerned in the matter; like every parent, and especially every Hindu parent, he was anxious that his children should get settled in life before his own exit from the world. In casting about for a suitable wife for Govinda, their attention was naturally directed to the daughter of Padma Pál, who was by no means opposed to the alliance. Everything almost had been settled, except a formal betrothment, before the harvest—though neither Govinda nor Dhanamani had any inkling of the matter. After the harvest had been gathered, and the rice-cakes eaten, the actual betrothment took place with all its formalities, and an auspicious day was fixed in the month of Phálgun—the *gameliôn*, or marriage-month of Bengal—for the celebration of the nuptials. The reader need not fear that we are about to inflict on him another description of a wedding, though if we did we could hardly be blamed, as Bengal is *par excellence*, the land of marriages. The same ceremonies as at the marriage of Málati and Mádhava were gone through; the same exclamations of *ulu! ulu! ulu!* were uttered; there were the same lavish use of turmeric, the same sort of musical, or rather unmusical *tom-toms*, the same gyrations round the plantain-trees, the same blows on the ill-starred back of Govinda, the same prayers, the same jests of the women, the same kind of nuptial chamber scenes, the same feastings and merry-makings—though these last were on a grander scale, as all the relations and friends of both the bride and the bridegroom, who were natives of the same village, were on the spot. All the relations of Govinda were there, and amongst them Málati of Durgánagar, her son, Yádava, and her sister-in-law, Kádambini. Next to Badan, Alanga and Sundari, who were, during the days of the wedding, burdened with an infinite amount of work, the two persons who were excessively busy were Gangá the barber and Rám Dhan Misra the priest, the former doing all the menial and the latter the higher and more dignified sort of work. The spiritual guide himself was not present, as he was at the time elsewhere in his annual visitations; but he had sent his legate in the person of Prema Bhakta Vairági, but who, as will appear afterwards, was more busy in accomplishing his own private purposes than in assisting at the wedding. It is unnecessary to remark that the friends and companions of Govinda—his *sángat*, his *bandhu*, his *mitá*, and the rest, were in constant attendance every day, and partook of the general festivity. Ráma Rúpa, the pedagogue, also came with his crutch, to congratulate his pupil on his marriage, and received a rupée for his pains. Nor must we omit to notice the unfeigned joy of Rúpa's mother, the venerable midwife of Kánchanpur, on this occasion. During ten days she never went once to her own hut, but ate and slept in Badan's house, and was as busy as any member of the household, though being of an inferior caste she was prevented from doing all that she could have wished. She blessed the bride and bridegroom a thousand times, and often congratulated Alanga on her singular good fortune.

"You are blessed above most women," said Rúpa's mother to Alanga; "a woman is considered fortunate if she is blessed with a child, but your grandson is now married; and you have also seen your granddaughter's child! What a fortunate woman must you be! You must have been very holy in your former birth, otherwise, why this wonderful good fortune? The saying is fulfilled in your case—

Nátir náti,
Svarge báti.

[That is, he who sees his grandchild's grandchild lights a candle for himself in the heavens.]

Alanga. "I have seen only my grandchild's child, so the saying is not quite fulfilled in my case. The gods have, however, been very kind to me in keeping me alive so long."

"You must be very holy; you are mother Lakshmi herself."

"How holy? If I were righteous, would I have suffered so much trouble in my life?"

"What trouble? You are like a queen! Yea, more fortunate than a queen, for how few queens can see their grandchild's child!"

"O Rúpa's mother! why call me fortunate when that golden moon of a son, Gayárám, has been bitten to death by a snake? I must be a great sinner to have deserved such a dreadful calamity! The gods must have been very angry with me to have sent such a visitation. O my dear Gayá! my moon of gold! my lost treasure! where art thou? Where are you gone, leaving your mother here?"

"*Ginni* [mistress], don't think such thoughts at Govinda's marriage. Why grieve when you have Govinda on your lap? The gods spare his life, and he will yet have sons and daughters, and then your heart will overflow with joy."

"True, Rúpa's mother! but how can I forget my poor Gayá devoured by the ruthless serpent? My chest is going to split with sorrow."

"*Ginni*, leave off these sad thoughts. Now rejoice at Govinda's marriage. Bless him, and he will remove all sorrow from your heart."

"The gods make my Govinda immortal and perfectly happy! But as for me there is no happiness in store for me. I shall be happy when I die; the wind will then enter into my bones. My wish has now been fulfilled; I have seen my Govinda married. I have seen my Govinda's wife with my eyes. I have no further wish. I can now die in peace. Let me go now to some place of pilgrimage, and there end my wretched days."

"Don't say so, *Ginni*. Banish that thought from your mind. Get up and join in the merriment. You will yet see Govinda's child."

At this moment Badan came accidentally to the spot where the two old women were talking together, and seeing tears trickle down his mother's cheeks, said, "You are weeping, mother? You weep when everybody else is rejoicing!" Alanga replied, "These are tears both of joy and of grief." Badan, of course, understood that his mother was sorrowing on account of Gayárám's untimely death; he therefore said, "Mother! do not fill your mind with melancholy thoughts on such a joyful occasion. Gayá died because his rice had been finished. His *paramáyu* (allotted life) was over, therefore he went away. Who could reverse the fate inscribed on his forehead? All sorrow therefore is useless. Besides, you have your Govinda. Delight yourself in him. One Govinda will be found equal to seven Gayá's. Now, get up, mother! come with me; speak to those women who have come to rejoice with us. Come and look at the sweet face of Govinda's bride." So saying, Badan took hold of his mother's hand, and joined a company of women who were making themselves merry.

CHAPTER XXXIII.

THE SUGAR-CANE.

These ways of planting Nature did ordain,
For trees and shrubs, and all the sylvan reign.
Others there are by late experience found;
Some cut the shoots, and plant in furrow'd ground;
Some cover rooted stalks in deeper mould;
Some cloven stakes; and (wondrous to behold!)
Their sharpened ends in earth their footing place;
And the dry poles produce a living race.
The Georgics (*Dryden's Translation*).

LIKE every substantial husbandman of the district of Vardhamána, Badan had a sugar-cane plantation. When the paddy was gathered in, the sugar-cane was almost ready to be cut, but it is customary to allow the crop to remain in the field some time longer, in order that the juice may attain to consistency. The sugar-cane is therefore cut generally a month after the paddy harvest, that is to say, about the end of January or the beginning of February—at least, such is the custom in the village of Kánchanpur. As the sugar-cane is a valuable crop to the Bengal ráiyat, as its cultivation is attended with greater labour and pains than that of paddy, and as India has supplied the rest of the world, amongst others the Southern States of America, with the precious plant, we hope to be pardoned for saying a few words on the manner in which it is cultivated.

When in the previous year Badan had cut his sugar-cane, he had lopped off the upper parts of the cane, and planted them in nurseries on the edge of the tank near his house, whence they were to be transplanted into the field, when the soil should be ready to receive them. Unlike the paddy-field, which requires only to be slightly scratched to ensure a plentiful harvest, the soil for the sugar-cane needs careful and repeated ploughing. As early as the beginning of March, the soil is turned up. The field is ploughed three or four times, and sometimes oftener. It is then manured with cow-dung, the earth of crumbling walls, and mustard oil-cakes. After this, the field is again ploughed. The clods are then pulverised, and the field made smooth and level by drawing over every part of it, with the help of bullocks, a bamboo ladder, which serves the purpose of a harrow. The whole field is next covered with parallel ridges of heaped-up earth, between every two of which is dug a trench. In these trenches, the cuttings are planted at the distance of a cubit, with the fingers closed, from each other. At the time of planting, around each cutting is put a small quantity of pulverised oil-cake, as manure. As the cuttings are invariably planted long before the rains set in, they require to be kept wet by artificial irrigation from a neighbouring tank, whence water is brought by a sluice, and thrown into the sugar-cane-field by means of baskets. This operation is repeated every day for about a fortnight. Cow-dung and oil-cakes are again applied to the cuttings, and the earth round about them is turned up. Irrigation commences anew, and continues for four or five days; and when the water is absorbed by the soil, the earth of which the ridges consist is put round the cuttings. This may be considered as the first process.

Should the cuttings not take root and sprout, the process is repeated again and again, till the object is accomplished. When the plant rises about two feet from the ground, some of the useless leaves are torn off, and the rest tied round. Weeding also is carried on at this time; and should the plants become dry, they are again watered. As by this time Heaven sends rain in copious showers, the husbandman is relieved of the laborious and troublesome work of irrigation, and his attention is chiefly directed to weeding the garden, and to its general superintendence. Constant inspection is, however, necessary, as, not unfrequently, a peculiar species of insect attacks the cane, and makes the ráiyat's labours abortive. Care is also taken that the plantation is not robbed and spoiled by that nocturnal thief, the jackal, an animal which seems to be particularly fond of chewing the cane, and of swallowing its sweet juice. Such, in brief, is the mode of cultivating sugar-cane in the village of Kánchanpur.

In the village three varieties of sugar-cane are produced—the *Puri*, the *Kájule*, and the *Bombai*. The last sort, which is blackish in colour, is by far the longest and the stoutest of the three; but much of it is not grown at Kánchanpur, partly because it requires a more moist soil than that of the village, which is rather high and dry, and partly because the peasants are of opinion that though a single cane of that species gives out more juice than two of the others, it contains less saccharine matter. The *Kájule*, the colour of which is deep purple, is believed to contain the largest amount of saccharine matter of the three varieties; but it so often cracks of itself, through excess of juiciness, and is so apt to be attacked by worms and insects, that it is considered not economical to grow it to any great amount. The *Puri*, therefore, which is white in colour, tinged with a slight yellowishness, and which is about seven or eight feet in height, is grown largely, and, indeed, may be said to be almost exclusively cultivated in the village of Kánchanpur.

Early one bright morning in the delightful month of February, Badan, Kálamánik, Govinda and his father-in-law Padma Pál, and about a dozen other husbandmen, who were either neighbours or friends of Badan, were seen busy in the sugar-cane plantation and its immediate vicinity. Some were cutting the cane with the sickle; others were taking off the dried leaves covering the cane, and cutting off the upper part of the stalk; and others still were carrying the canes thus cut and prepared to the *áuksálá*, or sugar-cane house, which is a temporary hut erected at no great distance from the plantation, where the juice is pressed out of the cane and boiled down into molasses. This hut contains what is called a *báin*, or boiling-house, an immense furnace for boiling sugar-cane juice in large earthen vessels. It is often a mere thatch of straw supported by bamboo posts, but sometimes the boiling-house is constructed in the open air, where the spot is shaded with mango or other trees. Just outside the boiling-house is the press for squeezing the juice of the sugar-cane. It consists of two massive wooden cylinders, cut into notches all over, and furnished at both ends with wheels, or rather simple spokes, for the spokes are not surmounted by a felloe. The cylinders are placed so close as almost to touch each other; and it is through this interstice between the cylinders that the canes are inserted and crushed, the juice falling into a large earthen receiver placed below. Two persons sitting opposite to each other insert the cane between the cylinders, which are kept in perpetual motion by four persons. As the cylinders are placed very close to each other, the friction produced is very great when the canes are inserted between them; strong men are therefore made to work at the spokes. Kálamánik was the best sugar-mill turner in the whole village. There he was now, with his two long legs placed firmly on the opposite side of the trench, tugging away at the spokes with almost superhuman strength, now pressing his lips together when making a grand pull, and now hallooing his associates to excite them to get on briskly. Our hero, who had now developed into a strong, well-built *Ugra-kshatriya* peasant, was also working at the spokes. Badan and Padma Pál were inserting the canes between the cylinders. Nor is this an easy task; indeed, it is the most perilous of all, since it not unfrequently happens that the fingers get jammed between the cylinders. The juice, taken out of the receiver, is put into the boilers, beneath which a glowing fire is kept up by two firemen on opposite sides of the kiln, the fuel being chiefly the dried leaves of the sugar-cane itself. Near each boiler stands a peasant, whose duty is to stir the boiling juice, and to skim it off by means of large wooden spoons or ladles.

It must not be supposed that the sugar-cane house and press, which we have now described, were set up only for Badan's purposes. It was the affair of a joint-stock company composed of all the husbandmen who grew sugar-cane living in the northern and eastern divisions of Kánchanpur. The sugar-cane of each of these was crushed and turned into *guḍ* or molasses in succession. We say turned into *molasses,* for Bengal husbandmen never manufacture sugar, that being the work of another caste, called the *modaka,* or the confectioner. Another sugar-cane house, with its attendant sugar-mill or press, was set up in the southern outskirts of the village for the benefit of the husbandmen of the southern and western divisions. I may state here that certain religious ceremonies are always gone through when Hindu ráiyats set up the boiling house. At the setting up of Badan's press, his family priest, Rám Dhan Misra, consecrated it. Prayers were offered chiefly to two divinities—Lakshmi, the Indian Demeter; and Agni, the god of fire. The first was not so much thanked for past favours as prayed to for future ones; and the second was earnestly besought to preserve the sugar-cane house from fire, for it sometimes happens that through the negligence of the firemen the sugar-cane house becomes reduced to ashes.

We have said above that a great deal of friction is produced in the sugar-cane press when the canes are inserted between the cylinders. The consequence of this is that the press makes an unearthly noise. The noise is quite deafening in the neighbourhood of the machine, and can be heard at the distance of two or three miles. Day and night—for the operation goes on all night—for three or four weeks together are the inhabitants of Kánchanpur regaled with this delicious music—a music which can be compared only with the "jarring sound" produced by the opening of the gates of hell, which "on their hinges grated harsh thunder," and shook Erebus to its lowest bottom.

But though the village *áuksálá* has this drawback, it has also its advantages. The paddy harvest-field is, as we have seen, a scene of rural joy, but the sugar-cane house is a scene of still greater joy. It is visited every day by every little boy and girl in the village, each of whom receives one sweet cane as a present from the kind-hearted peasants. Every day loads of sugar-cane are given away to children and Brahmans; but the peasants give them away with cheerful hearts, believing that Mother Lakshmi will bless them the coming year with a more abundant crop; and the name of the niggardly and impious husbandman who sends away children and Brahmans empty-handed from the sugar-cane house is held in execration by the whole of the village community.

Not only is the cane given away, but quantities of the juice while boiling are dealt out to children, who come provided with vessels for the purpose; and not unfrequently brinjals (egg-fruit) and other vegetables are thrown into the boilers, and then taken out and eaten with infinite relish by the children, multitudes of whom are seen, at all hours of the day, loitering about in the precincts of the sugar-cane house, to the great detriment of the village school, which during those days has a thin attendance.

CHAPTER XXXIV.

ÁDURI BECOMES A VAISHNAVI.

No finer dish
Than broth of fish;
Nothing is sweeter
Than lap of spinster:
With joy all ye the name of Hari shout.

Nityánanda.

THE reader has doubtless got some inkling of the religion of Badan and his family; but as religion forms a prominent part of the social and domestic life of Bengalis—the agricultural and working classes not excepted—we should be hardly excused if we did not speak of it at some length. The Hindu population of Bengal may be ranged under two classes, the Sáktas and the Vaishnavas: the worshippers of Sákti or the Divine Female Principle, and the worshippers of Vishnu, or rather of Krishna, for though the Hindus in general take the latter deity to be only a manifestation of the former, the Vaishnavas of Bengal regard him not as a part of God but as *Púrna Brahma:* that is, the full and complete divine essence itself in human shape. The Bengal Vaishnavas, however, are the followers of a Bengali reformer of the name of Chaitanya, whom they worship as a god, or, more strictly speaking, as an incarnation of Krishna. Images of Chaitanya, made of clay painted, and of the size of life, and those of his two chief associates, Nityánanda and

Advaitánanda, are worshipped by them; and in the village of Kánchanpur a life-size image of Chaitanya is adored, under the name of Syáma Sundar, by hundreds of the inhabitants. But the chief divinity of the Bengal Vaishnavas is Krishna, the cow-herd of Vrindávan near Mathurá (Muttra); and his mistress, Rádhá, the principal *gopi* (cow-herdess) amongst sixteen hundred women of the same occupation, receives equal adoration to himself. The sports and amours of Rádhá and Krishna form the subject of the Vaishnava's daily meditation; and there is no Vaishnava who has the slightest pretensions to piety that does not repeat the name of Hari or Krishna at least one hundred and eight times on a bead-roll made of the stem of the sacred *tulasi* (basil) plant. This institution of the repetition of the name of Hari is called the sacrament of *Harináma.* It is observed by elderly men and women, especially widows. Alanga observed it punctually twice every day—once before her noon-day meal, and again after sunset. The words of this formula of devotion are as follows:—

Hare Krishna!
Hare Krishna!
Krishna, Krishna!
Hare, Hare!
Hare, Ráma!
Hare, Ráma!
Ráma, Ráma!
Hare, Hare!

Áduri also occasionally told her beads, but not so punctually as her mother-in-law.

The visiting of holy places is another part of Vaishnava devotion. The three holiest places of Vaishnava pilgrimage are the groves of Vrindávan near Mathurá, where the divine neat-herd Krishna romped about when a lad with the milk-maids; the temple of Jagannátha at Puri in Orissa; and Dváraká in Gujaráṭh, once the residence of Krishna. But in the district of Vardhamána itself and its borders there are three places of some sanctity. These are Navadvípa, the residence of Chaitanya, Ambiká (Culna), where Nityánanda lived for some time; and Agradvípa, famous for the shrine of Gopináth, the lord of the milk-maids.

We have seen that Alanga felt that her cup of earthly felicity had become nearly full at the marriage of Govinda. She had now nothing brighter to look to. She could now sing her *Nunc dimittis* and calmly devote the rest of her life to religion and to pilgrimage. She therefore made up her mind to visit first the holy places of the Vardhamána district, and afterwards at some convenient opportunity to set out on the distant and somewhat perilous pilgrimage to Jagannátha. Áduri expressed great desire to accompany her mother-in-law. She said that as a widow she had no earthly object to live for; it was therefore her intention to devote the remainder of her life to pilgrimage. Though Badan and Kálamánik doubted the sincerity of her professions, yet they did not think it proper to put any obstacles in the gratification of her religious wishes, they therefore complied with her request, and the rather as their mother would thus have a companion in her peregrinations. In the company of two other women of the village, who went on the same errand, Alanga and Áduri set out on pilgrimage. Their plan was first to go to Ambiká, next to visit Málati at Durgánagar which was not far from it, then to go to Navadvípa, and last of all to Agradvípa, whence they resolved to return home direct. Our pilgrims, each of whom had a bundle containing one or two pieces of cloth, a quantity of rice, a small earthen pot of mustard oil, and one brass vessel, reached Ambiká in two days. They went to the house of the Gosvámis, bowed down before Syáma Sundara, worshipped the foot-print of Nityánanda under a tree, and bathed in the holy Bhágirathi. From Ambika to Durganaga was an easy journey of about eight miles. We need not say that Málati was delighted at her grandmother's visit, and made the party as comfortable as she could. After stopping there a couple of days they went to Navadvípa, the birthplace of Bengal Vaishnavism. There was not much to see there, for they were told that the house in which Chaitanya lived was in the middle of the Bhágirathi, as the river had since changed its course and washed away a good part of the old town.

From Navadvípa (the new island) they proceeded to Agradvípa (the fore island), where the great festival of Mahotsava (literally, the great rejoicing) had already commenced. Vaishnavas had flocked thither from all parts of the country. Vairágis, Báuls, Ňágas, Neḍas, and Neḍis, in their grotesque habiliments, were all there. The music of the *khol* or *mridanga* and of the *karatála* was heard day and night. They sang the praises of Gopinath in merry groups through the village. They danced with wild excitement.

> Now pursuing, now retreating,
> Now in circling troops they meet;
> To brisk notes in cadence beating,
> Glance their many tinkling feet.

They shouted the names of Rádhá and Krishna till their throats became hoarse; they foamed at the mouth; they cut religious somersets; men and women danced together promiscuously, the latter excelling the former in the violence of their gestures; many *mridangas* and *karatáls* were broken through violence of striking; and many women had fits of devotional fainting. The excitement among the pilgrims—and their number was about fifty thousand—was immense. The joy of Alanga and Áduri knew no bounds. They seemed to be translated to Vaikuntha, the Paradise of Vaishnavas.

While Alanga, Áduri, and their two companions were one day—for the festival lasted several days—going round the parti-coloured groups of regular, that is, mendicant Vaishnavas, they were attracted to one particular group, where the music and the singing were more vociferous, and the dancing more violent than the rest. There was one actor on this scene to whom every eye was turned, partly on account of the violence of the music—if music that could be called, which was dissonance itself—which his *karatála* sent forth, and partly on account of the vehemence of his devotional dance. He was in a state of primitive nudity, save and except a small bit of rag, called *kaupin*; a red cone-shaped cap was on his head; and his neck was encircled with a three-fold bead roll. He was singing, dancing, and shouting at a tremendous rate; now falling to the ground, now jumping up, and now twisting his body in varied contortions, as if in convulsions; in a word, he was conducting himself in such a manner that anyone not acquainted with the manners of the Vaishnavas would think that the man had gone "daft." But the madder a Vaishnava is, the holier he is deemed by the people. As he was going through all this buffoonery, to the edification, doubtless, of the spectators, his eyes met those of Áduri. Suddenly he fell down on the ground as if perfectly senseless, foaming at the mouth, his body trembling and moving like a fish hooked by an angler. His friends immediately gave out that he was possessed of *dasá*, that is to say, was under supernatural influence. When he lay thus stretched on the ground, Alanga and Áduri at once recognised him to be Prem-Bhakta Vairági, the same who often came to their house for alms, and who acted as their *guru's* legate on the occasion of Govinda's marriage. His companions lifted him up, and put a little water on his lips. Being still in a state of *dasá*, he was asked what he had seen. He said he had a sight of Gopináthji, who had revealed to him the interesting fact that there was one woman there standing amongst the group who was destined to be one of the most glorious of mendicant Vaishnavas. With a view to the identification of this favoured person, Gopináth had told him that the woman in question was a young widow, who had come to the festival in the company of three other women, and who was at that moment standing under a tree in the north-east corner of the area. All eyes were turned to the foot of the tree; and sure enough four women were standing there, one of whom, Áduri, was a young widow. The leader of the Vaishnava group went up to Áduri, acquainted her with the subject-matter of the revelation vouchsafed to Prem-Bhakta, congratulated her on her singular good fortune, and added that, under the circumstances, it was her duty to take *bhek,* that is to put on the garb of a mendicant nun and to join the Vairági order. Alanga did not know what to make of the affair. The idea never occurred to her simple soul that any imposture was practised; and yet she felt it difficult to part with a friend whom she loved and who was a member of her household. Other Vaishnavas now came forward, and poured their oily eloquence into the willing ears of Áduri. After a few moments' hesitation she consented to take the *bhek.*

As religious bigotry allows of no delay in swallowing its victims, Áduri was there and then made to go through the ceremonies, and admitted into the order. Vairágis, as men who are destitute of passion—for that is the meaning of the term—of course never marry; neither are female Vairágis given in marriage, they being like the angels in heaven; yet a pious Vairági has a religious female companion, who is to him a sort of helpmeet, and an invaluable auxiliary in devotional exercises. For this holy purpose Áduri was entrusted to the care of Prem-Bhakta who was the instrument of her conversion.

Poor Alanga, though a sincere Vaishnavi, could not help shedding tears at the calamity which had befallen a member of her household. With a heavy heart she started the next morning with her two companions, on her homeward journey. She had scarcely reached the door of her house at Kánchanpur when she set up a loud cry lamenting the loss of Áduri. Sundari and Dhanamani rushed out on hearing Alanga's cries, led her into the house, and, on hearing of the fate of Áduri, joined their lamentations to hers.

CHAPTER XXXV.

ALANGA GOES ON PILGRIMAGE.

> Than longen folk to gon on pilgrimages,
> And palmeres for to seken strange strondes,
> To serve halwes coutho in sondry londes;
> And, specially from everie schires ende
> Of *Bengala*, to *Jagannath* they wende.
>
> *Prologue to Canterbury Tales.*

"The *Sethuyá* was just here," said Alanga to Badan, as the latter returned from the fields; "he said I must be ready to start the day after to-morrow early in the morning. It is an auspicious day; and all the *yatrís* of this village and of the neighbouring villages will start on the same day."

Badan said, "So you have made up your mind, mother, to go? I am very sad; Sri Kshetra is at a great distance; it will take you about four months to go and come back and to stay there. And the way is long and tedious. My chest is almost breaking to think of what may be in store for us."

So saying the old husbandman burst into tears like a child. Alanga, wiping his eyes with the skirt of her *sáḍi*, said,

"Bábá Badan, don't cry. I am going on religious duty, and not on pleasure. The gods will take care of me in the way; Jagannath will protect me. Don't be sad. And besides, you know whatever is written on my forehead will surely come to pass. Who can undo the writing of Vidhátá?"

At this moment Kálamánik and Govinda came in, and were not a little surprised to see Badan weeping. On being acquainted with the cause Kálamánik said,

"Mother, if you go I will also go with you. If you be sick in the way, who will put water into your mouth? How can you go alone?"

"I am not going alone, Bábá," said Alanga; "you know six women of Kánchanpur are going; they will take care of me; and the Sethuyá will also take care of me."

"The Sethuyá has hundreds of people to take care of, and as for the six women of our village, they can hardly take care of themselves. Let me accompany you, mother."

"How can you come with me? If you come, who will till the fields? My son Badan is getting old and feeble, and Govinda is but a child; you, my Mánik, the treasure of seven kings, are the prop and stay of this house. If you come with me how will this family get on? No, child, you must not come with me. Mahá Prabhu will protect me."

Govinda, joining in the conversation, said, "But, grandma, what is the use of your going at all? you can worship Jagannath here in the house. Every man's mind is a temple of worship. I do not see the use of going to distant places to worship God. God can be worshipped in the mind."

"You have become a Pandita," replied Alanga; "you have got wisdom by conversing with Khonda Mahásaya, and by reading the books the Vardhamána Padre Saheb gave you. But I am an ignorant woman. I think there is great merit in going to Sri Kshetra."

"So there is," rejoined Govinda; "pilgrimage

is good for those who can afford it. But how can you, grandma, leave my mother alone in charge of this house; as for *bou* she is but an infant."

"I know that, Govinda; but I hardly do anything for the house; all the work is done by your mother and your wife. I only eat and sleep, that is all. You will not miss me. You have got a golden wife, Govinda. She works day and night. She is Lakshmi herself in flesh and blood; and because she is so active and energetic I am emboldened to go on pilgrimage. As for my safety, don't be anxious about it; Jagannath will protect me. Don't prevent me from going. My mind is made up, and won't be quiet. I have almost become mad for going."

Yes, indeed, it is a sort of religious madness which takes possession of old Hindu women, impelling them to go on distant pilgrimages, utterly regardless of the pains and troubles connected with the journey. The *Sethuya*, or the pilgrim-guide, had for many days past been visiting Alanga, describing to her the glories of the temples of Jagannath at Puri in Orissa, and expatiating on the ineffable merit of visiting those holy shrines. Alanga's imagination was set on fire. She made up her mind to go. In her dreams every night she saw the armless deity in all his glory. Nothing would dissuade her from going. The auspicious day scarcely broke, when the *Sethuya*, long before sunrise, came to the door of Badan's house, and shouted, "*Jagannáthji ki jaya.*" "Victory to Jagannath." The members of the household had been up long before—as for Alanga, she had had no sleep through excitement. Alanga took up a small bundle of rice, clothes, and two brass vessels, tied a few rupees at one extremity of her *sáḍi*, and hid it in her waist, and bade farewell to all those that were dear to her. She embraced and kissed Sundari and Dhanamani, and put her right hand on the heads of all and blessed them. They all gave vent to tears, Sundari and Dhanamani crying aloud, as if they were never to see Alanga again. Alanga, choked with tears, at last pronounced the words, "Sri Hari! Sri Hari!" and the *Sethuya* shouted out, "*Jagannáthji ki jaya!*" They both rushed out of the house, and Alanga did not look back, as that would have been an unfavourable omen.

It is superfluous to remark, that Alanga, like the hundreds of thousands of pilgrims that annually visit Jagannath, went on foot. The plan is to travel every day between twenty and thirty miles, and sometimes more, and stop at places called *chatis* or *áddás*, that is inns, or huts, where are sold rice, *dál*, salt, mustard oil, fried rice, treacle, and a few other necessaries of Bengali life. As hundreds of pilgrims may be stopping at the same inn the same night, there can be no room for them all to sleep under sheds; hence the great majority of pilgrims bivouack on the bare ground under the open sky, or at best under trees. It is easy to conceive that, under these circumstances, travelling all day and exposure at night generate disease, and numbers of *yátris* or pilgrims die before they reach the holy city. It is not our purpose to relate all the incidents connected with the pilgrimage of Alanga to Puri, but briefly to indicate the stages of her journey. The *Sethuya*, Alanga, and the six other women of Kánchanpur, went to Vardhamána, and from that place to Medinipur (Midnapore), through Chandrakona and Khirpai. At Medinipur they met with hundreds—it would be more correct to say thousands—who had come from all parts of Bengal, Behar, and the North-west, and who were on their way to the temple of the "Lord of the World." It was at Medinipur that Alanga's troubles commenced. After a weary day's travel of thirty miles or more, she had to assist in the evening at the cooking of the evening and the only meal, and then at night to sleep on the bare ground under the open sky. An hour or two before dawn the march again commenced, and did not end till near nightfall. Day after day did she pursue her wearisome journey, and night after night did she sleep on the bare ground. From Medinipur the pilgrims went to Náráyanagaḍ, then Chhatrapál, then to Pátna Jalesvara, and then to Rájghát, where they bathed in the Suvarna rekhá, or the Golden Line. From Rájghát they marched on to Valesvara (Balasore), the many temples in the neighbourhood of which they visited; then going by Panchagaḍ, they went to Bhadraka, near which they crossed the Vaitarani, the river of death, the Brahmani, and the Mahánadi. They then came to Kaṭaka (Cuttack), or the "Middle of the Mountains," for the spurs of the Vindhya Hills make their appearance there; and then passing through Gopináth Prasád, Balavanta, Sri Rám Chandra Sásana, and Hari Krishnapur, they came to Puri, or *the city*, by way of pre-eminence.

As we have brought Alanga to Srikshetra (or the Holy Field), we think it proper to inform the reader why the ground is holy, and briefly to recite the legend of Jagannath. Once on a time there lived a pious king of the name of Indradyumna, who, after he had performed great religious austerities, was told by the god Vishnu to form an image of Jagannath, and put in it the bones of the god Krishna, who had been killed by the chance arrow of a hunter, and whose bones had been put into a box by some person. On being asked as to who should be the architect of this image, the king was told that the image should be constructed by Visvakarma, the World-maker; so the king prayed to the World-maker, who agreed to make the image on the condition that, if he should be disturbed in his work, the image would be left incomplete. In one night the mighty World-maker built a magnificent temple on Niláchal, or the Blue Mountain—that is, Orissa; and then proceeded leisurely to construct the image of Jagannath, or the World-lord. But the pious king became impatient. Fifteen days had elapsed, and yet he had not heard of the completion of the image. In an evil hour he went to the spot to see what the World-maker was about. The architect, agreeably to the terms fixed on, immediately ceased from working, and the image was left without hands or legs. The king became very sad; but he was assured by heaven that the image, incomplete though it was, would become world-famous. The king invited all the gods to assist in the consecration and deification of the image. Brahma, the supreme god, himself officiated as hierophant on the occasion, and endowed it with the power of vision and a living soul; and the bones of Krishna were put into it. This is the image of Jagannath placed in the temple of Puri, called the Pagoda by Europeans; and it was to worship this legless and armless deity that Alanga, along with about two hundred thousand pilgrims, plodded on her weary way through hundreds of miles. What Alanga did at Puri must be described in the ensuing chapter.

CHAPTER XXXVI.

THE CAR FESTIVAL.

> All around, behind, before,
> With frantic shout and deafening roar;
> And the double, double peals of the drum are there,
> And the startling burst of the trumpet's blare.
> And the gong that seems, with its thunders dread,
> To stun the living, and waken the dead.
>
> SOUTHEY'S *Kehama.*

NEVER had Alanga seen so many human beings crowded together in so small a space as at Puri. She had been to Agradvípa, and had seen thousands of devotees worshipping the "Lord of milk-maids;" but they were as a drop compared to the ocean of human heads which she saw in the Holy Field. There were pilgrims from all parts of India; from Bengal, from Behar, from the North-West, from the Central Provinces, from Madras, from Bombay, from the Deccan; devotees of every religious persuasion were there, especially Vaishnavas of all orders and habiliments. The utmost enthusiasm prevailed amongst the pilgrims. They spent their time in visiting all the temples in the neighbourhood, and especially in loitering about within the precincts of the great Pagoda, near which, within an enclosure of stone wall, there are no less than one hundred temples. The attractions of vice were not wanting. The number of courtesans and women of easy virtue was immense; and in the purlieus of the holy temple itself dwelt women who were destitute of all sense of shame. To Alanga, however, who sincerely believed in the divinity of Jagannath, and was diligent in the discharge of every religious duty, the scene was one of high devotional enjoyment.

The worship of Jagannath is always associated with that of his brother Balarám, and of his sister Subhadrá. The image of each is a rudely constructed and ill-shapen wooden bust, of about six feet in height. The image of Jagannath is painted white, that of Balarám black, and of Subhadrá yellow. Jagannath has mere stumps of arms, while Subhadrá is destitute even of those stumps. On the whole, the two divine brothers and their sister are the ugliest of all the deities in the Hindu Pantheon. But though the ugliest, they are the most luxuriously fed of all the gods and goddesses. At the time Alanga visited Puri, Jagannath had the largest establishment of any prince in India. It consisted of 3,000 families of servants and dependants, of whom 400 families were cooks. The deity's daily bill of fare was as follows:—"220 pounds of rice, 97 pounds of *kalái* (pulse), 24 pounds of *mug* (another sort of pulse), 188 pounds of clarified butter, made from buffalo's milk, 80 pounds of molasses, 32 pounds of vegetables, 10 pounds of sour milk, 2½ pounds of spices, 2 pounds of sandal-wood, some camphor, and 20 pounds of salt." During high festivals, the 400 families of cooks, of whom we have spoken, are all engaged in preparing food for the pilgrims, who buy cooked food; and it is believed that within the court of the temple itself food for about 100,000 pilgrims is daily cooked and sold. No Hindu ever buys cooked food in any place, but the Holy Field is an exception to the rule.

Boiled rice in large quantities is bought by the pilgrims, is dried and taken to their respective homes, under the name of *maháprasád;* and in all parts of India, but chiefly in Bengal, one grain of this dried holy rice is eaten every day by every devout Vaishnava, male or female, before ordinary food is tasted.

The first great ceremony which Alanga witnessed at Puri was the Snán Yátra, or the Bathing Festival. The image of Jagannath was brought out from the temple in great state by the Pánḍás, or priests, and placed in an open terrace, amid the deafening shouts of "Jaya Jagannáth! Jaya Jagannáth!" "Victory to Jagannath! Victory to Jagannath!" raised by myriads of spectators. Holy texts were then chanted, and water was poured on the head of the "Lord of the World;" the deity, thus bathed, was wiped, and presented with offerings by innumerable votaries; and was taken back to his abode.

The other festival, the greatest of all the festivals of Jagannath, which Alanga saw, was the Ratha Yátrá, or the Car Festival. On the appointed day—and it usually takes place in June or July—the three idols of Jagannáth, Balaráma, and Subhadrá, were brought, or rather dragged—for they are actually pulled by means of cords fastened round the necks of the images—from their thrones in the temple, and taken out at the Sinha-dvár, or the Lion Gate. When the deities made their appearance at the gate, shouts of "Jaya Jagannáth! Jaya Jagannáth!" rent the air. The images were then dragged in the same irreverent manner as before, by means of ropes, up an inclined plane, into the *rathas*, or cars. The cars are huge vehicles, five stories high, with a number of wheels, turrets, and flags. The car of Jagannath is 43½ feet high, having 16 wheels of 6½ feet in diameter, and a platform 34½ feet square; the car of Balarám is 41 feet high, with 14 wheels; and that of Subhadrá, 40 feet high, with also 14 wheels. After the stumps of the idols had been put in their places on the cars, hands, feet, and ears (all made of gold), were supplied to them; and orders to drag the cars were issued. It is impossible to describe the enthusiasm of the people at the first movement of the cars. From myriads of throats issued the shouts of "Jaya Jagannáth! Jaya Jagannáth" "Hari bol! Hari bol!" accompanied by the harsh dissonance of hundreds of so-called musical instruments. To touch the holy ropes, or hawsers, by which the sacred vehicles were pulled, is reckoned an act of high merit; hence the rush towards the cars is always great. In former days, men and women used voluntarily to fling themselves under the wheels of the ponderous chariots, and were crushed to death. But, thanks to the humanity of the British Government, that murderous practice has been stopped. The gods remained eight days in their cars, receiving the adorations and offerings of their devotees. On the ninth day they returned to their temples. Soon after their return, the two gods and their sister were put to sleep, and as their sleep extends generally from about the middle of July to the middle of October—a shorter *siesta,* by the way than that enjoyed by the earthly divinities of the Calcutta Government House, on the sublime heights of the Indian Olympus—the pilgrims commenced returning to their homes.

It is when the pilgrims return from the Holy Field that the horrors of pilgrimage appear in their full magnitude. Owing to constant exposure, day and night, to the heat of the sun, to the rains pouring every now and then in copious showers, and to night dews—for most of the pilgrims sleep in the open air for want of accommodation in the inns; owing to the immense mass of human beings crowded into a small space; owing to the badness and insufficiency of food—for most of the pilgrims spend nearly all their means of subsistence before they set their face homewards; owing to imperfect sanitary arrangements in the sacred city and its environs; owing to these and other causes, no inconsiderable a proportion of the pilgrims fall victims to fever, to dysentery, and to cholera. The tract of country in the immediate vicinity of Puri becomes a vast Golgotha. Dead bodies are met with everywhere. The little river which flows near it is often covered with corpses. The great road from Puri towards Kataka (Cuttack) may be traced by funeral piles on which dead bodies have been burnt, or by bones left by jackals or vultures; while in the inns on the roadside may be heard every hour of the day and of the night the groans of dying men. On the pilgrim road to Puri, if anywhere, may be witnessed the shocking scene described by the poet:—

He saw the lean dogs
Gorging and growling o'er carcase and limb;
They were too busy to bark at him.
From a pilgrim's skull they had stript the flesh,
As ye peel the fig when the fruit is fresh;
And their white trunks crunched o'er their white skull
As it slipt through their jaws when their edge grew dull;
As they lazily mumbled the bones of the dead,
When they scarce could stir from the place where they fed;
So well had they broken a lingering fast
With those who had fallen for that repast.

Poor Alanga left Puri with the seeds of disease sown in her system. On the second day after her arrival at nightfall at an inn, she discovered all the symptoms of malignant cholera. The six women of Kánchanpur who had accompanied her did as much for her as they could under the circumstances; in other words, they did nothing, for they could do nothing. They did not succeed in getting shelter for her in a hut. She was laid down under a tree all night. There was no doctor, no medicine. The six women resolved next morning to leave Alanga to the tender mercies of dogs and vultures. Early in the day, however, Prem Bhakta Vairági and Áduri, who had come on pilgrimage, and who were returning home, accidentally came to the tree under which Alanga was lying. The Vairági, who pretended to have some knowledge of medicine, made her swallow some drugs. But in vain. Alanga died the same afternoon, after an illness of less than twenty-four hours. No firewood could be procured for the purpose of cremation, and the rest may be imagined. Such was the end of Alanga, a woman estimable both for her intelligence, considering her station in life, and for her character.

CHAPTER XXXVII.

BENGAL FEVER AND THE VILLAGE LEECH.

Learned he was in med'cinal lore,
For by his side a pouch he wore,
Replete with strange hermetic powder,
That wounds nine miles point-blank would solder;
By skilful chymist, with great cost,
Extracted from a rotten post.
Hudibras.

"I HEAR your father is sick, *sángát*," said Nanda to Govinda one morning, as the latter was sitting on his haunches on the threshold of the door of his house and enjoying his smoke.

"Yes, last evening when he returned from the fields he was in a strong fever. And all night the fever was upon him and has not yet left him."

"You should take care, as the fever this season is of a very bad type; are you thinking of calling a Voidya?"

"What's the use just now? I hope the fever is of a slight character; it may go off by fasting one or two days."

This, in truth, is almost the universal practice in the villages. In the first instance, in case of fever, no medicines are taken, but the patient is made to abstain from all food; and, as to drink, a few drops of water are given at long intervals, and only when the sick man loudly calls for drink. Two days had already passed, and there was no remission of the fever, indeed it was every day increasing in strength, and the patient had already become very weak. Kálamánik and Govinda both felt that the case was becoming serious, and that it was high time to call in the aid of a doctor. By the advice of neighbours they delayed one day longer, as it was imagined that if the fever were of a light kind it would go off after three days—the three being a magical number among Bengalis—but if it did not leave the patient on the morning of the fourth day, it would be necessary to call a Kaviráj. The morning of the fourth day dawned, and Badan was worse. Kálamánik therefore at once went to call a doctor.

There were several families of the Voidya or medical caste at Kánchanpur, the male members of which have in succession been practising medicine from time out of mind. They were all called Kavirajes, or lords of poets, though none of them ever perpetrated poetry in their lives. The most eminent physician in the village was Mritunjaya, or the Conqueror of Death, though to speak the truth, he seldom cured any serious case which he took in hand. Bengali physicians have been facetiously divided into "killers of ten," "killers of hundreds," and "killers of thousands;" and it is to this last class of heroes that Mritunjaya belonged. It might have been truly said of him:—

> Nor engine, nor device polemic
> Disease, nor doctor epidemic,
> Tho' stored with deletery med'cines,
> Which whosoever took is dead since,
> Ever sent so vast a colony
> To both the under worlds as he.

This trifling circumstance, however, did not detract from his reputation as a first-rate physician; for it is argued that a physician can only apply proper remedies; he cannot annul the decrees of fate; and if it is written on the forehead of a patient that he should die of a certain disease, no doctor in the world—not Dhanwantari himself—could cure him. That Mritunjaya had a collection of the best and rarest medicines was a fact admitted by every one in the village. He had the ingredients of several excellent aperients composed of five, ten, and eighteen different sorts of vegetables. Metallic medicines of various kinds, especially a famous one made of gold dust; *rasásindhu* of the first quality; poisons of serpents of various species of the cobra; and oils of an infinite variety. But the richness of his laboratory was his least merit. For many miles round no Kaviraj had such perfect *Dhátujnan*, or knowledge of the pulse, as Mritunjaya; and this must be acknowledged to be perhaps the most difficult part of the practice of medicine. Nor was he less profound in his knowledge of the diagnosis of disease. It is well known that he never made any mistake in ascertaining the nature of the disease, though it must be acknowledged that he was seldom successful in grappling with it. The wonderful insight which he had acquired into the nature of diseases was chiefly owing to a diligent study of those renowned medical treatises in Sanskrit which were written several centuries ago, and which showed such a miraculous knowledge of both diseases and their remedies, that he believed them, along with all his brethren of the craft in Bengal, to have been composed by divine inspiration—indeed, to have been written by the finger of Mahádeva himself. For modern medicine, and especially European medicine, he had a perfect contempt: and it was one of his constant sayings that European doctors did not at all understand the treatment of Indian fever. He admitted the superiority of English to native doctors in surgery, but then it was his opinion that surgery formed no part of the functions of a medical man, as surgical operations belonged, properly speaking, to the province of the barber.

In our accomplished physician there was only one drawback, and that was that he was an inveterate opium eater. He began with swallowing every day a dose of the size of a pea, but the modicum increased gradually, till at last he used every day to gulp down a quantity sufficient to kill a horse. Owing to this habit he was seldom in a perfectly wakeful state; whenever he sat for five minutes his eyes were almost always half-closed. As his practice was not large, and as a doctor's fee is very little in the villages—generally a rupee for curing a patient, who may require attendance every day for a fortnight or upwards, and in case of non-recovery nothing at all—he was often in pecuniary straits. But whether he had his daily *Dál* and *bhát* or not, the supply of his daily modicum of opium was absolutely necessary, and sometimes when the exact hour had passed away without his swallowing that precious drug, he became so sick as to seem almost to be in a dying state. Such was the redoubtable physician who now accompanied Kálamánik.

On feeling Badan's pulse Mritunjaya found him in strong fever, and therefore prescribed one of those aperient mixtures or *pánchans*, which goes by the name of *Dasmúla*, so called from its being a composition of the roots of ten different vegetables; but before the mixture could be prepared he made him swallow a couple of pills—a large number of which he always carried about with him in his pouch—mixed with the juice of a *pán* leaf. The *Dasmúla* had no effect; and there was no remission of the fever. Various other mixtures and pills were tried successively, but with little effect. *Rasásindhu* was applied, but with the like result. Badan was evidently in high fever. The members of his family were alarmed, and Rámdhan Misra, the family priest, was requested to come to the house, and offer every day to the gods one thousand leaves of the sacred *tulasi*; and various forms of prayers called *Swastyayanas* were offered, with a view to averting the displeasure of the gods and the recovery of the patient. Vegetable and serpent poisons were next tried by the Conqueror of Death, but no signs of victory were forthcoming. As a last resource the patient was made to swallow a deadly poison, which passed under the name of the *hukáwálár gundo*, or the *powder of the Hubble-bubble seller*, so called from its having been invented by a dealer in hookahs of the town of Vardhamána. All these poisons, instead of contributing to Badan's recovery, only made him worse. He became delirious. It was evident he was fast sinking, and there was not the remotest chance of his recovery. In order to prevent the spirit from departing from the body in a room, Badan was taken down one evening from his bed-room to the open yard, where shortly he breathed his last, amid the loud cries and lamentations of all the members of the household. That very night the corpse was taken to a tank called *Náráyan Sil*, on the embankment of which it was burnt, as it is considered inauspicious to keep the corpse for a long time in the house.

CHAPTER XXXVIII.

THE SITUATION.

They perished—the blithe days of boyhood had perished—
And all the gladness and all the peace I knew!
Now have I but their memory, fondly cherished—
God, may I never, never lose that too.

Longfellow.

The morning of life, like the prime of day, is unquestionably the pleasantest and happiest period of a man's existence. Devoid of all care and anxiety, having no experience of the asperities of life and the roughness of the world, the thoughtless youth eats and drinks, and takes his pleasure and rejoices in everything about him.

Govinda had hitherto lived a life of ease and quietude. It is true he had none of the elegant comforts of polished life; it is true he laboured every day in the field, either at the plough, at the barn, or the field; it is true he dined off only boiled rice and pulse, a vegetable or two, and some miserable looking fish, and washed down that food, not with wine, but with simple rain water; yet he felt himself as comfortable and happy as the proudest English nobleman who rolls in wealth and magnificence, and to furnish whose table with delicacies, earth, ocean, and air are laid under contribution. What though Govinda ate only *Punya Sák (Basella lucida)* along with his coarse rice, and slept on a palm-leaf mat spread on a mud floor, his stomach was not the less filled, neither was his repose the more disturbed on that account. Govinda's usual article of clothing, it is true, consisted of a single *dhuti* wrapped round his waist, and dangling down perhaps a little below his knees, while both the upper and lower regions of his frame remained in a state of primeval nudity; yet who shall tell me that the man who is covered in *kinkob* and gold brocade is, on account of that circumstance, happier than he. As a peasant youth he spent most part of his time under the canopy of Heaven, inhaling the fragrant breeze of the fields, and holding communion, such as it was, with the beautiful, if somewhat uniform, scenery of his native land; and though education was wanting to enable him fully to profit from his daily contact with external nature, yet there was nothing in paddy-fields and mango-groves and hedge-rows, as in towns and cities, to corrupt his heart and to brutalise his nature.

In most countries marriage brings in its train all sorts of cares and anxieties. It is not so in Bengal. Govinda got married, and even begat children, but he took no thought for the support of his wife and his children. It was Badan's business to provide for his daughter-in-law and his grandchildren. The family treasure, such as it was, was in the hands of Badan. He kept in his own possession all the money obtained by selling paddy and molasses, and the small sums he realised every month by selling milk and some of the products of his fields, like pulse, brinjal, *palval,* and other vegetables. He paid rent at fixed periods to the zamindár, or landlord, for the ground on which his house stood, and for the fields which he cultivated. He borrowed money from the *mahájan*, or the money-lender, when funds were a *minus* quantity; and though he consulted sometimes with his son, the task of making both ends meet never fell on the shoulders of Govinda during the lifetime of his father.

Next to Badan, Alanga had had the largest share of care and anxiety in the management of the family; indeed, it is no exaggeration to say that Badan did nothing without consulting his mother, who was endued with no little amount of common sense. Sundari, though the wife of the master of the house, had never been its mistress. That post was always filled by Alanga, without, however, the slightest jealousy on Sundari's part; indeed, Sundari often expressed her thankfulness for the privilege of being under the guidance of so wise and so affectionate a mother-in-law.

But all this now underwent a change. Badan has been gathered to his fathers, and Alanga has fallen a victim to the "Moloch of the East." According to Hindu manners and customs, it was Kálamánik's business to take Badan's place in the household; but though he was a brave fellow, and the sturdiest ploughman in all Kánchanpur, his defective intelligence incapacitated him for the task. Govinda therefore became the master of the house, and his mother Sundari the *grihini* or mistress. Hitherto Govinda had lived without anxiety. The colour and complexion of his life underwent a change immediately on the death of his father. How to support the family entrusted to his care became now the problem of his life.

At such a time it may not be deemed unseasonable briefly to glance at the situation in which

Govinda now found himself. There has been no change in his homestead. There is the same big hut, with its two compartments, one serving as a dormitory, and the other as a refectory, or rather store-room; there is the hut, in the verandah of which is the homely pedal; there is the third hut, which now serves the double purpose of a kitchen and a sleeping-room for Kálamánik; and there also stands the cow-house as before. It is unnecessary to remark that death had made havoc of the family. Gayárám had been bitten to death by a serpent; Badan had been carried off by fever; and Alanga had died on the "holy field" of Orissa. Málati was in her husband's house at Durgánagar, and Áduri, having become a mendicant, was wandering about the country in the company of her pious lover Prem Bhakta. There remained now our hero, his mother Sundari, his wife Dhanamani, and his uncle Kálamánik, who was still living in single blessedness.

The fields which Govinda cultivated were precisely those which his father had tilled; there was neither increase nor diminution in the number of *bighás*. Govinda, however, commenced life with one serious drawback. His father had bequeathed to him the legacy of a small debt, which had been considerably increased by Govinda having had to celebrate in succession the funeral ceremonies of his father and grandmother. What made the burden of the debt galling was that it was contracted at a heavy rate of interest, namely, two pice a rupee per mensem, that is, thirty-seven and a half per cent. per annum, though the rate, as it was the usual one, was not regarded as extravagant by any *mahájan* or money-lender.

CHAPTER XXXIX.

THE ZAMINDÁR OF KÁNCHANPUR.

Our laird gets in his racked rents,
His coals, his kain, an' a' his stents;
He rises when he likes himsel;
His flunkies answer at the bell.

The Twa Dogs.

ONE morning as Govinda was sitting at the door of his house, smoking and engaged in thought, he was accosted by a person who had a thick bamboo club in one hand and a bit of paper in the other. The person who came up to Govinda was of stalwart size, being six feet in height, with a fine pair of moustaches which joined the whiskers descending from the temples, and a thick beard brushed upwards. It was evident from his dress and features that he was not a Bengali, but a native of the North-Western Provinces. Hanumán Singha, for that was the name of the person who accosted Govinda, was one of the officers, or *nagodis*, of the zamindár of Kánchanpur, whose business was to bring them over to the *gomastá*, who received rent and gave receipts.

"And what is that in your hand, Hanumán Sing?" asked Govinda.

"In this paper is put down your share of the *máthot* which is being levied from every ráiyat on account of the approaching marriage of the son of the zamindár in February next."

"*Máthot!* dear me! how can I pay *máthot*, when

I am in arrears to the zamindár for rent, and largely in debt to other parties, chiefly on account of the funeral obsequies of my father and grandmother?"

"It is not much you will have to pay; and besides it is only once in a way, as the Raya Chaudhuri's son is not going every now and then to get married. You, along with other ráiyats, are to pay only two annas for every rupee of rent you give to the *Talukdár*. The amount of your rent is forty rupees per annum, and surely it is not too much for you to give five rupees."

"My dear sir, I am not in a position now to give any *máthot* or *abwab*. It is all very well for persons well-to-do to pay their cesses. But surely the zamindár ought not reasonably to expect me to pay anything of the sort, since now I am in great distress. You speak of five *tákás* not being too much, I cannot give five cowries."

"But you must give. It is the order of your zamindár. Any how, you must produce the five rupees either by begging, or borrowing, or mortgaging the ornaments of your wife, or selling your brass vessels."

"You go and tell the *gomastá* that I am unable to pay."

"What a fine fellow you are! You have become wiser than your father, who regularly paid every *máthot* demanded by his landlord. Come now, and get me the five rupees."

"Am I joking with you, Hanumán Sing? I have no money in the house. If you make a diligent search through the house you will not find even five payasás. Go and tell the zamindár when I have means I'll pay; at present I can't pay."

"Well, then, you yourself come and tell the zamindár. And if you don't come willingly, I have orders to take you by force."

Govinda, perceiving that resistance was hopeless, agreed to go. He put away the hookah, took his *gámchhá*, put it on his left shoulder, and went with Hanumán Singha.

The house of the zamindár was the largest and best building in the village. Its entrance faced the south, like most houses in this part of Bengal, as the object is to avoid the sharp, cold, north wind in winter, and to get the benefit as much as possible of the delicious south wind which blows during summer. The outer gate of the mansion was built of solid masonry, with a colossal door of *sál* wood, studded with huge nails, surmounted with the figure, in stucco and plaster, of a lion. As you go within through the gate, you see before you a courtyard of about sixty feet square, on the north of which is a large hall, and on the east and west suites of small rooms, extending from the sides of the hall, and meeting the long and high wall, in the middle of which is the gate. This part of the house, including the courtyard, the hall, and the suites of rooms on the sides, is called *Káchhári báḍi* (Cutcherry-house), where the zamindár holds his court, and transacts all affairs regarding his zamindári. The hall is covered with *satranajas*, or Indian carpets, in the middle of which sits the zamindár, propped up by pillows on all sides; the *divána*, the *gomastá*, and other officials squatting at distances varying according to their rank. Beyond this hall, and further to the north, is another courtyard of equal area with the first, in front of which is a spacious hall, called the *dálán*, supported by arches, and on the two sides of which are covered verandahs, two stories high, consisting of several small rooms. This part of the house is called the *Báhir-bádi* (outer-house), or the *Dálán-báḍi*. The *Dálán,* properly so called, is used only on great religious festivals; the images are placed there, and all sorts of dramatic and pantomimic exhibitions are made in the open courtyard below, which on such occasions is covered with a large cloth canopy, called *chandrátapa* or moonshade. The hall of the *Káchchári-báḍi* opens into the courtyard of the *Dálán-báḍi;* but the regular entrance into the latter is by a lane on the left of the hall. Beyond the *Dálán-báḍi* is a third courtyard of exactly the same area with that of the other two, which is built round on all sides with covered verandahs similar to those in the *Dálán-báḍi,* two stories high, containing a large number of small rooms, with very few windows. This part of the house is called the *antahpura,* or the *andar-mahal,* or the zenana, properly so called. There are the women's apartments, visited only by the light of the sun.

Govinda passed through the lion-gate of this huge pile of brick and mortar, walked on to the door of the hall, and putting his sheet round his neck, made obeisance to the zamindár, who was leaning on one of those bolsters called *tákiás,* but which looked more like a huge bale of cotton than a pillow. The zamindár was a large-built man, taller than ordinary Bengalis, and proportionately corpulent. He was sitting like a lion couchant. His eyes first attracted the notice of every one that approached him. Bright, large, and rolling, they seemed to be sending forth every moment flashes of lightning rage; and the sturdiest peasant of Kánchanpur has confessed that there is no standing the fire of those two dreadful batteries. His voice was singularly powerful, of immense volume, and sounded, when he was in a tempest of rage, like the artillery of heaven. The silver streaks in his hair showed that he was between forty and fifty years of age. Jayachánd Ráya Chauduri (for such was the name of the zamindár of Kánchanpur) was, strictly speaking. not a zamindár, but a middle man, for he only held a *Pattanitáluk* under his Highness the Mahárájá of Vardhamána; but though he was only a *Pattanidár*, he was usually called the zamindár of Kánchanpur and of scores of other villages lying round about. He paid 2,000 rupees a year to the Mahárájá for the village of Kánchanpur: but it was generally believed that he himself realised in rents about three times that amount. For the whole of his zamindári, or rather *pattani*, he gave eighty thousand rupees to the Raja, but he himself has admitted that after paying the *Sadar Jamá*, his own net profit amounted to the round sum of two lakhs, or £20,000 a year. Such immense profit could only be obtained by a system of rack renting, of illegal extortion, and of cruel oppression; and it must be admitted that Jaya Chánd belonged to a class of zamindárs who were the greatest curses to their country. Not having had the benefit of an English education, unacquainted with Sanskrit, and possessing only a smattering of his mother tongue, he was an ignorant man; and the natural selfishness of his character made that ignorance dangerous to those husbandmen who had the misfortune of being his tenants. Unscrupulous in his character, he did not hesitate to have recourse to any means, however illegal or dishonourable, to screw out of his ráiyats as much money as he could. Of the *Haptam* and the *Pancham* he often took advantage; and many were the ráiyats who were ruined by his oppression. By forgery, by chicanery, by all sorts of fraud—for Jaya Chánd stuck at nothing—he deprived many a poor man of his *lákhráj*, and though by religion a Hindu, he did not hesitate to rob many a poor Bráhmana of his *Brahmotra*. He was the object of universal dread. His name was never pronounced by his ráiyats except with execrations; and he was so much feared that it is said that at his name the tiger and the cow drank water at the same *ghát*. Such was the man in whose presence Govinda now stood with folded hands, and with his sheet round his neck.

"Who is there?" asked Jaya Chánd Ráya Chaudhuri, of his diváná.

"He is Govinda Sámanta, the son of Badan," answered the diváná.

"He is the son of a worthy father. What does he want?"

Hanumán Sing, advancing in front, said, "Mahárájá! He refuses to pay the *máthot* for the marriage of your worship's son. I have therefore brought him before Khodáwand."

"Refuses to pay *máthot!* Is there any ráiyat of mine who dare refuse to pay any *máthot* I choose to impose? Did you not say, he is the son of Badan Sámanta? Badan was one of the best and most obedient of my ráiyats. Is this fellow his own son? Who has put such high notions into his head?"

The diváná now whispered to his master that he had heard Govinda had as a boy attended the same schoolmaster's *páthsálá* for some years. The zamindár, darting a fierce glance on Govinda, said, "So you have become a *Pandita,* and your eyes have got opened, therefore you refuse to pay the *máthot.* I must forbid Ráma Rúpa to teach any peasants' sons; if he persists in doing it, I must break his other leg, fool that he is."

Govinda said in a faint voice, "O, Incarnation of Justice! I have not refused to pay. I dare not refuse. I only said I am unable to pay at present. On account of the funeral ceremonies of my father and grandmother, I have got largely into debt, and my rent will be again shortly due. I will pay the *máthot* afterwards, when I am able."

"Now, hold your tongue. This is my order. Within three days you must pay the *máthot.* If you fail to pay within that time, you shall be brought here with your hands tied. Remember that. Divána, let the fellow go."

I beg the reader not to run away with the idea that all zamindárs of Bengal are like Jaya Chánd Ráya Chaudhuri, of Kánchanpur. Amongst land-holders, as amongst every class of men, there are black sheep as well as white. Before this story is wound up I hope to present to the reader the picture of a just, humane, and philanthropic zamindár—the father of his people; but the lines of our hero had fallen on unpleasant places, and it was his fate—so Govinda expressed himself—to have his homestead in the zamindári of a man who was a Bengal tiger in human shape.

CHAPTER XL.

POLITICS AT THE SMITHY.

> Low lies that house where *tobacco* inspired,
> Where grey-beard mirth, and smiling toil retired,
> Where village statesmen talk'd with looks profound,
> And news much older than their weed went round.
>
> *The Deserted Village.*

It is evening. The sun has long ago gone in his fiery car behind Mount Sumeru; the cows have returned from the fields, and have been shut up in their house; the birds have slunk into their nests; the women of Kánchanpur have "shown the lamp" in all the rooms of their houses, to scare away ghosts and other evil spirits which might lurk in them; and most of the peasantry, after the day's toil, are either smoking in their huts or making preparations for their supper. Kavera, however, and his son Nanda, are busy as in the day; for their toil knows no intermission except in the dead of night. It is true that the people who frequented the smithy during the day for little jobs are no longer there, but their place has been taken up by friends who have come to enjoy an evening chat. But, friends or no friends, the father and son are never unmindful of their own business. Vulcan senior and junior have just taken out of the forge a large piece of iron, glowing and red-hot, have put it on the anvil, and are belabouring it with their hammers and scattering about particles of incandescent matter. *Swish! swish! swish!* go the paternal and the filial hammers, till the sound becomes changed, after the iron had cooled and been dipped in water, into *dhip-dháp! dhip-dháp! dhip-dháp!* While Kuvera and his son were at this exciting work, four or five people were sitting on a mat in the room. There was Kapila, the carpenter; Madan, the grocer; Chatura, the barber; Rasamaya, the confectioner; and Bokárám, the weaver. After the hammering had stopped and the piece of iron had been again put into the forge, Kapila said to Nanda—"Have you heard that Govinda was taken this morning before the *jamidár*" [Hindu Bengali peasants always call the landholder *jamidár*, and not *zamindár*], "and warned that if he did not pay the *máthot* within three days, he would be handcuffed and taken before the *jamidár?*"

"Yes, *sángát* told me on his return from the jamidár's house. It is a great shame that poor people should be oppressed in this way. I do not think, however, that *sángát* should yield in this matter. What have we to do with the marriage of the son of the jamidár? That is an affair of his own. Why should we pay its expenses?"

"But is it prudent not to pay? The jamidár is a rich man; he has a band of *láthiáls* [club-men] under him. How can a poor man, like *bandhu,* cope with him."

Nanda, greatly excited, took hold of his hammer and said, "I wish I could give a blow of this on the jamidár's fat belly and send him to the house of Yama [the king of death]. What have we to do with his son's marriage? What have we to do with *máthots* or *abwabs?* We will only pay the rent fixed by the *Kompáni Báhádur* [The East India Company]." Chatura, the barber, giving a sarcastic smile, said—"Well done, Nanda! You are a great hero! You show your heroism in the corner of your hut. You are a true 'palm-leaf Sepoy'—a very cheap sort of a hero! But here comes Govinda."

Govinda. "*Sángát!* You are very indiscreet. Don't you know that the jamidár's spies are all about? If what you said just now were reported to him by an enemy, it would go hard with you. Don't speak so loud, for aught I know somebody may be listening from behind the wall."

Nanda. "I don't care if it is reported to the jamidár. It is impossible to bear all this oppression. His injustice knows no bounds. Is there no God in the heavens? All the ráiyats have got their bones fried through oppression. The Bráhmanas are cursing him loud, taking the sacred *paita* in their hands, and looking up towards the sun. It is time we all made a *dharmaghaṭ* and refused to pay the iniquitous *máthot*. What say you, *sángát?*"

Govinda. "What you say, *sángát*, is all true. It is no doubt a terrible oppression. But what can we do? He is rich and powerful, and we are poor people. How can we fight with him?"

Nanda. "Then I suppose you mean to pay the *máthot?*"

Govinda. "I have no choice in the matter. If I refuse to pay, he will ill-treat me, perhaps imprison me, and possibly set my house on fire; and it will be impossible to get justice done."

Nanda. "I say, is there no one above? Will He not punish the wicked jamidár?"

Govinda. "I believe the gods punish wicked men. But we do not see that in this life. Perhaps in his next birth he may be punished. But I see no hope of his being punished in this life."

Kapila. "Friend, you are quite right. There is no use opposing the jamidár. You should anyhow pay down the *máthot.* You cannot prevail against the mighty."

Madan. "No one is more against the iniquitous *máthot* than I am. The jamidár has no right to impose this cess on us. But how can we successfully fight against him? Therefore my opinion is that we should quietly pay the cess."

Nanda. "But why not make a *dharmaghat?*"

Govinda. "That is easily said; but with whom will you make *dharmaghat?* Will all the people of the village agree with us? Don't you know that fifteen annas (fifteen sixteenths), of the people through fear of the jamidár will not join us, if we refuse to pay? And of what use will a *dharmaghat* of half-a-dozen persons be? You are very bold, *sángát,* but you want discretion."

Bokárám. "I don't understand about *dharmaghat* or *farmaghat.* I know this, that, if we don't pay the *máthot,* we shall be ruined. Besides, it is useless fighting against fate. It is his fate to be a jamidár, and it is our fate to be his ráiyats; we must, therefore, submit to his exactions, whether just or unjust."

Nanda. "Well said! you, Bokárám, are a true hero. *Sábásh! sábásh!*"

Bokárám. "You need not ridicule me. I do not see any difference between you and me. In talk, you are as big as a mountain, but in action, you are like a mustard-seed. I know your father will at last pay the *máthot.* Then of what use is this boasting?"

Nanda. "If my father pays the *máthot*, it will be without my consent; and, as he is the head of his family, he can certainly do whatever he likes; but his paying or not paying will not alter my views. But, here comes uncle Mánik, I am much mistaken if he consents to Govinda's paying the *máthot*. What say you, uncle Mánik?"

Kálamánik. "What about, Nanda? don't bother me with questions just now. Let me first take a whiff."

Govinda was smoking at the moment Kálamánik entered the room, and he immediately put the hookah into his uncle's hands. Amongst the higher and middle classes, it would be deemed bad manners for a young man to smoke in the presence of his father's brother, but it is not considered so amongst the labouring classes, and chiefly for this reason, that, as they always work together in the field, where there can be no privacy, and, as tobacco is the only refreshment they enjoy, they are obliged to smoke in the presence of their superiors.

Kálamánik gave three or four hard pulls with his mouth at the hookah—indeed, the pulls were so hard that the *kalika* blazed up—and then turning towards Nanda, enquired on what subject he wished to have his opinion.

Nanda. "What other subject can it be, uncle Mánik, except the all engrossing one, of the *máthot*? I wish to know whether you are going to pay the *máthot* or not."

Kálamánik. "I thought you knew me too well to ask such a question. I consider the *máthot* to be a most unjust imposition, and, as such, I can never submit to it. Forsooth! because his son is going to get married, therefore we, poor people, must pay the expenses of the wedding! When the sons of poor ráiyats get married, pray who pays the expenses! Does the jamidár pay one cowrie? On the contrary, does he not on such occasions expect, and actually receive, presents? Such is the way of the world! On the head which is already saturated with oil, more oil is poured, whereas we poor folk go entirely oilless."

Nanda. "Well said, uncle Mánik. I quite agree with you. We should not submit to injustice."

Kálamánik. "That is what I say. But Govinda is like his father. He is a man of peace; he has already made up his mind to pay. He is quite frightened by the jamidár's threats. If I were he, I would refuse to go again to the jamidár's cutcherry and crack the skull of the first fellow that came to catch hold of me."

Govinda. "But, uncle, would not that be foolhardiness? I quite agree with you that the imposition is unjust and oppressive. But what can I do? and what can you do? If I beat any of the jamidár's servants, I shall be without doubt put in jail. Living in water, how can I quarrel with the alligator? The best plan is to live on good terms with him. If I resist, I am ruined."

Chatura. "That is speaking like a wise man. How can we, poor and weak as we are, contend with the jamidár? Dwarfs as we are, how can we hope to catch the moon with our hands? Govinda is wise in making up his mind to pay."

Kálamánik. "People say that I am rash, and have not much sense. But it is said of over-sensible people, that a string is——you know the proverb. No, no; I do not wish to be wise like you all. I should like to see the fellow that dares come to me asking for *máthot.* Won't I make him drink sour milk on the spot, and perhaps send him to the house of Yama."

Govinda. "Take you good care, uncle, what you do. By your boldness you may bring ruin upon our family. You are the strongest and bravest man in the village, but you cannot fight singly against one hundred men; and the jamidár can muster five hundred men against us."

Kálamánik. "Don't be apprehensive of me, nephew. I am not a fool; I will not bring ruin upon you."

Kapila, the *bandhu,* or friend of Govinda, who had been all this time quietly listening to the above conversation, said, "Is it not extraordinary that the *Kompáni Báhádur* allows all this injustice to be inflicted upon us? *Kompáni Báhádur's* rule is in many respects better than the rule of the Mussulmans; but how is it that in this respect it is worse? How can *Kompáni Báhádur* see without concern all this oppression of its own subjects by wicked jamidárs?"

Chatura. "What a sheep you are, Kapil! you think *Kompáni Báhádur* cares either for our weal or for our woe! Not a bit of it. All that it cares for is the regular payment of the *Jamá.* So long as the jamidár regularly pays the *Sadar Jamá,* the *Kompáni Báhádur* does not enquire how he collects it, or how much he collects. Has not the *Kompáni Báhádur* armed the jamidár with those dreadful weapons, the *haptam* and the *pancham,* to the ruin of all its raiyats?"

Madan, Govinda's *mitá,* said: "But I have always heard old people say that the *Kompáni Bahádur* is just and merciful. How then can it allow the jamidárs to oppress the ráiyats so much? The *Sadar*

Jamá which the jamidár pays is the blood-money of the ráiyats."

Govinda. "The fact is, though the *Kompáni Báhádur* is just and merciful, it has made laws on the supposition that the jamidárs have common honesty and humanity. The *Kompáni Báhádur* never dreamt that jamidárs would be so wicked."

Basamaya. "But you don't mean to say that all jamidárs are wicked. The jamidár of my maternal uncle in Zilla Hugli is said to be a very good man. My uncle says that that jamidár is the father of his ráiyats. He not only does not exact illegal cesses, but in a season of drought, or of inundation, he exempts the ráiyats from paying rent."

Nanda. "I daresay there are a few jamidárs of that sort. But fifteen annas of them are tyrants. I should say fifteen annas three paysas out of the rupee are of that sort. They rob the poor, deprive Bráhmanas of their rent-free lands, and burn the houses of their ráiyats. Why does Mother Earth suffer these miscreants to remain in her lap?"

Govinda. "*Sángát*, you are always hot. Some crow will carry your words to the jamidár."

Nanda. "I don't care if it does."

The conversation detailed above was followed by a game of cards called *Grábu*—Nanda and Govinda being partners on one side, and Chatura and Madan on the other; the rest of the assembly ranged themselves under the one party or the other as spectators. As Chatura was the best player of them all, his party won, having hoisted no less than three sixes and two fives to the disgrace of the other party. When the winning party hoisted a six, great was their joy, which they expressed by a loud clapping of hands. Not a drop of wine or any spirituous liquor had ever gone down the throat of any of these rural players—their only refreshment was the hookah, which ever and anon went round. It was almost midnight when our village statesmen arose and went to their houses.

CHAPTER XLI.

BEFORE THE ZAMINDÁR.

I've noticed, on our laird's court-day,
An' mony a time my heart's been wae,
Poor tenant bodies, scant o' cash,
How they maun thole a factor's snash:
H'll stamp an' threaten, curse an' swear,
H'll apprehend them, poind their gear;
While they maun stan', wi' aspect humble,
An' hear it a', an' fear an' tremble.

The Twa Dogs.

THE next two days Govinda spent in earnestly debating in his mind whether he should pay the cess or not, and he found no little difficulty in making up his mind. In his own house he had talk on the subject with his mother and his uncle, and they were of opposite views —the mother urging him to pay, and the uncle insisting on not paying and on abiding the consequences. The arguments of Sundari may be thus summed up:— "It is a dangerous thing to incur the displeasure of a powerful man, and especially of one's rájáh. The jamidár can ruin us, can seize the crop in the field on pretence of arrears of rent, can carry away our cattle, can sell our houses, can imprison us, can kill us. How can you, then, my son, incur the displeasure of such a man? Fishes cannot afford to be on bad terms with the alligator of the tank." Kálamánik, on the other hand, thought it would be great cowardice to submit to so iniquitous an exaction. He broke out against the zamindár in a most violent manner, calling him his brother-in-law (wife's brother), and describing him as the greatest sinner upon earth. Govinda's father-in-law, Padma Lochan, was of the same opinion with his mother, thinking it madness not to pay. He moreover told Govinda that he must not put faith in the empty declarations of people, some of whom, though they use tall language, submit at last; and that not a few people were mischievously inclined towards him, dissuading him from paying the *máthoṭ* only that they might witness Govinda's ruin. On the whole Govinda thought it wise and expedient to make up his mind to submit to the zamindár's exaction, but at the same time he determined to tell the landlord to his face at the time of payment that the imposition was illegal and unjust.

On the appointed day, at about eight o'clock in the morning, Hanumán Singha called at the house of Govinda, and said that he was wanted at the zamindar's cutcherry. Tying the amount of the *máthoṭ* in his *dhuti* round his waist, he followed the *táidgir*. The zamindár was seated in his usual place, surrounded by the divána, the gomastá, and others. Govinda, putting his bathing-towel round his neck, made obeisance to him by touching the ground with his forehead. The divána said,

"Well, Sámanta, have you brought the *máthoṭ* with you?"

Govinda. "If the divána *mahásáyá* were to forgive me I should feel greatly obliged, as I am largely in debt."

Zamindár. "You scoundrel, you still talk of being excused? It is only in consequence of your father, who was a good tenant, that you escaped with impunity three days ago, when you refused to pay the cess. I mean to punish you well for delaying to pay, and for doing an infinite deal of mischief among my tenants, whom you were trying to dissuade from paying."

Govinda. "O, Incarnation of Justice! I never attempted to dissuade anyone from paying."

Zamindár. "Harámzáda! I am well informed, you did try. Did you not hold nocturnal meetings to discuss this subject? And did you not use threatening language towards me?"

Govinda. "I never used threatening language towards your worship."

Zamindár. "You did, you rascal; and if you again deny it you will be beaten with shoes. You mean to say you did not hold meetings at night for abusing me?"

Govinda. "I do not know of any meeting especially held for the purpose of discussing the subject of the *máthoṭ*, or of abusing your lordship."

Zamindár. "Were you not present in the shop of Kuvera the blacksmith two nights ago? and did you not abuse me then?"

Govinda. "I happened to be there that night, as I am there almost every evening, but there was no meeting especially called; and I never said one word against your worship, O Incarnation of Justice."

Zamindár. "I repeat, if you deny it, you will immediately get shoe-beating."

The divána now suggested that perhaps it was not Govinda, but some other person at the meeting that abused the zamindár, though he must have heard it with approbation.

Zamindár. "No, I am sure it was this wicked

fellow who used threatening language. Well, if he did not, let him name the party who did."

Untruthfulness not being regarded by the Bengal ráiyat as dishonourable, especially in dealings with landlords, Govinda had no hesitation in saying that no one at the meeting abused the zamindár. The zamindár, who had ıeceived from some unknown person an account, with considerable additions, of the talk at the smithy, became now furious, and was almost going to strike Govinda, when the divána interposed, and represented that he was too mean a person to deserve the distinction of being beaten personally by the great zamindár himself. The divána then ordered Govinda to pay down the *máthot* and go away. While in the act of untying the money from his *dhuti,* he said, "I am paying the cess; but the imposition is an unjust one. It is contrary to the laws of the *Kompáni Báhádur.*" The zamindár could no longer restrain his anger, but got up, and taking into his hand one of his own slippers, struck Govinda with it, abusing him at the same time somewhat in the following strain: "You, wife's brother, ungrateful wretch, you accuse me of injustice! You, ghost of a peasant, you pretend to be versed in law; you dare teach me my duty! I will shorten your mouth by shoe-beating. This is only the beginning of your misfortunes. Worse calamities are in store for you. I will ruin you till dogs and jackals weep and howl at your misery." Govinda had not courage enough to make any reply to this castigation and this outburst—indeed, he had already shown more than the average courage of Bengali peasants. He quietly bore the castigation and swallowed the insult, wiped his eyes and that part of his body to which the shoe had been applied, paid down the cess, and left the cutcherry.

The zamindár and the divána now entered into a conversation as to the extent of dissaffection created in the village, and both of them dwelt on the necessity of severely punishing Kálamánik who, it was said, was doing more mischief than any other man. The gomastá mentioned the name of the young blacksmith as another dangerous fellow, who was always speaking against the zamindár; but the divána, who was kindly disposed towards Kuvera, Nanda's father, represented that the lad was indiscreet, using always high-flown words, but that he did no mischief, as he exercised no influence in the village. There was no doubt, however, of the guilt of Kálamánik. It was only through his representations that Govinda had at first refused to pay the cess, and there could be no reasonable doubt that he was endeavouring to prejudice the other ráiyats against their landlord. But how was he to be punished? He was a most determined and obstinate character; and as to personal strength, he had such an uncommonly powerful body, that he was more than a match for any three men in the village. It was deemed necessary, however, that he should be somehow punished. The zamindár immediately ordered Hanumán Singha, who was in attendance, to go in search of Kálamánik, and to tell him that his landlord wanted to see him. The divána said that Kálamánik was not likely to obey the summons, and that it would be necessary to send at least a dozen men to catch hold of him. The zamindár replied that should Kálamánik refuse to come, severer measures must be resorted to; but it was expedient in the first instance to have recourse to less coercive measures.

Hanumán Singha, accordingly, went in search of Kálamánik, whom he found in the field busily engaged in watering a field of sugar-cane. Seeing the zamindár's *taidgir*, he said, "Hallo, Hanumán Sing! what brings you here?"

Hanu. "I have come in search of you, Mánik Sámanta."

Kála. "In search of me! What have you to do with me?"

Hanu. "The jamidár wishes to see you."

Kála. "The jamidár wishes to see me! What have I to do with the jamidár? I owe him nothing He may have to do with Govinda; but what on earth have I to do with him?"

Hanu. "I do not know the reason why he has sent for you. I simply obey orders."

Kála. "I am not the jamidár's servant that I should go to him at his bidding. Go and tell him I am watering my fields, and have now no leisure to go to the cutcherry."

Hanu. "I advise you to come with me. Why should you incur the displeasure of the jamidár for nothing? There is, surely, no harm in going to him. He will not eat you up."

Kála. "Eat me up! I should like to see him try to eat me up. Should he succeed in swallowing me up, he would die of a pain in his stomach. Whereas I can swallow and digest many jamidárs like Jaya Chánd Ráya Chaudhuri. Mánik Sámanta is too tough to be easily digested. Do you go and convey my reply to his summons."

So saying, Kálamánik went on, with greater energy than before, with the work of irrigation.

CHAPTER XLII.

THE INDIGNATION MEETING.

> Thou knowest the discontent,
> The ill-pent murmurs, which this man's oppression,
> His cruelty and avarice, hath provok'd
> Amongst all honest hearts in Schwytz.
>
> SCHILLER'S *Wilhelm Tell.*

AMONGST the peasantry of Western Bengal there is not a braver nor a more independent class than the Ugra-Kshatriyas, or Águris, the caste of which our hero was a member. Somewhat fairer in complexion than Bengal peasants in general, better built, and more muscular in their corporeal forms, they are known to be a bold and somewhat fierce race, and less patient of any injustice or oppression than the ordinary Bengali ráiyat, who is content quietly to submit, even without a protest, to any amount of kicking. The phrase *Águrir gonár,* or the "Águri bully," which has passed into a proverb, indicates that the Águris are, in the estimation of their countrymen, a hot-blooded class; that they are fearless and determined in their character, and that they resent the slightest insult that is offered them. Fewer in numbers than the Sadgopa class, which constitutes the bulk of the Vardhamána peasantry, they are a compact and united band; and there is amongst them a sort of *esprit de corps* which is hardly to be found in any other class of Bengalis. Naturally stronger and more industrious than other husbandmen, the Águris, as a class, are in better circumstances than the rest of the peasantry, and, in consequence of their superior wealth, display a correspondingly higher spirit of independence. Hence it is not to be wondered at that the zamindár's treatment of Govinda should rouse the indignation of all the Águris of Kánchanpur. Shoe-beating is looked upon as a most degrading punishment, fit only for the lowest classes of the people; and by how much the Águris deemed themselves to be better than *Bágdis, Doms,* and *Háḍis,* by so much was their indignation roused at the insult offered to one of their tribe. Kálamánik, when on his return from irrigating the sugar-cane field he heard of the shoe-beating, became almost insane with rage; he broke out into the most violent language, called the zamindár all sorts of names, and vowed revenge to wipe out the blot with which the honour of the family had been tarnished. In the course of the day and the ensuing evening, almost all the Águri peasants of the village visited Govinda and Kálamánik in their house, expressed sympathy with them, regarded Govinda's cause as their own, and resolved to harass the landlord in every way they could. And yet what could they do? There were not more than twenty-five families of Águris in the village; and if their number were larger, how could they hope to be successful in a contest with a zamindár, whose ráiyats numbered by thousands, and who had an organised *láthiál* band of at least one hundred able-bodied men? Nor were the *Sadgopas* and other classes of husbandmen on the side of the Águris. Accustomed as many of them were to be daily beaten, cuffed, and kicked by the zamindár and his deputies, they were strangers to that sense of honour which animated Govinda and his caste-men. So far from sympathising with them, they looked upon the Águris as a very thin-skinned class, who made much ado about nothing.

In the days of which we are treating (and it is about twenty-five years ago), it was hopeless for a ráiyat, or any number of ráiyats, to cope successfully with zamindárs. The zamindárs were armed with tremendous powers by the British Government, especially by Regulation VII. of 1799 and V. of 1812, which empowered them not only to distrain the crops and cattle and all the property of tenants who are in arrears of rent, or supposed to be so, but to compel them to attend their cutcherries, and to imprison them. And the zamindárs of those days were not generally an honourable class. They made false charges against their tenants, refused to give receipts for rents received, and had recourse to perjury, chicanery, forgery, and the thousand and one arts of knavery for their own aggrandizement and the destruction of the peasantry. Nor were the peasantry spirited enough to oppose the landlords in their high-handed measures. We have represented the Águris to be a spirited and brave class; but it must be remembered that they were spirited compared only with other Bengali ráiyats, and Bengali ráiyats are, as a rule, a sheepish and submissive race. Were Bengal peasants like Irish cottiers, Orangemen, Ribbonmen, and the rest, zamindari oppression would be impossible. An old husbandman of the Águri caste, speaking in reference to the mode in which they should endeavour to harass the zamindár, said—"As most of us have already paid the cess, it will not do to prevent the rest from paying it. In what precise way, then, should we vex the landlord?"

Kálamánik. "In my opinion, the best mode would be to deliver by one stroke Mother Earth of so heavy a burden as the wretch whom we call our rájá. I could undertake by one blow of my club to dash out his brains."

The Old Peasant. "Mánik Sámanta, I fear you will by your rashness bring all of us into great trouble. Should you kill the jamidár, you will get yourself suspended from the gallows at Vardhamána, and some of us will perhaps be imprisoned for life or transported beyond the Black Water."

Kálamánik. "Mánik Sámanta will never do business in such an awkward manner as to imperil either his own life or the lives of his friends. The act will be done, but the hand that will do it will not be seen."

The Old Peasant. "My son—I am old enough to be your father—dismiss such a horrid thought from your mind; do not imbrue your hand in the blood of a fellow-creature. The gods will punish him. It is not for us to anticipate the decree of fate. We should content ourselves with giving him all sorts of petty annoyances."

Kálamánik. "But have you heard that I have personally given mortal offence to the jamidár? He sent for me through Hanumán Sing, and I refused to go."

The Old Peasant. "What did he send for you for? Did Hanumán Sing not tell you the reason why you had been called?"

Kálamánik. "No reason was given, and it was therefore I refused to go. But I know the reason why. Some mischievous fellow, some tale-bearer, must have reported to either the jamidár or the divána, what I said the other night at Kuvera's shop. I am supposed to be the ringleader; and the creator of disaffection."

The Old Peasant. "You were quite right in refusing to go. If you had gone you would perhaps have been dishonoured. You might have been beaten with shoes or imprisoned."

Kálamánik. "Ah well! let me see. If my name be Mánik Sámanta, the jamidár will have to rue his treatment of Govinda."

The Águri husbandmen of Kánchanpur, however, did not determine upon the mode in which they should wreak vengeance on the zamindár. But Kálamánik seemed to revolve some scheme in his mind. From the next day he seldom went to work in the field, but was seen to go about much in the neighbouring villages. Not unfrequently he left Kánchanpur early in the morning, long before sunrise, and returned at night. Govinda could not but notice this circumstance, but as Kálamánik kept quiet when questioned about the matter, he thought it proper not to make any further inquiry.

CHAPTER XLIII.

FIRE! FIRE!

Why flames yon summit—why shoot to the blast
Those embers, like stars from the firmament cast?—
'Tis the fire-shower of ruin.

Campbell.

ONE night when Govinda and the women were fast asleep, and when Kálamánik lay half-awake on his bed, tossing from side to side, partly on account of the sultry heat of the weather, and partly on account of the bite of that little creature (the *Cimex lectularius*) which infests in shoals the dormitories of poor people in Bengal as in England, but whose inodorous name in vernacular Anglo-Saxon we dare not mention in this history, in the event of some English lady honouring it with a perusal—I say when Kálamánik was in this state, his half-drowsy ears were assailed by the loud barkings of the house-dog Bághá. As Bághá was not in the habit of setting up such a loud howl at the dead of night, Kálamánik thought it strange; and the idea suddenly crossed his mind that some burglar might be, with a view to theft, making a hole in the wall of the big hut where the valuables of the house were deposited. Finding that the barking was becoming louder and louder, he got up from his bed, took in his hand his bamboo-club which stood in a corner, opened the door, and went softly and slowly into the lane behind the huts. Scarcely had he entered the lane when two men rushed past him in great haste, and ran away with as great speed as their heels could carry them. One of these men he distinctly recognized—for the moon was still in the heavens though not far from the horizon—to be Bhima Katál, the head of the zamindár's band of club-men. Kálamánik called out and said, "Bhime! Bhime! Thief! Thief." But at that dead hour of night no one responded to the call, as all his neighbours were asleep. He at first thought of pursuing the two men, but finding they had already gone a great distance alongside the tank far into the mango-grove, he gave up the idea, and went round to the back-side of the big hut to see whether any hole had been bored. On going to the south-east corner, he found to his horror that the thatch was on fire. His first thought was to save the lives of Govinda, of his wife and children, who were all sleeping in the very hut the thatch of which was blazing. He rushed back into the house, knocked at the door of the big hut with his club, at the same time bawling out with all his might, "Govinda! Govinda! get up! get up! fire! fire! the house is on fire!" Govinda, startled with the loud noise at the door, and the crackling noise of the thatch overhead, was on his feet in a moment, wakened his wife, and rushed out of the room with their children in their arms. Kálamánik rushed into the room, and seizing with both hands whatever clothes and other valuables he could find, brought them out into the open yard. He then ran towards the huts of his neighbours, and raised the cry of "Fire! fire! get up, neighbours!" Having succeeded in rousing some of his neighbours, he, before their arrival, rushed back into the house, and ordered Govinda, who by this time had scarcely realised the horror of his situation, to bring *kalsis* of water from the tank which, as the reader knows, lay near the house, while he himself went up to the thatched roof of the big hut, part of which was blazing with fire. When Govinda brought the first *kalsi* of water, some of the neighbours arrived and assisted in the work of putting water on that part of the hut which the fire had not yet reached. One of these neighbours stood at the *ghát* of the tank and filled the *kalsi* with water; it was then carried by a relay of men from shoulder to shoulder to the top of the bamboo ladder where Govinda was standing. Govinda put the *kalsi* into the hands of Kálamánik, who poured it over the thatch. *Kalsi* after *kalsi* of water was in this manner brought and poured on the thatch. But the attempt to save a part of the hut was in vain. The fire had spread itself to the highest part, which is the middle of the thatch, and, in spite of the frequent effusion of water, was making rapid progress. Kálamánik was obliged to come down from the thatch, and resign the hut to the flames. Lest the other huts should take fire, they were copiously watered in the manner we have described. The bullocks and the cows were taken out of the cow-house, and put at as great a distance as possible from the fire, for it is looked upon as a great sin if any member of the bovine species is allowed to be burnt; indeed, the penance which a householder has to submit to in the event of such a catastrophe is far severer than the penance he has to submit to if his wife or children are consumed in the flames. In the meantime the whole of the big hut, which was the best, was on fire. The smoke ascended far into the heavens; the light which the blazing hut produced, lit up half the village; the sounds of "*phut, phut, doom, doom,*" which the burning bamboos and palmyra-beams sent forth, were heard from a great distance. The news of the fire was carried to every part of the village, and people from all directions came running to see the spectacle. All of them expressed much lip-sympathy, but few lent a helping hand. Agni, the god of fire, was, however, satisfied with consuming one hut, and the conflagration was stayed. Govinda, Kálamánik, and the other members of the little household, spent the remaining hours of the night in the open yard in front of the fire yet blazing. They had the company of a few sympathising friends like Nanda the blacksmith, Kapila the carpenter, Madan the grocer, Padma Lochan, Govinda's father-in-law, and a few other Águris. They had not succeeded in saving anything excepting those few articles which Kálamánik had brought out. Whatever valuable things they had—and they were certainly very few—were burnt, including of course all the papers and documents belonging to the family. Kálamánik told them the events of the night, how the dog barked, how he got out of his room suspecting a burglar was at his work, how he had met Bhima Kotál, the zamindár's head *láthiál*, and another, how they ran away, and the rest. All came to the conclusion that the hut had been set on fire by Bhima Kotál, doubtless at the bidding of the zamindár. Next morning Kálamánik went to the *Phánḍidár*, or police-constable of the village, informed him that his big hut had been reduced to ashes, and that Bhima Kotál was the incendiary. Bhima Kotál was sent for by the constable. Bhima's wife sent word that her husband was away a couple of days at his father-in-law's house, which was in a village five miles distant, and that he had not yet returned. Khoda Bux, the village *Phánḍidár,* asked Kálamánik how he reconciled his own statement with the fact that Bhima was not in the village the last two days; but he and other Águris who were with him maintained that Bhima was certainly in the village yesterday, and that his wife's statement was false. The next morning Bhima returned to Kánchanpur, for he had certainly been away after setting Govinda's house on fire; an investigation was held by the *Phánḍidár,* and it was deposed by more than a dozen witnesses amongst the zamindár's retainers that Bhima was not in the village the last three days, and witnesses from Bhima's father-in-law's village for the last two days; the *Phándidár* therefore dismissed the case, and, at the bidding of the zamindár, did not send any report of it to the Daroga of Mantresvar, his official superior. Most inhabitants of the village, however, notwithstanding this investigation, believed that poor Govinda's house had been set on fire by Bhima Sardár by the order of the zamindár. The indignation of the Águris was roused still more than ever, and Kálamánik, gnashing his teeth in anger, thirsted for vengeance.

CHAPTER XLIV.

THE MAHÁJAN.

> Go with me to a notary; seal me there
> Your single bond; and, in a merry sport,
> If you repay me not on such a day,
> In such a place, such sum or sums as are
> Expressed in the condition, let the forfeit
> Be nominated for an equal pound
> Of your fair flesh, to be cut off and taken
> In what part of your body pleaseth me.
>
> *The Merchant of Venice.*

How to reconstruct the best hut, reduced to ashes by the zamindár, now formed the great subject of Govinda's anxiety. The walls only were standing; the straw-thatch, the bamboo frame-work, the palmyra posts and beams, had been all burnt down. The cost of erecting such a cottage—and cottages in the Vardhamána district are probably better built than those of other districts in the country—including the raising of the walls, could be hardly less than one hundred rupees; but, as the walls and the flooring remained intact, the roofing and the palmyra supports would alone cost about fifty or sixty rupees. Whence could Govinda get such a large sum? In his money-box—for he had a small wooden box, of about the length of a span—there was hardly anything, excepting perhaps one rupee and a few *payasá*, as it is reckoned ominous to keep the money-box quite empty. A peasant, however well-to-do, and Govinda was confessedly poor, has no ready money at any time, all his silver being in the shape of ornaments, on the persons of his wife and children. A ráiyat's wealth consists almost wholly in his *marái* of paddy, *pálai* of straw, and in his cows and bullocks. In all cases of pecuniary difficulty, the ráiyat's only resource is the iron chest of his *mahájan*, that is, by way of eminence, the "great man"—the man of all men in the village, who gives help to the distressed husbandman in the hour of his need. We have selected for the motto of this chapter, the words of Shylock; but the reader must not suppose that all mahájans of Bengal are as hard-hearted and inhuman as Shakspeare's model Jew. It is true that all mahájans, without exception, take usurious interest, but the husbandman gladly pays it; and we do not believe that, in Bengal at least, the money-lender is so much detested by the peasantry as a portion of the Indian press represents him to be. Indeed, but for the good offices of the mahájan, many a Bengal ráiyat would have to cool his heels in the cells of some prison-house. The very next day after his house had been burnt down, Govinda paid a visit to his mahájan, who lived at no great distance from the smithy of Kuvera.

Golaka Poddár, for that was the name of Govinda's mahájan, was by caste a *Suvarna vanika*, that is, the banker caste, though of a lower order than that to which the Malliks of Calcutta, and the Láhás, Silas and Maṇḍals of Chinsurah belong. He was not a *svarnakára*, or goldsmith, by caste, though his chief business was to make gold and silver ornaments; and he had the reputation of being the best ornament-maker for many miles round. But he was a master-goldsmith, having under him a number of workmen whom he superintended. He also bought and sold ingots of gold and silver. He lent money on mortgage of silver and gold ornaments, or on interest. He had a shop in the town of Vardhamána in the immediate precincts of the Mahárájá's palace, where business was carried on by two of his sons. The people all declared that Golaka Poddár was the richest man in the village, though nobody would have thought so from the sort of house in which he dwelt or from his style of living. His house was, certainly, surrounded by a high brick-wall, the top of which was stuck with broken pieces of bottle, to make it difficult for thieves and robbers to climb; but there was not on the premises a single brick-built room; there were only several cottages of mud thatched with straw, though, it must be admitted the frame-work was of superior workmanship. He spent so little upon himself and his family, performed so few religious ceremonies requiring some outlay of money, bestowed so little charity on either Brahmanas or beggars, that he was looked upon as a miser of the first water; and his name was never pronounced of a morning by anyone, lest the unhappy pronouncer should be deprived that day of his dinner for having taken on his lips so unlucky a name. Nevertheless, Golaka Poddár was a most respectable man; he never cheated any one, and was honest and upright in his dealings.

When Govinda entered his mahájan's house, he saw Golaka sitting on a mat on the verandah of a neat cottage, with a touch-stone in his hand, and a piece of gold which he was rubbing against it, in order to ascertain its quality. He was dressed in a simple *dhuti*, the upper part of his body being quite naked. He looked like a man more than fifty years old; his chest was largely covered with hair; he had spectacles on; and his hair was mottled grey. Raising his head and taking off his spectacles, he looked at Govinda and said—"Well, Sámanta, what's the news? I am sorry to hear that your big cottage was burnt last night. Has the whole of it been burnt, or only a part of it?"

Govinda. "The whole, Poddár *mahásaya.* Not a bit is remaining. It is all ashes."

Golaka. "Who could have done such a wicked deed?"

Govinda. "What shall I say, sir? The poor are always oppressed. My uncle saw Bhima Koṭál running away towards the mango-grove in the company of another man, immediately after the fire had taken effect."

Golaka. "Bhima Koṭál! and did you inform the *Phánḍidár* of it?"

Govinda. "Yes, Uncle did. But you know very well, the *Phánḍidár* is in the palm of the jamidár's hand. The jamidár's people came and gave witness that Bhime was that night and two days before in his father-in-law's village five miles distant; so the case was hushed up, and no report of it was sent to the Dárogá of Mantresvar. Poor people never get justice."

Golaka. "Aye! aye! So it is, Sámanta. It is a wicked world. I have seen enough in my day That is one reason, Sámanta, why I have taken no lands for cultivation; I do not wish to come in contact with any jamidár."

Govinda. "You, sir, can afford not to rent land, as you have plenty of gold and silver. But what are we husbandmen to do? Land is our life."

Golaka. "True. What is to be done now?"

Govinda. "Nothing, so far as punishing the burner of the house is concerned. But the hut must be thatched again. And who is to befriend me on this occasion except yourself? You are really my *annadátá*—the giver of rice."

Golaká. "Sámanta! You already owe me a considerable sum of money, and though I never have had recourse to the law-courts for recovering my money in any case, yet you must pay back the money to me soon. How can you afford to borrow more money?"

Govinda. "But if I don't borrow, how can I get on? Shall my wife and children sleep at night in the open air? If you don't give me money the house cannot be built."

Golaka. "Well, let me see; how much do you want?"

Govinda. "Less than sixty *tákás* will not do."

Golaka. "Sixty *tákás!* What do you want such a large sum for? The walls must be all there, the flooring is there, and perhaps some of the posts; and you must have plenty of straw in your *pálai;* and then, near the tank, you have some clumps of bamboo. Thirty *tákás* will, I think, be quite sufficient."

Govinda. "Not one cowrie less than sixty *tákás.* All the posts have been reduced to ashes; the straw in the *pálai* is barely sufficient for the cows and bullocks; and as for the clumps of bamboos near the tank, there is not in them one single bamboo fit for building purposes, they are all young and unseasoned."

Golaka. "I can give you the money, certainly; but what I am thinking of is that the interest of the former debt, added to the interest of the present debt, will make a large sum and press heavily on you. You must, of course, pay interest at the rate of two *payasá* per *táká* a month."

Govinda. "Of course, the interest will be heavy. But there is no medicine for this disease: I must somehow bear it."

Golaka Poddár brought out a piece of paper, wrote on it a regular receipt, which was signed by Govinda as well as by two workmen as witnesses. The silver was then counted out.

On receiving the money Govinda and Kálamánik immediately set to work. Palm trees were bought and cut; bamboos were brought from a village several miles distant, were slit, and turned into *bákháris*. In these and other operations Govinda and Kálamánik were materially assisted by Nanda the blacksmith, and Kapila the carpenter; the former doing gratuitously all the necessary iron-work in the shape of nails, hooks, &c., and the latter preparing the palmyra posts, the beams, and rafters.

CHAPTER XLV.

THE VILLAGE GROG-SHOP.

Pass where we may, through city or through town,
Village, or hamlet, of this merry land,
Though lean and beggared, every twentieth pace
Conducts the unguarded nose to such a whiff
Of stale debauch, forth issuing from the styes
That law has licensed, as makes Temperance reel.

Cowper.

SOME days after Govinda's big hut had been reduced to ashes, Babu Jaya Chánd Raya Chaudhuri was sitting in his Cutcherry, or rather half sitting, half lying down, his elbows resting on a huge bolster, and smoking, by means of one of those monstrous pipes called snakes, "which extended long and large, lay floating many a rood;" when Jaya Chánd was sitting in this interesting position, surrounded by the pomp and circumstance of landlordism, by his divána, his gomasţa, and mohurirs; Bhima Sardár, the captain of his clubmen, stood in front of the room, and made a profound bow. Jaya Chánd raised his head a little, took off the snake from his mouth, and said, "Well, Bhima Sardár, what's the news?"

Bhim. "Mahárāj! everything is right. In Mahárája's dominions nothing can go wrong."

Jaya. "You managed the thing rather neatly, the other night. But you were almost caught, and if the fellow had once seized you, it would have been all over with you; for the rascal is not only as black but as strong as Yama."

Bhim. "That fellow catch me! Maháráj, by your blessing I have strength enough to fight alone and unaided with half-a-dozen fellows like him."

Jaya. "Ah, well, I don't know about that; you are exaggerating your strength. That fellow must be stronger than you. If you are Bhim, he is Arjjuna. However, you did your work successfully. You deserve some *bakshish* (reward)."

Bhim. "Maháráj! everything I have is your lordship's. In your lordship I live and eat and drink. What more could I expect?"

Jaya Chánd ordered the treasurer to give to Bhim Sardár two rupees. As the treasurer threw the rupees on the floor, the zamindár said to the Sardár, "Take that *táká*, and enjoy yourself with your companions." The Sardár made another profound bow, repeating the words, "Ráma, Ráma! Maháráj," and went away.

Leaving Jaya Chánd and his ministers to their confabulations, with the reader's permission, we will accompany the Sardár and see how he and his friends enjoy themselves. He, along with about a dozen of his companions, went to a grocer's shop and bought some quantities of *muḍi, muḍki, bátás, phuṭ-kalái,* and *páṭáli,* and went towards the tank Krishna Ságara, below the high embankment of which lay the only grog-shop in the village.

I suppose there were grog-shops in the country before its occupation by the British, but there is no doubt that the increase of drunkenness in the land is chiefly owing to the operation of the Ábkári system of the Government. That three thousand years ago the Aryan settlers in India were, as may be inferred from the Rigveda, hard drinkers and staunch beef-eaters, is probably true, but it is equally true that the inhabitants of India have been for centuries the soberest people in the world; and it is sad to think that amongst this remarkably temperate people drunkenness should be introduced and extended by the foremost Christian nation in the world. It is all very well to say that the excise on spirits, which it is the office of the Ábkári Department to collect, has a tendency to repress and not to increase the sale of spirits, as it makes them dearer than before; but anyone who is acquainted with the working of that department must be aware that the practice belies the theory. The aim of the Ábkári, like that of every other branch of the fiscal service, is to increase the public revenue; but the revenue from spirits cannot be increased without an increase in their sale. It is therefore the aim of all Ábkári officers to establish as many grog-shops as they can in the country. To this State interference we owe it that there are at this moment, in the year of grace 1871, more grog-shops in the country than it ever had since it was upheaved from the universal ocean. Now every village almost has a grog-shop, and the larger villages more than one; though things were not in so bad a state in those days when the scene of this story is laid as at present.

But to proceed. Bhim Sardár and his dozen friends went to the grog-shop, which was a small mud hut thatched with straw. They sat on the ground and ordered some *kalsis* of an intoxicating liquid called *dheno,* prepared from *dhán,* that is, paddy. In those days no European wines, spirits, or liquors could be had in the village grog-shop. Only two sorts were sold, one prepared from treacle, and the other from paddy. The spirit distilled from treacle was rather dear for the poorest classes, who alone drank, as it was sold about eight annas or a shilling a bottle; whereas *dheno*, or, as it used to be jocosely called, *dhányesvari* (that is, the goddess of paddy), which is simple fermented paddy and water, a gallon could be had for a trifle. A large *haṇḍi* of *dhánesvari*, which is as much as any human stomach can contain, was sold for one *payasá*, which is a little less than a halfpenny. The thirteen club-men, including Bhima Sardár himself, sat in a row on the floor on their feet, without their bodies touching the ground, lifting up their heads and keeping their mouths open, as if they were going to catch the rain. The *sunḍi* (wine-seller), with a *kalsi* of *dhánesvari* in his hand, approached them, and into the open mouth of the first person in the row he poured as much liquid as he wished to drink. In this manner the whole company, thirteen in number, were served. After all had had a drink, they opened their store of provisions, which consisted of *muḍi* and *muḍki*, *bátása*, *phut-kalái*, and *pátáli*, and fell upon them with the utmost fury. The *muḍi* and *muḍki* were in such large quantities that when put on a piece of cloth on the floor they made a hillock. But in a short time the whole was demolished. As they ate the *phut-kalái* they became very jolly, and cracked many a joke; some of them rolled on the mud floor, and thus gave unmistakeable signs of intoxication. After the provisions had been all demolished, they again called for *dhányesvari*, and the *sundi* again served them in the manner I have already described, pouring into their upraised throats as much of the liquid as they wanted. They now prepared their hookahs and smoked tobacco,

> Sooty retainer to the vine,
> Bacchus' black servant, negro fine.

With hookah in hand, some half-tipsy, and some entirely so, they left the grog shop, and passed through the village, dancing and wild with merriment. I have heard it said by some of the inhabitants of Kánchanpur, that of an evening respectable Bráhmans of the village sometimes visited the grog-shop. I believe the statement is true, but still there is no doubt that the grog-shop was visited mainly by the lowest class of inhabitants, a class lower than that to which our hero belonged.

CHAPTER XLVI.

THE INDIGO-PLANTER OF DURGÁNAGAR.

> He finds his fellow guilty of a skin
> Not coloured like his own; and having power
> T'enforce the wrong, for such a worthy cause
> Dooms and devotes him as his lawful prey.
>
> *The Task.*

THE reader will perhaps recollect that, a long time ago, we left the little family of Durgánagar, giving his first rice to the infant Yádava, the son of Mádhava; since then no noteworthy event had happened, excepting that Málati once paid a visit to Kánchanpur on the occasion of the celebration of the usual purificatory rites, which, amongst the Sudras, always take place one month after the death of an individual. When she first heard of her father's dangerous illness, she was anxious to come to Kánchanpur, but her mother-in-law dissuaded her from the journey; when subsequently the tidings of her father's death reached her, she hastened to her native village to be present at the purification. Her stay, however, had been short; and she had returned again to her own house at Durgánagar, of course walking all the way on foot, as her husband was too poor to pay for a *pálki,* the only vehicle used by the wealthier classes in the country, where the roads—where there are such—are in such a state, that no four-wheeled carriage can possibly pass on them. Mádhava and Málati, the most affectionate couple at Durgánagar, were happy in each other's company, but as no earthly state is susceptible of unalloyed happiness, each had a cross to bear. The crook in Málati's lot, as the reader knows, was the unhappy temperament of her mother-in-law, who, true to her name, was every hour of the day distilling nectar, in the shape of cross words, rebukes, threats, and ill-natured language of every sort, to the never-ending torment of Málati and Kádambini. These nectarine outbursts could be tolerated if they were occasional, but the Wise man's saying was realized in Sudhámukhi, that, "a continual dropping in a very rainy day, and a contentious woman are alike;" and poor Málati felt with the said Wise man that, "it was better to dwell in the wilderness, than with a contentious and angry woman." And to the wilderness she would have fled, or would have, like Áduri, turned a Vaishnaví, if if she had not been either a wife or a mother; but her conjugal and maternal ties chained her to her homestead, made, however, uncomfortable by the ebullition of an unhappy temper. The crook in Mádhava's lot was of quite a different sort; it consisted in his relation to the indigo planter of Nildángá.

Nildángá (that is, the "Field of Indigo") was not, properly speaking, a village, as it consisted only of an indigo factory, together with scores of huts, in which dwelt the Buná coolies (chiefly the natives of Chota Nagpore, and the Sonthal Pergunahs) who worked in the factory. The residence of the planter was a fine-looking house, with an immense compound, in which there was a beautiful avenue of the stately fir, introduced into the country since its occupation by the English. In front of it there was the factory properly so called, where were carried on the complicated operations of indigo manufacture. Round about the factory, but at some distance, stood miserable huts, in which lived the Buná coolies of whom we have spoken. The planter was an English gentleman of the name of John Murray, who, though not the proprietor of the factory, was its manager and superintendent, the factory itself being the property of the East India indigo concern, one of the richest indigo joint-stock companies in the lower provinces, and which supplied the English market with the largest quantity of the blue dye. As the ráiyats of Bengal find it difficult to pronounce English names aright, they generally lengthen and widen them agreeably to the genius of their mother tongue, and make them correspond to some Bengali names or sounds. By this interesting process, Campbell is turned into *Kambal* (a blanket); Larmour into *Lál Mohana* (a sort of Bengali sweetmeat); Sibbald into *Subol* (a Bengali personal name); Saunders into *Sandes* (a sweetmeat); Brown into *Varuna* (the Neptune of the Hindu Pantheon); Maskelyne into *Maskil* (trouble); and Baldwin into *balad* (that is, a bull). Agreeably to this system of metamorphosis—each instance of which is as remarkable as any sung by Ovid—Mr. Murray, the planter, was called *Mári*, which in Bengali means either flogging or the plague. And, truly, when we consider the relation in which Mr. Murray stood to hundreds of the peasantry in the neighbouring villages, we think he merited the cognomen, for he was constantly in the habit of beating refractory coolies and ráiyats with a sort of cat-o'-

nine-tails, which he christened under the name of *gadádhár*, or the *club-wielder*. He was, for this and other reasons, looked upon as the plague or the pestilence. Mr. Murray, though a young man of about thirty-five years of age, had a sunburnt complexion, for he was constantly out in the fields inspecting the plantations. Early in the morning—that is to say about seven o'clock—he had his *chhotá házri* (breakfast), which consisted of a cup of tea, a slice of bread, and a half-boiled egg; mounted on his Bucephalus, and rode many a mile, with his inseparable companion, *gadádhár*, in his right hand. He did not return home till about ten o'clock, when he held a sort of court, hearing petitions from coolies and ráiyats, and giving decisions on them. At about one o'clock he had his breakfast, properly so called, when he consumed quantities of claret and brandy. In the afternoon he again rode out, more for pleasure than for business, and had his dinner at about eight at night. It is also certain that he compelled unwilling ráiyats to take contracts for indigo, forcibly seized the lands of poor and helpless husbandmen, and sowed them with indigo seed, burnt the houses of many, imprisoned them in his factories, and employed his *láthiáls* (club-men) to plunder villages. And yet if anyone saw and conversed with Mr. Murray, it was difficult to believe that he could be capable of such acts. He was a gentleman of good family and of some education. His manners, especially to Europeans, were exceedingly pleasing. He kept an open table, and his hospitality to Europeans was proverbial. He paid a monthly subscription of ten rupees to an English school established in a neighbouring village for the education of native youth; he had a large medicine chest out of which he used to deal out freely quinine and other drugs to the sick people of the villages, and his name, I believe, has been found in the subscription lists of the Tract and Bible Societies, and even in the reports of one or two missionary societies carrying on their operations in Bengal. How all this tallies with his barbarous inhumanity towards the peasantry, his oppressive measures, and his acts of spoliation, I do not pretend to understand, but there is no doubt that both these classes of facts are true; and it is the business of a philosopher — not of a matter-of-fact historian like myself—to reconcile them. Mádhava's father, Keśava, had in an evil hour taken *dádan,* as it is called, that is, advance-money, from Mr. Murray, for cultivating indigo in his fields, and ever since, he had been supplying the factory with many cart-loads of the plant every year, till the day of his death. He often tried to get out of the muddle, but that was impossible. Whoever once touched the indigo planter's advance, became a slave for evermore. Somehow or other, whatever quantities of the indigo plant Keśava gave in at the factory every year, he always remained a debtor to the planter. For the debt of one year he was obliged to sow indigo the next year, and the sowing went on every year simply because the debt was never cleared. A ráiyat's debt to the planter descends from generation to generation. No matter what heaps of the indigo plant the ráiyat brings into the factory, the debt has the singular faculty of never getting cleared off. Agreeably to this self-perpetuating faculty of the factory debt, Mádhava felt himself bound hand and foot to the planter. Though he hated the name of indigo, yet sow he must, as against his name in the factory books there was the everlasting debt. He would have gladly paid off the debt in the shape of money, in order to rid himself of the incubus. But the planter would not receive it. The debt was not an ordinary one, which could be paid off by specie; it was advance-money—originally it was so with Mádhava's father—and must be paid off by so many bundles of the indigo plant; and as Mádhava's bundles of the plant which he raised in his own fields had the singular faculty, when taken to the factory, of never coming up to the prescribed measure and quality, his debt went on increasing and increasing, till it became something considerable for so poor a peasant as he was. The planter, like the Old Man of the Sea in the Arabian Nights' Entertainments, never left those upon whose shoulders he had once got up till he ruined them. Before concluding this chapter, however, it is as well to remark that we do not regard every Bengal ráiyat as a saint, and every indigo-planter as a blue devil. Some planters are benevolently disposed, but the system which they follow, being pernicious in the extreme, is sufficient to convert the gentlest of human beings into ferocious tigers, unless, indeed, they choose to bring ruin upon themselves. And even more than this. There are some indigo-planters in Bengal who are not only not hated by their ráiyats, but loved by them, and looked up to as their *Ma-báp*, that is, *mother and father*. But the planters of whom we speak are not Europeans, neither are they natives. They are rich East Indian gentlemen—they are confined to the district of Purneah—not birds of passage, like the Europeans, whose only object is to make money and then run away to merry England as fast as steam can carry them; but men born and bred in the country, and who purpose also to be buried in it. They are kind to their ráiyats, and their ráiyats look up to them as benefactors. Such planters—alas, that their race is dying out!—are like the better sorts of zamindárs. And as for the ráiyats, no doubt some are dishonest, trying to evade cultivating indigo after taking advances, and sometimes taking advances from two planters, if they be sufficiently near each other, for the same crop. But making every allowance for the dishonesty of the ráiyat, there is not the slightest doubt that a fearful amount of injustice and oppression has been exercised upon the helpless cultivator by the powerful indigo-planter.

CHAPTER XLVII.

THE ADVANCES.

> And from his coffers
> Receive the golden earnest of our death.
>
> *King Henry V.*

THERE are two systems of indigo-planting, the *nijábád* and the *ráiyati*. In the former, the planter cultivates the plant on his own lands, of which he is either the zamindár or which he has taken on lease from a zamindár; and in the latter, he gives advance of money to the ráiyat on condition that he should cultivate the plant on his own lands and sell it to the planter at the factory rate. In the *nijábád* system there is not much room for oppression, for the planter cultivates the plant on his own land by his own men and at his own cost; and if there be any oppression, it is not extended to the peasantry, but is confined to his own servants and coolies. The *ráiyati* system is the fruitful mother of innumerable evils. In this system the ráiyat enters into a contract, in which he stipulates to supply the planter in the season of manufacture with a certain quantity of the plant at fixed rates, and obtains advance of money in order to help him in the cultivation. No doubt there are cases in which dishonest ráiyats, after receiving the advance, do not produce the plant at the proper time; but these cases are few and far between, owing chiefly to the fact that the planter is infinitely more powerful than a single ráiyat or a number of ráiyats, and can maintain his rights by law or by force. It is the ráiyats who suffer most. The contracts are very generally forced upon ráiyats who are unwilling to take them. To the English reader this may appear strange, but it is a simple fact; and it will not appear strange when we consider that the peasantry of Bengal are weak and spiritless, and are unable to resist the all but omnipotent planter. The unwillingness of the ráiyats to take contracts for the indigo plant arises from the fact that indigo cultivation is not remunerative to the ráiyat. It exhausts the soil more than other crops. The rate at which the ráiyat is paid for the indigo-plant which he cultivates is, though nominally -ust, in reality ruinous. When the husbandman takes his plant to the factory, it is measured by an officer of the planter called *ojandár*, or weigher, or rather measurer. This officer is provided with an iron chain six feet long, which he puts round the girth of the plant, and whatever quantity of the plant this chain encloses is, in the language of the factory, called a *bundle*. The *bundle* is six feet not only in girth but also in length, and as generally, unless in an exceptionally good season, the plant does not attain the requisite length, it is placed on the ground and put end to end with the stalks outwards, and the whole is pressed with the utmost force of the measurer, who is selected for the strength of his arms. The ráiyat who measured the plant in his own field and found it to be, say, six bundles, finds to his astonishment at the factory that it has become reduced by the Procrustean process to which it is subjected to only two bundles. He wrings his hand in despair; he weeps. But there is no help for it. The *ojandár* has found it to be only two bundles. At this rate the ráiyat, of course, is never able to produce his full tale of the plant, and is accordingly put down in the planter's books as a debtor by the difference. This happens every year, and the debt is ever on the increase.

One day towards the end of March, Mádhava was ploughing his field, when Mr. Murray in the course of his morning ride made his appearance, and stood under a tree which was not far off. Mádhava immediately put the plough into the hands of his companion, and advancing towards the planter, made a profound bow after the Hindu fashion, that is, bending down his head and touching the forehead with joined hands.

"Well, Mádhava," said the planter, "I see your land is ready for sowing. Are you going to sow indigo in this field?" "Hazúr," said Mádhava, "if I sow indigo, what will my family eat? I have prepared this field for paddy, but if indigo be sown in it, I shall be without food." "You don't mean to say you are not going to sow indigo! You must come and take advance to-morrow! besides, you owe me some money. As long as that debt is not discharged you must cultivate indigo."

"Khodáwand! I will pay my debt in silver. What can I do? I will borrow the sum from the mahájan and pay Hazúr."

"Pay your debt to the factory in silver! Who ever heard of such a thing? I suppose Nava Krishna Banerjea has been tampering with you."

"Gurrib Purwar! no one has been telling me anything. I find that by cultivating indigo I only lose; I do not get any profit, and my granary of paddy remains empty."

"By cultivating indigo you only lose! Who has put this bright idea into your head? Your father cultivated indigo for me every year; he never lost anything by it; you have become wiser than your father! I find a great many husbandmen of this village are refusing to take advance. There must be meaning in all this. The wicked zamindár must be at the bottom of it all. I must teach you all and the zamindár a lesson. You must come to the factory to-morrow and take advance. If you do not, you will feel the consequence."

"Khodáwand! forgive me this year. I am unable to obey Hazúr's order."

"Take care, fool, what you do; don't be led away by the evil counsels of designing men. Come and take advance, and cultivate indigo."

"Excuse me, Khodáwand! this year I will pay Hazúr in cash. Have pity upon me, O Incarnation of Justice, and grant my petition!"

"You are a great fool, Mádhava! You are rushing headlong into destruction with your eyes open. I tell you, when I am angry with you, no *sálá* (wife's brother), not even the zamindár, will be able to protect you."

"I know Hazúr is omnipotent, like the gods. Who is able to contend against Hazúr? How can I make Hazúr angry, and live? Have mercy upon an innocent man."

"You an innocent man! I believe you are the ringleader of all the malcontents of this village. You have been dissuading them from taking advance, and the zamindár has been promising to support you. But I shall see who supports you."

"Khodáwand, I never dissuaded any one from taking advance. I am too insignificant a person to have any influence upon other people. I look upon Hazúr as my protector. I pray Hazúr will be pleased to grant my humble petition."

"Your petition cannot be granted. You are a dishonest fellow. You owe money to the factory, and you now refuse to sow indigo. But I will see to it that you do sow indigo in your field."

"Khodáwand! be pleased to consider that the debt, properly speaking, is my father's, and I am quite willing to pay it in full in silver."

"You are very kind! Dare you say that you are not bound to cultivate indigo for the factory, when your name is in the factory books as a debtor? If you say that again, you will get something on your back immediately. Now, listen. Come to the factory to-morrow and take advance. If you do not, your ruin is certain; and not only your ruin, but the ruin of all the *sálás* of this village who refuse to sow indigo. Now, remember what I have just now said. You know Murray Saheb means to do what he says."

"Hazúr!——" Mádhava was going to say something, when Mr. Murray, turning his horse's head, said, "No more words; no more of your impertinence!" and cantered off.

CHAPTER XLVIII.

THE ZAMINDÁR OF DURGÁNAGAR.

He is a noble gentleman; withal
Happy in 's endeavours; the general voice
Sounds him for courtesy, behaviour, language,
And every fair demeanour an example:
Titles of honour add not to his worth,
Who is himself an honour to his title.

Ford.

THE reader will have gathered, from the conversation between Mr. Murray and Mádhava that several peasants in the village of Durgánagar had refused to take advances for cultivating indigo in their fields. As such refusal on the part of poor and spiritless ráiyats was quite unusual, at least in those days, Mr. Murray was right in supposing that they had been promised support by the zamindár. The fact is, the village of Durgánagar was the property of the Banerjeas, or Banḍujes as they were called, a wealthy zamindár family of Dakshinpalli, a large village situated on the Bhágirathi a few miles distant. The old zamindár, who had jogged on well with Mr. Murray, had lately died, and his son now managed the property. This young man, Nava Krishna Banerjea by name, was quite different from his father. His father belonged to the old school, had received no English education, and was somewhat loose in his principles. He cared not for the welfare of his ráiyats, and therefore did not interfere with the indigo-planter in his tyrannical career. He felt that Mr. Murray was a powerful planter, having scores of club-men under him, and that he was in high favour with the Deputy Magistrate, the Magistrate, and the Collector of the district, who sometimes partook of his hospitality; he therefore took care not to quarrel with him. Nava Krishna, on the other hand, was not unacquainted with English; he had studied for some years in the *Hindoo College* of Calcutta, and become animated with liberal and patriotic sentiments. From his childhood he had heard and seen a good deal of the oppression exercised by Mr. Murray and his predecessor at Nildángá on his father's own ráiyats, and often regretted that his father did not afford them sufficient protection. The histories of Greece, of Rome, and of England, which he read at College, introduced him to a new world of ideas, and as he grew in years his hatred of the oppressors of the peasantry began to increase. At Debating Societies, which were numerous in those days, he used to denounce the oppression of the indigo-planters, and sometimes sent anonymous letters to the Calcutta newspapers praying for justice to poor and ill-treated ráiyats. After leaving College, he became a member of the British Indian Association in Calcutta, where he used usually to reside, and frequently spoke at its meetings, advocating measures for putting a stop to the oppression of the planters. Nor was he unaware of the oppressive conduct of several zamindárs. He regretted this for the sake of the poor peasantry, and for the sake of the class to which he belonged, as he looked upon those zamindárs as a disgrace to their order. Nava Krishna was, it thus appears, one of those few zamindárs who know the duties attached to their station, who was actuated by public spirit, who was inspired by liberal and patriotic sentiments, who had sympathy with the down-trodden ráiyats, and who was honourable in all his actions. The number of such zamindárs was very few in those days, but, thanks to the spread of English education in the country, it is daily on the increase. On his accession to the *gadi* he made a general proclamation throughout his estates that there was to be thenceforth an end of all injustice and oppression, so far as he himself was concerned, in his zamindári; that might would not be allowed to prevail over right; that he would protect, to the utmost of his power, all his own ráiyats from the unjust interference of strangers and outsiders; that all *abwábs, máthots, salámis,* and other cesses, which were illegal, should cease; and that he was determined, according to the measure of his means and ability, to promote the welfare of all his tenants. The accession of Nava Krishna to the landlordry of Dakshinpalli was greeted by the peasantry of the district with an enthusiasm similar to that of the people of Ayodhyá on the consecration of Ráma to the regal office. The joy of the people knew no bounds. The oldest inhabitants wept through excess of delight when they heard the words of the proclamation. They compared the new zamindár to Ráma the son of Dasaratha; they said that they now had the prospect of dying in peace, leaving their children and grandchildren free from all oppression, and happy in the enjoyment of their rights; and the old women of a hundred villages lifted up their hands towards heaven and blessed the young Rája (for such they styled him) who had now mounted the zamindári throne. Nor was Nava Krishna satisfied with merely issuing a proclamation. He strictly enjoined on all his servants, from the corpulent and well-greased diväna to the piyádás, to be just and honourable in all their dealings with the ráiyats, to avoid all unjust demands in the shape of *salámis*, *abwábs*, and *párbanis;* adding at the same timo that any of his *amlas* that disobeyed his injunctions would be dismissed from his service at the first offence. The diväna, who was an old sinner of the most orthodox type, and who had done no little work in his day in the line of ráiyat oppression, remonstrated against the impolicy of such a procedure. He represented that lying, knavery, chicanery, and even forgery, were necessary to the successful management of a zamindári, that without such weapons the estate would be a losing concern; and that if his young master persisted in so insane a policy, the zamindári would soon be brought to the Collector's hammer. Nava Krishna remained deaf to these remonstrances, and indeed hinted that if the diväna could not manage the estate according to the policy he had adopted, his services might be dispensed with. From this time the diväna not only remonstrated no longer, but became loud in the praise of the policy which his master had initiated. The subordinate *amlas* took their cue from the diväna, and all seemed apparently to be convinced of the superiority of justice and right over injustice and oppression. But this was not all. Nava Krishna, for the education of his tenants of every description, established several vernacular schools, on the model of Lord Hardinge's schools, in his zamindári, and at Dakshinpalli set up an Anglo-vernacular school, at the head of which he put a class-fellow of his in the Hindoo College. He also set up a dispensary for the gratuitous distribution of medicines among his ráiyats, at the head of which establishment he placed a graduate of the Medical College of Calcutta, on a salary of 100 rupees (£10) a month, whose business it was not only to superintend the dispensary, but also to attend professionally to as many sick people as chose to come to that establishment for help. He also wrote to Mr. Murray, the planter, with whom he had formed acquaintance in his youth, a friendly letter, in which he dwelt on the poverty and helplessness of the ráiyats, and urged upon him the equity as well as the good policy of treating them with justice and clemency; and concluded with expressing the hope that his own tenants at any rate would not be compelled, contrary to their wishes, to take advances for sowing indigo on their own fields. It was on this account that Mr. Murray said to Mádhava that he had been encouraged by the zamindár. Such was the zamindár of Dakshinpalli, the representative of a class of Bengal landlords which, I am glad to say, is every day on the increase.

Shortly after the last harvest in December, about forty ráiyats of Durgánagar, including in the number our friend Mádhava, had been to Babu Nava Krishna Banerjea, whose tenants they were, represented to him the utter unprofitableness of indigo cultivation, and the injustice and oppression to which they are invariably subjected, and begged protection from him as their landlord. Amongst those forty there were ráiyats who had been cultivating indigo for a number of years, others who had been the previous year forced to do so, and others still who had not hitherto cultivated the plant, but who had been warned that they must take advances immediately, otherwise they should be subjected to ill usage. There was nothing new in all this to the zamindár, for he was well acquainted with those practices. He warmly took up the cause of the ráiyats, especially as they were his own tenants, with whom the indigo-planter had nothing to do whatever; advised them to decline taking advances to cultivate indigo on their fields if they thought that cultivation was prejudicial to their interests; and offered his willingness to lend any sums of money to those ráiyats who were in debt to the planter. It was after this conference with the laird and his tenants that the conversation between Mr. Murray and Mádhava took place, which I have recorded in the preceding chapter.

As Mr. Murray had used threatening language towards the ráiyats of Durgánagar, Nava Krishna thought it necessary to keep a number of men on the spot to prevent the outrage. At the same time he thought it proper to send to the Dárogá of Ságarapur, within whose jurisdiction the village of Durgánagar lay, a representation to the effect that the planter of Nildángá had used threatening language towards the husbandmen of the above-mentioned village, and that a raid upon the ráiyats was highly probable. He further requested the Dárogá, in pursuance of his duty, to prevent the outrage. Having sent this representation to the Thána (Police Station) he made some preparations and told his men to be on the alert

CHAPTER XLIX.

ALL ABOUT INDIGO.*

Why did all-creating Nature
Make the plant for which we toil?
Sighs must fan it, tears must water,
Sweat of ours must dress the soil.
Think ye, masters iron-hearted,
  Lolling at your jovial boards,
Think how many backs have smarted
  For the *gains* your *weed* affords.

Cowper.

WHILE Mr. Murray is devising measures for the punishment of the recalcitrant ráiyats of Durgánagar—whose only crime was that they refused to engage in a cultivation which was notoriously disadvantageous to them—and while Nava Krishna is making preparations for the prevention of any violence upon those ráiyats by the planter, I may take this opportunity to tell the reader all about that wonderful plant, the dye of which is so highly valued in the markets of Europe, and the production of which has been always attended with so large an amount of human suffering.

The indigo plant, which must have been growing in a wild state ever since the upheaval of the Indian continent from the bed of the universal ocean,

* For much of the information contained in this chapter, the author is indebted to Mr. Colesworth Grant's elegant treatise, entitled "Rural Life in Bengal."

was hardly turned to any profitable account till English skill was applied to its cultivation and manufacture. There are two ways of cultivating the indigo-plant; *first*, by the ordinary method of cultivation, that is, by ploughing the land and sowing the seed; and *secondly*, by a process called *chhitáni.* In order to explain this second mode, it is necessary to remind the reader that, owing to heavy rains in Bengal, the rivers, whose name is legion, overflow every year, and inundate both banks to some distance. At the end of the rains, when the waters recede and the rivers fall, there is left on the banks, as on those of the Nile, a deposit of loam, which is taken advantage of by the Bengal ráiyat. These *chaḍás* (*churs*), as they are called, are ready-made fields, where the seed can be scattered without the preliminary processes of ploughing and harrowing, provided the sowing takes place when the mud is soft. The process is called *chhitáni,* or scattering, since the seed is merely scattered over the mud by the hand, without preparing the ground. Hence the sowing of the *chaḍás* must take place immediately after the receding of the waters, that is to say, in the month of October. The sowings on the ordinary lands cannot take place before the month of February, or March, or even April, long after the paddy crop has been gathered in, the ground ploughed and harrowed, and the early rains, called by Anglo-Indians the *chhotá barsát* (the little rains), have moistened the soil. Though there is an interval of about five months between the two sowings, the crop of both the low and the high lands is reaped nearly at the same time, the harvest of the high lands being gathered, at the utmost, only four or five weeks later than the crop of the low lands; and both the reapings take place before the heavy rains set in in June or July.

The indigo crop, though it exhausts the powers of the soil, and is in every respect unremunerative to the ráiyat, does not require much labour. Human exertion is hardly necessary, "boon Nature" doing nearly the whole. Two days after it is sown, the seed germinates, and in the course of a week the whole field is covered with an infinite number of plants about half an inch in height. In June the plant becomes about five feet high, when it is considered to be full-grown. It is then cut. In *nijábád* cultivation, the planter cuts his own indigo and brings it to the factory in carts or in boats, according to the situation of the plantations. In *ráiyati* cultivation, the husbandmen, who have taken advances and have cultivated indigo, must cut the plant and carry it to the factory at their own expense. Then begins the process of measuring, which has been described in a previous chapter, and in which so much injustice is done to the poor cultivator.

The plant is next put in the vats. The vats, which are solid masonry, are a range of brick buildings, or rather pits, open at the top. They are always in pairs, a higher and a lower series, the higher ones communicating with the lower ones by means of openings which may be stopped with plugs when necessary. The vats are generally twenty-one feet square, with a depth of about three feet and a half. In Mr. Murray's factory at Nil-dángá, which was a large one, there were no less than twelve pairs of vats. The upper vat is now filled with the indigo plant, which must be done soon after it is cut, otherwise it will rot. The plant is then pressed by means of a number of bamboos put upon it. Over these bamboos, at right angles to them, are placed large beams of *sál* wood, which serve further to press down the plant and bring it to a general level.

Then commences the important process of steeping the plant in the vats with water. The water is brought from a river through aqueducts and Chinese pumps, till the plant is completely steeped. It is allowed to remain in this state for about twelve hours. The plug of the upper vat is now removed, and the liquid, saturated with the colouring matter of the plant, is let off into the lower vat, into which no plant had at all been put. The dead plant, technically called *sithi*, whose colouring essence has mixed with the water, is then removed and spread out to dry; but it is not completely dried till after the lapse of two or three months, when it is stacked, to serve in future the purpose of fuel for the factory boiler and of manure for the fields.

We must now attend to the liquid in the lower vat. It is first subjected to the process of *beating*. A number of men go down into the vat, each furnished with a piece of bamboo about five feet long, flattened at one end, like the oar of a country boat. With these bamboo sticks the blue devils of the vat beat about the liquid in a most picturesque manner, ranging themselves in a variety of positions, putting their bodies into every conceivable posture, and often regaling themselves during the operation with singing in a chorus—the object of the whole being to separate the colouring matter, technically called the *grain*, from the liquid. The beating, which lasts usually about two hours, is put a stop to when the grain is found to be separated from the liquid, and ready to precipitate. The liquid is now allowed to rest for two hours, when the grain precipitates and subsides to the bottom of the vat. The water, now separated from the bluish grain, is drawn out of the vat by means of a series of plugs, and carried through an aqueduct into the river. The liquid colouring matter is then carried through another aqueduct, pumped into the boiler, and subjected to the process of ebullition by means of huge furnaces fed with the *sithi* of last year's manufacture. Then follows the process of *straining*, which is effected by means of a monstrously large piece of American sheeting. The thickish liquid is then pressed in a variety of ways, till all the water is drawn out, and the grain formed into solid blocks, which are then cut into cakes. The cakes are next stamped with the name of the factory, and exposed to dry in a room furnished with bamboo shelves. They take about three months in drying; after which the cakes, weighing eight ounces each, are packed in boxes, taken down to Calcutta, and shipped off for the Indigo Mart in Cannon Street in London. Such is a brief account of indigo manufacture, as it is carried on in the indigo districts of Lower Bengal and of Behar.

CHAPTER L.

BENGALI HEROISM.

Some village Hampden, that, with dauntless breast,
The little tyrant of his fields withstood.

GRAY'S *Elegy*.

THE day following that on which Mr. Murray had given notice to the peasants of Durgánagar that they should either immediately accept advances, or be prepared for the worst, Mádhava, having nothing particular to do in the afternoon, put his bathing-towel on his shoulder, and, taking in his hand the hookah, the cup of which was diffusing around the sweet odour of tobacco, wended his way to a *vakula* tree growing in the middle of the village. On the brick-built platform around the tree he found four husbandmen sitting; he joined them; others dropped in; and in the course of a short time the number of peasants under the tree amounted to about twenty. They were all dressed in *dhutis,* which went down as far as the knees, the rest of the body, both upward and downward, was, of course, naked. Some of them had the *gámchhá,* or bathing-towel, on their shoulders, and others had it not; but considerably more than half the number had each a hookah in his hand. A great deal of smoking, coughing, and expectorating went on in the midst of talk on various subjects; but the chief burden of the conversation was the threat of the planter. Mádhava, addressing a peasant whose hair was silvered over with age, and who had just finished one of those long fits of coughing into which he invariably fell whenever he applied his lips to the hookah, said,

"And what say you, Murabbi?" (The word *murabbi* is equivalent to the English word "Governor" in colloquial English.) "What is to be done at this time of difficulty?"

The old peasant answered,

"What shall I say, *bábá* Mádhava? I have become old; three stages have already past, and the fourth and last stage only is remaining; a few days more and my body will be reduced to ashes. I am for peace. The whole of my life I have been cultivating indigo for the Sáheb of Nildángá; I have suffered much. What is the good of resisting the Sáheb now, at the fag end of my life? You are young; you have before you many years of enjoyment and of trouble. If you be successful in your resistance I shall be glad—not for my sake—but for the sake of you all. But I doubt whether your resistance will be successful."

"It is not our resistance, murabbi. Who are we? We cannot prevent Mari Sáheb from doing anything. Our kind Rájá has promised to assist us."

"It is all very well for the jamidár to promise to assist us, but you will see that he will not be able to protect us. All *topiwálás* (hat-men, that is, Europeans) are brothers to each other. The magistrate and the judge will always decide in favour of their white-skinned brother."

"What are you driving at, old man?" said a third party, in a somewhat angry tone. "Do you advise us to take Mari Sáheb's advances, and go on cultivating indigo till the day of our death? Old age seems to have taken away your sense."

"Don't be angry," said the old man, "I have seen enough of opposition, in my day, to the Sáhebs of *Nilkuthis* (indigo factories); but those Sáhebs can never be put down. They always come off victorious from the struggle. I say, therefore, it is useless to contend. It is wisdom to submit."

"It would be madness to submit," said a fourth peasant, who seemed to be somewhat better dressed than the rest, and to exercise some sort of authority over the assembly, "it is better to die than to cultivate indigo. The moment you touch the cursed gold of the planter, you are done for. Your debt is never liquidated. It increases year by year. The best portion of your fields is selected by the planter for sowing indigo. When the plant is cut and taken to the factory, it is found always less than when you measured it in the field. You get less paddy than is sufficient for the support of your family; and thus eating the food of your own house, as the saying is, you drive buffaloes in the wilderness. Mari Sáheb is a merciless creature, like all indigo-planters. Provided he gets his indigo, he does not care whether poor husbandmen live or die. His only object is to make money, and then to go away to his native land. But there is justice in the heavens. The man that builds happiness on the ruin of other people can never prosper. Such is the decree of the gods. No, no, we must not submit. May the gods make Nava Krishna Bábu immortal! He has promised to befriend us. With his help we will oppose the wicked Feringi."

This speech of the respectable-looking husbandman, who in fact was the *mandal,* or headman of the village, elicited general applause from the audience, on which the old man wept. Mádhava, after the applause had subsided, said,

"What the *mandal* has just now said is exactly my opinion. We ourselves cannot contend against the *Nilkar* (indigo manufacturer), but, if the jamidár be on our side, what can Mari Sáheb do?"

The *mandal,* who had now worked himself up into great excitement, said in a loud voice,

"*Mari sáláke máro!*" (strike the scoundrel Murray,) "*Mari sáláke máro!* that should be our battle-cry. The indigo-planters have been the ruin of our country. Before those *sálás* came, this country was as happy as Ayodhyá in the time of Ráma. But now everything has gone to wreck and ruin. They oppress us; they beat us; they imprison us; they torture us; they kill us; they dishonour our wives and daughters. Down with the indigo-planters! Down with the blue monkeys! *Mari sáláke máro!*"

These words, which were repeated with great energy and fierce gesticulation, produced a tremendous sensation in the assembly, and all exclaimed, "*Mari sáláke máro!*" But the old peasant, who had hitherto been silent, could no longer contain within himself. He stood up, with the eternal hookah in his hand, and said—"We shall see, friends, how you beat Mari Sáheb. I have seen enough of the heroism of my countrymen. You are like mountains in words, but in action you are like the mustard-seed. You have big mouths, but little chests. You talk big, but when you see the face of a Sáheb you shrink into nothing. When Mari Sáheb comes with his bands, you will all run away like dogs, putting their tails between their hind legs." The assembly was greatly excited, and some of the young fellows proposed that the old man should be turned out of the place, when at that moment the *gomastá* of Bábu Nava Krishna Banerjea came to the spot. On seeing him they all stood up, and made him sit in the middle of the platform of masonry on a mat. He had come, he said, to inquire, in the event of a raid on the village by Mr. Murray, what amount of opposition the people could make. The people there assembled declared their readiness to stand on the defensive. There were no swords in the village, excepting a few owned by the *páiks*, or the village police. But though swords and spears were wanting, there was no lack of bamboo clubs; and the peasants all declared that they would be ready to wield their clubs at the bidding of the zamindár. The *gomastá* then addressed them in a short speech, in which he dwelt on the iniquities of indigo planting, and on the necessity of union amongst the peasantry with a view to put down all oppression. He also assured them of the earnest determination of the zamindár to stand by his tenants, to free them from the oppression of indigo-planters, and to promote their welfare in any way he could. The ráiyats were overjoyed at this announcement, and they shouted out—"May Nava Krishna Bábu become immortal! May he live for ever!" The peasants then went away to their houses.

CHAPTER LI.

THE AFFRAY.

> For why? Because the good old rule
> Sufficeth them; the simple plan,
> That they should take who have the power,
> And they should keep who can.
>
> *Wordsworth.*

Twenty-five years ago there was hardly an indigo-planter or zamindár in Bengal who had not a regular establishment of *láthiáls* or club-men. The keeping up of such an establishment was considered a necessary item of expense, as it was deemed impossible in those days to manage either an indigo factory or a zamindári without an armed force. Mr. Murray had the reputation, such as it was, of being the owner of one of the finest bands of *láthiáls* in the country. They were usually fifty in number, which was his peace establishment; but the number could be considerably increased on the occasion of an affray conducted on a large scale. These club-men were, for the most part, natives of Pharidpur (Furridpore) and Pabna—the two districts in Bengal noted for their excellent *láthiáls;* there was a sprinkling also of *goálás* (milk-men) of Sántipur, who are said to be amongst the most stalwart and spirited peasants in the country; and there were besides a few up-country-men, who were, however, used as a sort of reserve force for times of emergency. These last had been initiated into the mysteries of firing muskets, which were seldom used in ordinary village frays. The majority of the club-men were furnished with clubs made of bamboo. The *láthiáls* were also called *sarkiwálás,* that is, wielders of *sarkis,* which are bamboo clubs having at end an iron spear-head. These *sarkis* are used not only for striking the enemy at close quarters, but thrown at him from a distance. Hence in a fray a club-man is furnished with about half a dozen *sarkis,* one of which he keeps in his right hand, ready for use either at close quarters or at a distance; and the others he carries in his left hand successively to supply the place of the one in the right hand. Besides these *sarkis* the *láthiál* is furnished with a shield, which he carries in his left hand along with the *sarkis.* The shields are usually made of rattan, the Indian cane, covered with cow-hide; though a better class of shields are covered with the more valuable and less penetrable hide of the rhinoceros.

Early one morning, long before sunrise, about forty or fifty of Mr. Murray's *sarkiwálás,* suddenly emerging from a mango-grove beside a tank with lofty embankments, raised a loud shout, and approached the peasant huts of Durgánagar. Scarcely had the husbandmen washed their eyes after getting up from their beds, when the club-men fell upon them with fury. The zamindár's people were scarcely ready; but even if they had been quite ready they would have been no match for the practised club-men of Mari Sáheb. Not that Bengali zamindárs have smaller establishments of club-men than European indigo planters, but the fact is that the father of Nava Krishna Banerjea, having been prudent enough never to pick a quarrel with Mr. Murray or his predecessor, his club-men, for want of exercise, had become rusty, and had almost forgotten their vocation; and Nava Krishna himself was too enlightened and humane a zamindár to pay much attention to the improvement of his military resources. The peasants, who had no *sarkis,* could not offer determined opposition; and the club-men of the zamindár, unaware of the exact time of attack, were not in readiness. The villagers, however, soon assembled in large numbers, and pelted the foe with brickbats and pieces of broken *háṇḍis.* They also came out with their hoes, their axes, and their sickles. The veteran *sarkiwálás* of Mr. Murray, who was himself on the scene, riding on a milk-white Arab, and fortified with fire-arms, soon became masters of the field.

About this time, however, the *láthiáls* of the zamindár appeared on the scene of action, and rushed into the fight with great impetuosity. Both parties threw *sarkis* against each other; the combatants drew nearer and nearer till they came to close quarters. For a moment the zamindár's party seemed to be gaining ground, when Mr. Murray fired off two pistol shots, to the infinite consternation of his opponents. These latter now took to their heels. The factory people pursued them and the villagers to some distance, captured some of the ráiyats, entered into the huts of the peasants and plundered them. Several on both sides were wounded, but not seriously. The only person who had received a bad wound was our friend Mádhava. As the first fury of the assailants had been directed against his huts, he had defended himself with some spirit, and had in consequence been pierced by a *sarki.* Smarting with the wound, he had concealed himself in a thicket near his house. The *sarkiwálás* of the factory, on their return from the pursuit of the zamindár's men, found Mádhava in the bush. They caught hold of him and took him away, especially considering that he might die of his wound, which would greatly embarrass the planter. The prisoners, about twelve in number, including Mádhava and the *mandal*—the same who had spoken with vehemence against the planter—were handcuffed and taken away by the *sarkiwálás,* who rent the air with shouts of exultation, Mr. Murray himself bringing up the rear. On reaching the factory grounds the *mandal* and the other captives were confined in a large go-down, but Mádhava alone was taken, by the planter's orders, towards the river side.

It is but doing simple justice to Mr. Murray to state that he had not the least desire to kill or even severely to wound any of the ráiyats of Durgánagar; his object was merely to intimidate them into submission. Nor did he wish that their property should be plundered; but as he could not be present at the same time in every part of the scene of the conflict, his men plundered, without his knowledge, whatever valuable things came in their way. What became of the prisoners, and why Mádhava was separated from the rest, will be told in the next chapter.

CHAPTER LII.

WHAT HAPPENED IN FATHER-IN-LAW'S HOUSE.

And worse than all, and most to be deplored,
As human nature's broadest, foulest blot,
Chains him, and tasks him, and exacts his sweat,
With stripes, that mercy with a bleeding heart
Weeps, when she sees inflicted on a beast.

The Task.

In the high and palmy state of indigo-planting in Bengal, every factory had a large go-down-looking room, which passed among the men of the planter under the *soubriquet* of *Sasurbáḍi*, or Father-in-law's House. However it may be in other countries of the globe, in Bengal at least most men regard their sons-in-law with the utmost kindness and affection. Whenever a young son-in-law goes to the house of his wife's father, he meets with the warmest reception from every member of the family; he is coaxed and caressed beyond measure; he is presented with valuable gifts; and of feasting and jollification there is no end. Hence one's father-in-law's house is looked upon as the happiest and sunniest spot in this world of care and anxiety. The go-down in the indigo-planter's factory, which went under the name of father-in-law's house, had none of these attractions. It was not the sunniest, but the gloomiest room on the factory premises; no other presents were given in it than kicks, cuffs, shoe beatings, strokes of the cat-o'-nine-tails called *gadádhar*, racking pains produced by pressing the chests of prisoners against two bamboos; no music was ever heard in it except the wailing of distress and the sigh of despair; and as for feasting, the whole of it was comprised in a handful of *bhát* and *dál* once a day, just sufficient to keep the bones and flesh together. The fact is, the go-down is a veritable dungeon for incarcerating, on the planter's own authority, all defaulting and recalcitrant husbandmen, and was called *Sasurbáḍi*, or Father-in-law's House, in bitter irony. Of course there was no furniture in it, not even a mat to sit upon; there were only some instruments of torture, like bamboos, old boots, one or two *sarkis*, and a number of cane switches. There was only one small hole in the upper part of one of the walls, which was not a window but an apology for one. Such was the room in which the *mandal* of Durgánagar and his ten fellow villagers found themselves. They had not, however, been a quarter of an hour in it when they saw entering by the door the dreaded Mari Sáheb himself, his redoubtable divána, and two of those formidable looking *sarkiwálás* who had signalized themselves in the recent fight. The planter seated himself in a chair which was brought in, the divána and the *sarkiwálás* standing on either side of their august lord. Mr. Murray called the *mandal* to him, and thus addressed him:—"Well, *mandal*, you are now the *mandal* of a broken-up village, as the Bengali proverb has it. What has become of your boast—'*Mari Sáheb sáláke maro* (beat the scoundrel, Mr. Murray)?'"

Mandal. "Khodáwand, I never used these words! Some enemy of mine must have told you a lie in order to ruin me."

Planter. "You are a lying rascal, like the whole of your race. Do you think I do not know everything that passes amongst you? You and that other rascal, Mádhava, threatened to beat me, and persuaded the other husbandmen to oppose me and fight with my men. The zamindár *Sálá* promised to protect you. Where is now your father, Nava Krishna? Let him now protect you."

Mandal. "Hazúr is all-powerful; Hazúr can either kill me or save me. Khodáwand, show mercy to a poor peasant like me."

Planter. "You are guilty of such heavy crimes that you deserve instant death; and no father of yours can save you. But I will spare you under two conditions. One condition is that you immediately take advance for indigo; and the other condition is that when the police make an investigation of this affray, you affirm, with Gangá-water in your hands, that no affray did take place, that you were not brought by force into the factory, and that you willingly took the advances."

Mandal. "Dharma-avatár! (Incarnation of Justice!) I shall be ready to swear that there was no affray at all; but Hazúr will excuse my not taking advances."

Mr. Murray was highly incensed at these words, and ordered the *sarkiwálás* to put the *mandal* down on the floor, and to torture him with bamboos. These two messengers of *Yama* immediately caught hold of the prisoner, threw him down on the floor, and began pressing his chest with a bamboo.

The *mandal,* agonising with pain, shrieked—"O father! O mother! My life is going out! O save me!"

Mr. Murray, enjoying the scene, and being in a jocular vein, said—"Let me see which father of yours will now come to your help. Come now, why have you not kept your promise to beat Mari Sáheb? *Sarkiwálás*, get on smartly with the bamboo."

The *mandal* yelled out again in a yet shriller tone —"O father! O mother! My life is going, going, going! Give me the advance, Sáheb!"

The *sarkiwálás* immediately stopped in their work, the *mandal* was put in a sitting posture, and a tumbler of water was given him to drink.

Mr. Murray said he was glad the *mandal* had so soon been brought to his senses, and expressed the hope that the lesson might not soon be forgotten. The other ten prisoners, who were eye-witnesses of their friend's agony, when asked whether they would take advances, readily agreed to the proposal. They were all removed from the *sasurbáḍi* to the *daphtarkhána*, where papers of agreement were drawn up and signed, by the *mandal* in writing (for he could read and write), and the other prisoners by a cross mark; and advances were given. They were then dismissed by the planter, who warned them that if they gave evidence against him before either the Dárogá or the magistrate, he would, on an early opportunity, burn their houses and put an end to their lives. About noon they left the factory and went to their village.

As for Mádhava, the reader knows that, instead of being sent to *sasurbáḍi*, he was taken to the river-side; the reason was this. Mr. Murray perceived by a glance at Mádhava's wound, that, if not fatal, it was very serious; if the police got hold of him, they might make a serious case of the whole affair; hence it was necessary to shove him out of the way. I do not mean to say that Mr. Murray resolved to kill him outright; of such cold-blooded murder, I believe, though rough and inhuman in his dealings with the ráiyats, he was incapable. On the contrary, Mádhava's wound was dressed by a barber attached to the factory, who generally discharged the functions of a surgeon. After this, he was put into a boat, and sent away privately in one of the planter's own boats to a distant factory, away from the scene of the affray and the police investigation which was sure to follow.

CHAPTER LIII.

THE POLICE INVESTIGATION.

'Tis gold
Which makes the true man kill'd, and saves the thief;
Nay sometimes hangs both thief and true man. What
Can it not do, and undo? *Cymbeline.*

THE reader will doubtless recollect that the zamindár Nava Krishna Banerjea, had, before the occurrence of the affray, sent notice of the planter's threat to the Dárogá of the Thánà of Ságarapur, requesting him to prevent the outrage. But Nava Krishna had been forestalled by the indigo-planter. Mr. Murray had, on the very day of his conversation with Mádhava, sent word to the Dárogá that, in order to bring some recusant ráiyats of Durgánagar to their senses, he would be obliged to have recourse to some measures of intimidation; and that he must not, in consequence of any representations the zamindár might make, interfere with the planter's dealings with his defaulting ráiyats. The Dárogá jumped at this notice of Mr. Murray, as he knew it would bring him gain. There was always a good understanding between the indigo factory of Nildánga and the Thánà of Ságarpur; indeed, the indigo-planter could not have committed half the outrage he did commit, without the connivance of the police; and this connivance was obtained—*purchased* would be too vulgar a word—not, indeed, by bribes—for so honourable a gentleman as Mr. Murray must be presumed to be incapable of giving a bribe—but by presents of money, given either before, or immediately after, the perpetration of an outrage. Such being the case, the Dárogá was always thankful whenever he heard of an intended affray. In case of an affray, the Dárogá usually manages to get money from both parties; but, in the present case no money—call it a gift, a present, a donation, or a bribe, if you please—could be expected from Nava Krishna Banerjea, as he had sedulously set his face against corruption from the commencement of his administration. On receiving representations from both Mr. Murray and Babu Nava Krishna Banerjea, the Dárogá had no difficulty in adopting his course. "My best policy," said he to himself, "will be not to stir in the matter at all, but to wait till the affray is over, and then immediately after to repair to the scene of the conflict, and make the most of the business to enrich myself; and as that raw youth, Nava Krishna, inexperienced in the ways of the world, will, I fear, not give me a single *paysá*, I must screw from Mr. Murray as much as I can, especially as he will be victorious in the affray, and will doubtless cause much injury to the ráiyats." Such were the calculations of the Dárogá; and he was not mistaken.

Immediately after Mr. Murray had set free the captive ráiyats, he sent an express to the Dárogá, informing him of the result of the affair. The Dárogá forthwith ordered his pony to be made ready, and then proceeded in state with the *Baksi*, the *jamadár*, half a dozen *barkandázes*, and a score of *chaukidárs*. As his way lay through the village of Dakshinpalli, he had an interview with Nava Krishna, who gave him a detailed account of the affray, including the capture of the ráiyats, the tortures inflicted upon them, their subsequent release after advances having been forced upon them, and the disappearance of Mádhava, who perhaps had been killed in the fray. He denounced in forcible words the violent conduct and tyranny of the indigo-planter, and called upon the Dárogá to send a truthful report of the affair to the magistrate. The Dárogá quietly said that he must not form any opinion of the affair without holding an investigation on the spot; that in all affrays both parties are generally to blame, though the degree of criminality on one side may be greater than that on the other; and gently hinted that his sending to the magistrate a report favourable to the zamindár depended chiefly on the zamindár himself. Nava Krishna, though he understood the hint, took no notice of it, but urged on him the propriety of his sending, as a police officer, a truthful report to the magistrate.

The Dárogá was not disappointed, as he had not expected any *douceur* from Nava Krishna, and proceeded on his way more and more confirmed in his mind of the good policy of sending in a report favourable to the planter. There was one fact he learned from the zamindár which gave him great satisfaction, and that was the disappearance of Mádhava. He thought Mádhava must have been killed in the fray, and that the planter must have either thrown his body into the river or buried it in the factory grounds. The Dárogá deemed this fact to be a perfect God-send, as it would enable him to extort a large bribe from the planter.

Gloating over this unexpected good fortune—for police officers, as a rule, live on the ruin of the raiyats—the Dárogá proceeded on his journey, and reached Durgánagar in the afternoon.

The advent of a Dárogá into a village in Bengal, is regarded with the same horror as the entrance of a body of Prussian Uhlans into a town of France was regarded by the French during the late Franco-Prussian war. Requisitions become the order of the day. Soon after the Dárogá entered Durgánagar, the *barkandázes* and *chaukidárs* went on a foraging expedition. In the course of one short hour an incredible amount of provisions was obtained. From the Muhammadan inhabitants were extorted fowls by the dozen and eggs by the score; and the Hindus gave large quantities of unboiled rice, pulse, vegetables, mustard oil and clarified butter. The provisions which they collected must have sufficed the officials of the Thánā of Ságarapur for a whole month. Nor were provisions the only thing extorted. Timid ráiyats gladly gave copper, and even silver, in order to purchase the goodwill of the formidable myrmidons of the police.

The Dárogá held an investigation on the very spot where the affray had taken place, which was not far from the house of Mádhava. There was nothing to show that any affray had taken place, for the *sarkiwálás* of the factory had carefully abstained from making such depredations as might leave traces of the outrage. Besides the Dárogá and his subordinates, and the ráiyats themselves, there were present on the spot the *gomastás* of the planter and the zamindár, who were watching the case on behalf of their masters. Before the depositions were taken down, the *gomastá* of the planter drew aside the *Baksi,* who is a police officer next to the Dárogá, and, indeed, his right hand, and talked with him for a few minutes. The *Baksi* resumed his seat next to the Dárogá and whispered to him. What formed the subject of conversation between the planter's *gomastá* and the *Baksi* of the Tháná has not transpired; and I should be abandoning my character as a veracious historian were I to put down in this authentic narrative a guess of mine own; the *gomastá* of the zamindár, however, declared that the Dárogá was offered a large bribe through the *Baksi.* Be that as it may, the depositions began now to be taken down. The reader will scarcely believe me when I say—nevertheless it is a simple fact—that the ráiyats, one and all, including the *mandal* himself, swore that no affray had taken place, that no ráiyats had been captured, and that they had willingly received advances from Mari Sáheb. The reason why the ráiyats perjured themselves must be plain to the reader—they were afraid of Mari Sáheb, who had proved himself to be stronger than the zamindár. They believed the zamindár to be animated with the sincere wish of doing them good, but it was evident he was unable to cope with the planter. To lean on Nava Krishna would be to lean on a broken reed. They therefore at once denied that there had been any affray. One ugly fact remained to be accounted for. What had become of Mádhava? The ráiyats all declared they did not know; indeed, they had not seen him at all during the affray.

When all these depositions had been taken down, the Dárogá, with an air of triumph, turned towards the *gomastá* of the zamindár, and said, "What a lot of liars these Hindus are! (The Dárogá himself was a Muhammadan.) The zamindár's representations are now proved to be all false. I now see through the whole. From the beginning to the end it is a trumped-up case of the zamindár's. He has got up the story of the affray in order to involve Mr. Murray in trouble; and it is clear to my mind as noonday that the zamindár himself has concealed Mádhava in order to bring a heavy case against good Mari Sáheb." Agreeably to these views, the *Baksi* drew up, on the spot, a report for the magistrate to the effect that the Dárogá had been to the spot of the alleged affray, and examined every witness that could be brought forward, and found that there had been no affray at all. That the story had been evidently invented by the zamindár to bring Mr. Murray into trouble; and that it was highly probable that Mádhava had been concealed somewhere by the zamindár himself.

The Dárogá returned the same evening to the Tháná, after having had an interview with Mr. Murray at the factory, where his hand was well oiled.

CHAPTER LIV.

MÁDHAVA'S END.

The undiscovered country, from whose bourn
No traveller returns.

Hamlet.

THE ráiyats of an indigo district will tell you that one of the modes in which the planter punishes those whom he deems most dangerous is to make them "drink the water of seven factories." A ráiyat of some pluck, "some village Hampden," is spirited away, and sent from factory to factory—for one indigo concern has generally several factories—according to the circumstances of the case; and this mysterious translation from place to place ends in his exit from the stage of the world. We must do Mr. Murray the justice to remark that before the affray he had not the slightest intention to spirit Mádhava away, and send him the round of the factories; but the severe wound which he had unfortunately received in the *mêlée*, left the planter no choice. If Mádhava had been allowed to remain at Durgánagar after having been wounded, it would have been highly prejudicial to the interests of Mr. Murray, as the wound alone would have been sufficient proof of the affray; and if he had died in consequence of the wound, in the course of a few days, the planter's case would have been more serious. Hence the necessity of kidnapping Mádhava away. The first factory to which he was carried was ten or twelve miles distant, but here he was not kept for more than twenty-four hours. The magistrate, believing, on the strength of the Dárogá's representations, that there had been no affray at all, and that the zamindár had hidden Mádhava in some secret place in order to get Mr. Murray into trouble, had issued orders on the zamindár immediately to produce Mádhava, on pain of heavy penalties. Though the zamindár was as innocent in the matter as the unborn babe, he was obliged to take measures for ascertaining the whereabouts of the planter's captive. The police were also active in the search, not so much in obedience to the magistrate's orders as with a view to obtain illegal gratification from the party in whose custody the missing Mádhava might be found. The zamindár's spies and the *chaukidárs* of the Thána were forthwith set in motion, and they found out that the boat which carried Mádhava on board had sailed towards Kuládaha. On this circumstance being known to the assistant planter, the wounded prisoner was sent to the next factory on the Bhágirathi named Serpaḍá, which, though distant only a few miles from the former one, had the advantage of being situated in a different district, namely, Hooghly. But the spies and *choukidárs* followed the fugitive to that place; therefore it became necessary to remove Mádhava to some far-off factory in Eastern Bengal. The boat touched at several factories in the way, such as Krishnadhám, Rádhánagar, Chakradwípa, Sárisamudra, at each of which places the prisoner was taken ashore and kept a few hours, till he reached Maulaviganja, on the banks of the Ichhamati, the factory of which was determined to be his prison. Poor Mádhava, however, had not long to live. In consequence of his removal from place to place, his wound, which was utterly neglected, festered, and scarcely had he been landed at the *ghát* of the planter at Maulaviganja, when he died. His remains were neither burnt nor buried, but were simply thrown at night into the river, which carried them to the Bay of Bengal. Such was the end of Mádhava, the victim of the planter's cupidity.

It was after a long time that the news of Mádhava's death reached his family at Durgánagar. Immediately after the conclusion of the affray, his wife and mother supposed that he had been carried along with the other captives to the factory at Nildángá; but when all returned excepting Madhava, their grief knew no bounds. Consumed with grief, they waited day after day, and week after week, and yet no tidings came of the object of their affection. Málati wept by day and by night. She broke her silver ornaments and cast them aside; she often dashed her head against the floor through despair; she scarcely ate or drank anything. The mother of Mádhava became almost mad with despair. She became ten times more furious than ever: it was impossible for any human being to approach her. At last a chance traveller announced in the village the news of Mádhava's death. We will not attempt to describe the state into which the women were thrown on hearing the melancholy tidings. Sudhámukhi became insane, and hung herself one night on one of the bamboo rafters of her sleeping hut. Kádambini went to her late husband's relatives, who were not unwilling to support her. Málati sold off the huts and everything else she had, and, taking her son Yádava with her, came to Kánchanpur and took up her abode with her brother. Govinda was ill able to support his sister and her son. Nor was it necessary. By selling her late husband's property she had got about one hundred rupees, with part of which she traded, and part she lent out on heavy interest. The trade which she carried on was this. She bought paddy, turned it into rice, and sold it. The proceeds of this little trade, together with the interest of the money lent out, were sufficient to supply her wants and those of her son. The boy was also able in a short time to earn a little money, about a shilling a month, by tending the cows of neighbours and by gathering cow-dung every day, which Málati turned into cakes and sold as fuel.

As in the course of this narrative we shall not have occasion to mention the name of Nava Krishna Banerjea, the zamindár of Durgánagar, we may remark once for all that, though often opposed by the indigo-planter of Nildángá in his honest endeavours to protect his tenants and to ameliorate their condition, his exertions were crowned with complete success; and there is no name in the long roll of the zamindárs of Bengal which stands higher for philanthropy, liberality, uprightness of conduct, and public spirit than the honoured name of Nava Krishna Banerjea. Concerning Mr. Murray, of whom the reader will not hear again, we may state that the Rob Roy principle which he adopted—"the simple plan that they should take who have the power, and they should keep who can"—did him little good. His oppression created universal disaffection among the peasantry, and produced an outbreak some years afterwards; and he had so completely mismanaged affairs that the Bengal indigo concern, of whom he was a servant, were obliged to shut up shop and sell the factory to the highest bidder.

CHAPTER LV.

THE LARES AND THE PENATES.

Hail, Ceres, hail, by thee from fertile ground
Swift springs the corn, and plenty flows around.

Kallimachos.

THE reader will probably remember that, before speaking of the affairs of poor Mádhava and the indigo-planter of Durgánagar, we left our hero reconstructing the big hut which had been reduced to ashes. A peasant's cottage is not so easily built, or rather thatched in the present case, as the reader might suppose. One reason of the delay is that the materials cannot be had ready at hand; and even if they can be got ready, the peasant has not the means to buy them. Bamboos could certainly be had at Kánchanpur, but they were dearer than in some villages ten or twelve miles off, where they were cheap because they were plentiful. Kálamánik had to go to one of these distant villages, select some bamboos in a plantation, cut them down, and bring them to Kánchanpur; but as there were no roads for carts, the bamboos had to be brought on the backs of bullocks, and one bullock could hardly carry more than four long and stout bamboos. But the bamboos thus brought were not fit to be used immediately. It is always advisable to season them by keeping them some time soaked in water. The bamboos were therefore thrown into the tank near Govinda's house.

After they had lain for some days in water, they were taken up; some of them were cut for posts, and others were split and smoothed and turned into laths. Then the palmyra trees had to be cut, sawn, and smoothed for beams and rafters. Ropes and strings could certainly be purchased, if not at Kánchanpur at least in Vardhamána, but that would be too expensive for the poor family; Kálamánik and Govinda had, therefore, to spin them, by a reel of the primitive type called *ḍhera*, from the hemp which grew in their fields. Then again the paddy-straw, which was in the stack, and which was the food of the cows, was not fit to be used for thatching purposes unless it had been subjected to some process. The bundles were all loosened: bullocks, strung together in a line and tied to a post in the centre of the yard, were made to tread upon them in order, to remove from the straw any grain of paddy that might not have been thrashed out; and then the whole was tied again in long bundles of picked straw called *loṭ*. Day after day, week after week, did Kálamánik work incessantly at the thatching of their hut; and when the *maḍkachá* (the ridge of the thatch) was laid on, their joy was as great as that of the Jews when they saw the completion of the temple of Solomon.

The hut thus thatched was not used for human habitation without the performance of some religious ceremony. Uneducated and poor as Kálamánik and Govinda were, they had, like most Hindu peasants, a deep sense of religion. No new house, or an old one rebuilt, is in Bengal used without a religious ceremony. The Lares and the Penates had to be invoked and reinstated in their former seats. Besides, the case of the hut of which we are speaking was a peculiar one. It had been reduced to ashes by Brahmá, the god of fire; and though they knew that the act had been perpetrated by the orders of the wicked zamindár, it was looked upon by the superstitious family as a judgment from heaven. There were, therefore, especial reasons for consecrating it. When the last wisp of straw was put on the *maḍkachá,* and everything was complete, Rámdhan Misri, the family priest, held within its walls a solemn service, repeated *mantras,* and invoked *Ganesa* and the fire deities. But the deity chiefly worshipped on this occasion was Lakshmi, the goddess of prosperity, the Démeter of the Hindu Pantheon, whom Vishnu had obtained at the churning of the ocean. There is not a single Hindu family in all Bengal, however poor, which does not regard this goddess with peculiar veneration. She is the *Lar familiaris* of Bengali Hindu houses; all prosperity in life is owing to her auspicious influence, The favour of Lakshmi makes a man rich, her disfavour makes him poor. When a household is in affluent circumstances, Lakshmi is said to have taken up her abode in it; and when it is reduced to poverty, it is said to be *Lakshmi-chháḍá*—that is, deserted by Lakshmi. Hence she is worshipped in every house. She is usually represented as a handsome young lady, painted yellow, sitting on a water-lily. But it is not in this form that she is worshipped in every Hindu household, and especially in every Hindu peasant's household. Her more common symbol is a corn-measure, called *káthá,* painted with red-lead, filled with paddy, adorned with a garland of flowers, covered with a white cloth, and encompassed with a number of cowrie shells. This is the palladium of a Hindu household's prosperity—it is the Bengal ráiyat's most sacred symbol.

After the religious ceremony was over, a few Bráhmans were feasted—three, I think, was the number, as Govinda was too poor to entertain more—and presented with a little money called *dakshiná*. A few friends and relations were also feasted, and thus the feast of dedication was over. After this the hut was used for household purposes.

People may call this fetichism if they choose, but it is impossible not to have respect for that deep religiousness which underlies the Hindu character even in a common Hindu peasant. Though the rites are superstitious, they are not meaningless; they indicate the existence of an essentially noble and supersensual sentiment; they show that, even in an uneducated peasant, there is something which could not have been either inherited or developed from a monkey; they are an acknowledgment that human happiness is dependant on the smiles of an unseen power, and that all prosperity flows from the bountiful Author of all Good.

CHAPTER LVI.

A GALA DAY.

Therefore sacrifice they unto their net,
And burn incense unto their drag;
Because by them their portion is fat,
And their meat plenteous.

Habakkuk.

It was in the sunny month of Chaitra (half of March and half of April) that all the artizans of Kánchanpur had their day of worship and festivity. This was the *pujá* of Visvakarmá, the World-maker, the Hephaîstos of the Hindu Pantheon, the patron of arts and manufactures in the holy land of Bhárata. The celebration, like all Hindu *pujás*, was partly religious and partly social. On that day the sound of the hammer, which is never still, was not heard in the village, nor did any of the artizan class pursue their ordinary avocations. It was the yearly Sabbath of Bengali artizans. Visvakarmá, the engineer of the celestials, is represented by the figure of a man painted white, having three eyes, wearing on his head a crown, a necklace of gold, and bangles on his wrists, and holding a club in his right hand. But the image is seldom made, its place being supplied by the implements and tools in the various departments of mechanical labour. Every peasant, every artizan, worships the tools of his trade in his own house.

On that day Govinda set up in a corner of his house the plough, the hoe, the sickle, and other implements of husbandry; Nanda, his hammer, his anvil, and his bellows; Kapila, his axe, his wedge, his inclined plane; Chatura, his razors, his basin, and the sharp instruments for paring off the nails; Bokárám, his loom and shuttle; the fisherman, his nets, his rods, and lines; the oilman, his oil-mill; the potter, his wheel; the mason, his trowel and plumb-line; the shoemaker, his awl; the washerman, his beetle, his mallet, and his ironing instrument—they all washed and cleaned these implements, and set them apart for the day from ordinary use. The worshippers themselves, after performing their ablutions in the village tanks, were dressed in their holiday's best. The religious part of the ceremony was soon over. The prayers recited by the Bráhmanas expressed not only gratitude for past favours, but a desire for future ones. It is superfluous to remark that the implements of handicraft, which are set apart for the day and presented with flowers and offerings, are not themselves worshipped; and the best proof of this is found in the fact that those implements are not regarded with any degree of reverence on other days. The great Architect of the Universe, the Master Mason, is worshipped by these simple artificers without any other visible representations than the symbols of the arts; and we cannot but think that this periodical and public acknowledgment of the Creator by the working classes of Bengal is to be infinitely preferred to the absorbing secularism and practical atheism of the proletariat of some of the countries of Europe.

The religious ceremony is followed by festivity.

That day, the blacksmith, the carpenter, the weaver, the barber, the husbandman, eat better dinners than perhaps on any other day in the year. Nor does each one selfishly eat his own dinner by himself. The richer artizans give feasts to their poorer brethren of the same craft. Though the system of caste does not allow a blacksmith to dine with a carpenter, it does not seem to us to impede the flow of brotherly kindliness between members of two different guilds. There is no country in the world where the spirit of caste is not to be found in some shape or other. In India, caste is practically based on occupations, people who pursue the same trade forming one caste by themselves; in England, it is based chiefly on money, the richer class forming the Bráhmanas, and the poorer, the *Chandálas* of English society. In its practical working, though not in its theory, the Indian system of caste is hardly worse than the English system. In England, though a rich goldsmith dines with a rich cotton spinner, he does not admit to his table a very poor member of his own guild; in India, a rich goldsmith does not dine in the company of a rich cotton-spinner, but cheerfully admits to his table a very poor goldsmith. In our opinion, this particular phase of the English system of caste is a great deal worse than that of the Hindu system.

The feast over, the peasants and the artizans betake themselves to all sorts of amusements. As on the occasion of the Navánna, or the new rice, they engage at this festival in all sorts of sports; they play at *háḍu-guḍu;* they angle in the tanks; they play at *guli-ḍánḍá;* they shuffle cards; they sing songs, accompanied with instrumental music;

they form themselves into companies in different parts of the village, and sit, and smoke, and talk, under trees, on matters affecting their craft, or tell stories, of which, like all simple men, they are immensely fond.

CHAPTER LVII.

KÁLAMÁNIK.

> In the dust he fell :
> So nourished long in some well-watered spot,
> Crowned with green boughs, the smooth-skinned poplar falls,
> Doomed by the builder to supply with wheels
> Some splendid chariot, on the bank it lies
> A lifeless trunk, to parch in summer airs.
>
> *Homer.*

THE reader might have inferred from what we said in a previous chapter that ever since the time when Kálamánik incurred the zamindár's displeasure, he had been meditating on some dark design, and with this view had been visiting the villages round about Kánchanpur. As he never fully disclosed his mind to anyone, it is impossible to ascertain the exact nature of that design, whether it was an intended personal attack on the zamindár himself, or some scheme of daring robbery in the zamindár's house. But whatever its nature might have been, the hand of Fate prevented him from accomplishing his object.

Jaya Chánd Ráya Chauduri was seated one morning in his cutcherry when Bhimá Kotál, the leader of his club-men, approached him and made him obeisance. Jaya Chánd said—"You seem to be a worthless fellow, Bhime; you have not been able to do anything with that wicked fool, Kálamánik, who has defied my authority, and who seems to be sowing the seeds of disaffection among my tenants not only of this village, but of all the villages round about. Can't you get rid of him?"

Bhim. "O Incarnation of Justice! had I only known that such was your honour's wish, Mother Earth would long ago have been rid of him."

Jaya Chánd. "But did you not know that that was my wish? I have hardly pleasure in anything so long as that fellow walks about at large. He will do an infinite deal of mischief if he is not arrested in his course."

Bhim. "I thought your worship wished merely that that fellow should be beaten. But if I had known that the Incarnation of Justice wanted to get rid of him altogether, the deed would have been accomplished long ago. What cannot Bhim Sardár do if ordered by your honour? Order me to bring the milk of a tigress, and I shall do it. Give but the word, and Kálamánik's head will be brought this instant."

Jaya Chánd. "I do not want that exactly; but I wish the thing to be done without noise."

Bhim. "It will be done to-day, Khodáwand."

So saying, Bhimá Kotál went away from the cutcherry, consulted the zamindár's *goindás,* or spies, —for he maintained a regular system of *espionage*— as to the movements of Kálamánik in the evenings, and accordingly adopted measures.

It was evening when Kálamánik left the village of Kádrá, just four miles to the north-east of Kánchanpur, whither he had gone in the course of the day, for reasons known only to himself. The cows had all come home from the meadows, on which the shades of evening were fast descending. The tract of land between Kádrá and Kánchanpur was a plain, the like of which is to be found in many parts of the Vardhamána district. It was one vast paddy-field, interrupted by no hamlet or village, the only objects which disturbed the monotony of never-ending paddy were a tank here and there, and an *asvatha* tree on its embankments. The peasants of Kádrá told Kálamánik that he should spend the night with them, as night had already covered the plains, and there were no intervening villages. But Kálamánik would not be dissuaded from setting out. Conscious of his own immense strength, and naturally foolhardy, he laughed at the idea of *láthiáls* attacking him in the way. Wrapping his bathing towel round his *dhuti* on his waist, with his thick bamboo club in his right hand, he plunged into the encompassing darkness. There was no road, the path lay over paddy fields from which the harvest had been recently gathered. He went on rapidly, with giant-like strides. He met with no human being on the solitary plains, the birds even had taken shelter on trees which skirt the villages; and excepting the chirping of the grasshoppers and the occasional flight of some belated night-bird, there was no sign of life in the darkened plain. He had proceeded more than a mile when the moon emerged from the horizon, and shot forth her friendly beams. Kálamánik walked faster and faster. There was no fear in his dauntless breast. He had now nearly come half the way where there was a large tank, covered with aquatic plants, and a tall *asvatha* tree. At the foot of the tree Kálamánik descried from a distance, through the moonlight, the figure of a human being in a standing posture. As the nearest villages, on all sides round, were about two miles distant from the spot, he wondered who that person could be; but as he considered himself more than a match for half-a-dozen men, he fearlessly went on his way. No sooner had Kálamánik gone within about twenty yards of the tree, which lay in his path, than he heard the voice of Bhimá Kotál accosting him in the following style—"Welcome, brother Kálamánik! welcome! We have been waiting for you for a long time." Kálamánik, nothing daunted, said—"So, Bhime, you have come here to meet your doom;" and with that he sprang forward like a tiger and made Bhima's shoulder feel the weight of his Herculean club. In a moment Bhimá fell down, and lay sprawling on the ground. Before Kálamánik could give a second blow, he found himself surrounded by about a dozen club-men, who had been sitting on the water's edge. Dire was the conflict. Kálamánik maintained the struggle with superhuman valour, wounding many of his assailants. Victory for a long time hung in the balance, when Bhimá got up from the ground, and joined his comrades. A thump of Bhima's club brought Kálamánik to the ground; and as he lay stretched, like a palmyra tree felled by the woodman's axe, the *láthiáls* belaboured him with their clubs till Kálamánik was no more. As the club-men had, by anticipation, brought two hoes with them, they dug a trench on the side of the tank, threw in it the corpse of Kálamánik, and covered it up with earth and turf. For three days no one at Kánchanpur knew of the fate of Kálamánik. On the fourth day some passers-by saw the remnants of a dead body lying on the side of the tank half-way between Kánchanpur and Kádrá. The grave had been dug open by jackals, and the corpse half devoured; but it was not impossible for those who knew Kálamánik to make out that they were his remains. Through the influence of Jaya Chánd the affair was hushed up, and as the hands of the police officers were well oiled, no report on the subject was sent to the magistrate of the district.

CHAPTER LVIII.

THE PANCHAM.

> They covet fields, and take them by violence;
> And houses, and take them away;
> So they oppress a man and his house,
> Even a man and his heritage.
>
> *Micah.*

One day about noon, when Govinda was washing his feet in the tank adjoining his house, after returning from the field, a paper was put into his hands by one of the peons of Jaya Chánd Ráya Chaudhuri. The purport of the paper was a demand for some ninety rupees and odd, being the amount due to the zamindár on account of arrears of the rent of the fields which he cultivated. The paper also contained a *jamá másil báki*, a statement which exhibited the grounds on which the demand was made. Govinda was thunderstruck. To make use of an expressive saying in Bengali, "his hands and feet entered into his stomach" through fear. "I am in arrears," said Govinda to himself, "to the zamindár, and in arrears to the amount of ninety *tákás!* O gods! what is this? Am I awake or am I dreaming? Surely the paper is not intended for me. But sure enough my name is on it. Have I not paid every *payasá* of the rent? O gods, how can ye allow such injustice to be perpetrated on this earth?"

The fact is, that when the zamindár gave orders to Bhimá Kotál to burn the big hut of Govinda, it was not with a view merely to burn the hut itself, and thus inflict on him the loss of property, but chiefly with a view to reduce to ashes those receipts which the zamindár had given him on the payments of rents; and now that those receipts had been destroyed, Govinda was entirely at the mercy of his landlord. And Jaya Chánd was determined to stretch to the utmost those vast powers with which the law had invested him for the ruin of Govinda.

There were two Regulations in the Revenue Code, which were the dread of every ráiyat in the country. These were the *Haptam* (or the *seventh*), and *Pancham* (or the *fifth*), so-called from the numbers those Regulations bore in the Fiscal Code. The one was Regulation VII. of 1799; and the other was Regulation V. of 1812. The former Regulation empowered landholders summarily to arrest and to imprison any tenant who was a defaulter, or was supposed to be a defaulter; and the latter empowered them to distrain and sell off to the highest bidder the property of a ráiyat who was a defaulter, or who was supposed to be one. The object which Government had in giving such extraordinary powers to landholders was to enable them to realise their rents regularly, and transmit them punctually to the public exchequer; but, in consulting its own interest, the Government virtually consigned the entire peasantry of Bengal to the tender mercies of a most cruel and rapacious aristocracy. Happily, a more enlightened and humane legislation has taken away from the code those iniquitous regulations; but it is worthy of note that, for half-a-century, those horrible engines of oppression were allowed, by a Government calling itself Christian, to grind to the dust many millions of probably the most peaceful people upon earth.

Govinda was not in arrears to the amount of even a farthing. To Golak Poddár, the money-lender, he owed a considerable sum, but to the zamindár nothing. He knew the nature of the beast, and therefore took great care not to fall within his clutches. But Govinda had reckoned without his host. It mattered nothing to Jaya Chánd, though a tenant whom he wanted to ruin had paid up his rent; it was not difficult for him to make the tenant out to be a defaulter by the arts of chicanery, perjury, and forgery, in which he was so great an adept. And in the case of Govinda it was the easiest thing in the world, as all his receipts had been destroyed.

The property of Govinda was attached; his crops in the field, now ready for the sickle, his *marái* of paddy in the yard of his house, his cows, and all his personal property, were attached by a process of law. On the sixth day after the attachment, the *phoḍosh-ámin,* or Sale Commissioner, who was entitled to a commission of ten per cent. on the amount of money realised by the sale, gave notice of the sale of Govinda's property, fixing the day and the hour of the day. The terrible *Pancham* just left one little loop-hole for the escape of the victim; but that lay beyond Govinda's power. It provides that a tenant whose property has been attached, may, within five days, enter into a bond before the Collector or Sale Commissioner, with good security, binding himself to institute a summary suit, within fifteen days from the date of the bond, for the trial of the demand, and to pay whatever sum may be adjudged to be due, with interest. But where was this "good security" to be got? Govinda tried all Kánchanpur, but none was forthcoming.

At last the terrible day of the sale arrived. Govinda's crops of paddy, and sugar-cane, and other products, his store of paddy in the house, his cows, were all knocked down by the hammer of the ruthless *phoḍosh-ámin.* All his personal property was also knocked down. But the proceeds of the sale had not yet come up to the zamindár's demand, *plus* the commission of the sale-officer. It was given out that there was valuable property with the women and children, who had shut themselves up in one compartment of the recently rebuilt big hut. With the help of a police officer, who was in readiness, the door was broken open, amid the shrieks of the women and children. All the brass vessels were taken possession of, and put up to auction. The maw of law was now satisfied, and our hero was completely ruined.

CHAPTER LIX.

THE RÁIYATS' MAGNA CHARTA.

A bold peasantry, their country's pride.

The Deserted Village.

THE year 1859 witnessed a great change in the status of the Bengal ráiyat. Act X. of that year is justly regarded as the Magna Charta of the peasantry of Bengal; and though, owing to causes inherent in the ráiyat himself, namely, his ignorance and the consequent want of spirit, that celebrated piece of legislation has not done him all the good it is calculated to do, it must be admitted that it has effected his legal emancipation.

Anyone that has paid attention to the subject of the tenure of land in Bengal can hardly deny that that tenure is based on the right of labour. He who clears the land of jungle becomes its owner. It is true he pays a certain share of his profits to Government, or to the zamindár, who is usually a collector of tax appointed by Government; nevertheless the right of ownership lies with the clearer of the jungle and the occupant of the soil. This theory underlies all legislation on land in this country. It is implied in the protection given to casual occupants, and in the right with which the law invests an occupant for a certain period, to keep possession of the land on the payment of a customary rent. The zamindár, on the other hand, practically regards himself as the owner; and hence there has been, ever since the effecting of the Permanent Settlement, a perpetual struggle between the ráiyat and the zamindár, the one insisting on the payment of a fixed rent, and the other endeavouring to enhance that rent under all sorts of pretexts.

But periodical enhancement of rent was not the only hardship to which the Bengal ráiyat was subjected. Cesses, called *abwabs*, of various sorts were levied, though not authorised by law. The celebration of the marriage of the zamindár's son or daughter, or of the ráiyat's son or daughter, the performance by the zamindár of a *puja* or religious ceremony, or the observance of the thousand-and-one social customs of the land—all these were taken advantage of by the landlord to exact money from the ráiyat. The number of these *abwabs* was, and, we are afraid, still is in some parts of the country, so great that the amount of money extorted in this illegal way far exceeded in many cases the rent justly due for the occupation of the soil.

But this was not all. The zamindár was armed by law with extraordinary powers, which placed the ráiyat entirely at his mercy. One act allowed him to let the rent accumulate till it became so heavy that the ráiyat was unable to pay it, and was consequently ruined. Another law allowed him to distrain, merely on his own declaration that the ráiyat intended to abscond. And a third law empowered him to compel the ráiyat's attendance at his cutcherry, and to flog him almost to death. These two last Acts, usually called the *pancham* and the *haptam*, spread ruin and desolation throughout the country.

From this terrible oppression Act X., of 1859, delivered the Bengal ráiyat. That Act, passed through the exertions chiefly of Mr. Edward Currie and Sir Frederick Halliday, abrogated the hated *pancham* and *haptam*. It declared that any ráiyat who has occupied land for more than twenty years can never have his rent enhanced. It declared that a ráiyat, who has occupied land for more than twelve years, is entitled to receive a lease at a fair and equitable rate; and any enhancement of rent that is to be made, is to be made on certain conditions. It ruled that no enhancement can be made without a year's previous notice, with a view to enable the ráiyat to contest his liability. It made it compulsory on the zamindár to give a receipt for the rent he receives. And lastly, it declared the exaction of *abwabs* to be a punishable offence.

Such were the provisions of Act X., of 1859. If this act had been passed a few months earlier, Govinda would not have been ruined; but as the *haptam* and the *pancham* had their full swing, his property was sold to the highest bidder. Govinda was now perhaps in a more helpless state than at the time when his homestead was reduced to ashes by the orders of the zamindár. He had hardly recovered from the effects of that conflagration when he was plunged into fresh distress. Though his homestead was standing, he was rendered penniless. Inexpressible was his grief, when, the morning after the sale, he saw his house stripped, not only of the comforts of life—if a Bengal peasant can be said to have any comforts at all—but even of its necessaries. As Govinda was somewhat undemonstrative in his nature, he did not give vent to extravagant expressions of grief. He simply sat down on his haunches, and, crossing his arms on his knees, rested his head upon them, and silently wept bitter tears. The women, however, were not so quiet in their demonstrations of grief. They imprecated the wrath of the gods on the head of the zamindár, poured maledictions not only on him, but on his ancestors up to the fourteenth generation. They cursed the very gods themselves for taking pleasure in heaping calamity upon calamity on poor people like themselves; they violently struck their foreheads with the palms of their hands, and exclaimed, "Oh, Vidhátá! why did you write all this on our foreheads?"

Govinda, however, had no leisure to indulge in unavailing grief. He had to feed several hungry mouths, which, like the daughters of the horse-leech, were continually crying, "Give, give!" The wants of his family roused him from his momentary stupor, and impelled him to adopt every means in his power for the support of his wife and children. Of means he had scarcely any. He had, in fact, nothing to fall back upon except the good-will of the ever ready Golak Poddár, the money-lender. Golak kindly came to his rescue, and Shylock though he was, he was so greatly affected at Govinda's pitiable situation, that, on this occasion, he lent him money on less interest than formerly. It took Govinda, however, a long time to be restored to the state in which he had been before the *pancham* and the *haptam* were brought to bear upon him. The debt pressed upon him heavily; and it was not till nine or ten years had elapsed after the auction that he was able to pay off the debt. The history of those ten years, as it was a history of silent suffering and self-denial, I shall not here recount; thus much I may state, that when he paid his last instalment to the *mahájan*, he celebrated the event by giving a feast to his friends and relatives.

CHAPTER LX.

THE EPIDEMIC.

> **With his breath he draws,**
> **A plague into his blood ; and cannot use**
> **Life's necessary means, but he must die.**
>
> *The Task.*

We have seen in the last chapter that Govinda gradually extricated himself out of the wretched plight to which he had been reduced by the zamindár. It now seemed as if the cloud of adversity had been dissipated for ever, and as if Govinda was destined to pass the evening of his life in peace and prosperity. But Providence had determined otherwise. In the year 1870, Kánchanpur was visited by a terrible epidemic. That dreadful plague had years before manifested itself amid the marshes of the district of Jessore; and year after year it had been marching westwards, not only decimating the population, but depopulating entire villages and reducing them to jungles, the abode of the hyena and the tiger. It crossed the Bhágirathi, and fell upon the towns and villages pleasantly situated on its right bank, and hurried to untimely graves thousands of the population. It showed itself in the form of a wasting fever, which no medicines could allay. The demon of the epidemic stalked from village to village, from district to district; and its ghastly form spread dismay and consternation wherever it went. Of the origin of this "scourge of God," no rational account could be given. Some people ascribed it to the rank vegetation with which the villages had been covered; others to the accumulated filth of centuries; and others still, to the checking of drainage by the laying on of the iron road. But, whatever the cause, there could be no question but that the epidemic carried off a large per centage of the population.

East Burdwan had always been regarded as one of the healthiest districts in the country. The dryness of its soil, its comparative elevation, its proximity to that long range of hills which, under various names, stretches from one end of the Indian peninsula to the other, its freedom from rank vegetation, its want of stagnant pools and stagnant marshes, and its thorough cultivation, made it a delightful garden; and so salubrious was its air, and so medicinal its waters, that people from Calcutta and the eastern districts repaired to Burdwan as to a sanatarium. But all this was now changed. The malignant genius of the epidemic entered the district, and infected its air, and poisoned its waters, and the smiling plains of Burdwan were converted into scenes of suffering and desolation. When the first case of epidemic fever occurred at Kánchanpur, its inhabitants were filled with dismay, and though the case did not prove fatal, the consternation of the people did not diminish. The fever went from one end of the village to the other, killing some people, and reducing others to skeletons. Govinda had never seen so many people die in the village. Every day the solemn sound of "Hari, Hari bol! Hari bol! Hari!" was heard in the streets, and announced to the terrified inhabitants the exit of their fellow-villagers from this transitory scene. The fire at the burning tanks was not put out; when the remains of one man were reduced to ashes, those of another were ready for cremation. The oldest inhabitant declared that he had never witnessed such a dreadful visitatión. From nearly every house were heard the sounds of lamentation and weeping; and the people in the streets looked more like ghosts than human beings clothed in flesh and blood. The physicians of the village, who followed the ancient Hindu method of medicine, were powerless. A benevolent Government was sending native practitioners of medicine, according to the European system, to the infected villages; and Kánchanpur was fortunate enough in getting one. A charitable dispensary was established in the village, at which quinine was dealt out liberally. The native doctor was overwhelmed with work; he had no rest either by day or by night. Despite, however, his indefatigable exertions, the plague was not stayed.

The unwelcome visitant did not for a long time enter the homestead of Govinda; and as the rage of the epidemic was evidently abating, he congratulated himself on his escape. But his mother, Sundari, always regarded these congratulations as ominous. She would sometimes say, "Oh, my child, Govinda! don't say we have escaped. If you say so, we are sure to be attacked." Sundari proved a true prophetess. The epidemic fever was upon Govinda, and he lay prostrate for weeks. Other members of the family also got it, but they soon recovered. It was now Sundari's turn, and she fell a victim. The distress of the humble family at this calamitous event can be more easily imagined than described, especially as it took place at a time when Govinda himself had hardly regained his strength. "Oh gods!" cried he in extreme agony, "for what sin of mine are you punishing me so severely? What dreadful sin had I committed in my former birth that you are visiting me with such terrible afflictions? Why do you not make an end of me once for all? Why torment me after this fashion? Why cut my body, as it were, into slices, and put salt into them? Oh, Vidhátá! didst thou write all this on my forehead? Oh, my mother! my dearest mother! who never didst rebuke me, who never didst speak to me angrily once in thy life; Oh, thou, the best of mothers, where art thou gone? Where art thou gone, leaving thy Govinda in this forlorn state?" Such were the exclamations uttered by Govinda on this sorrowful occasion. He wept rivers of tears, and dashed his head on the ground. All this may seem extravagant to the English reader; but it is to be remembered that in Bengal, as in all India, the parental and filial affections are livelier and more intense than amongst the inhabitants of colder regions, and amongst nations who are not accustomed to the peculiar joint-family system of the Hindus.

Though Govinda's grief was sharp and poignant, it soon subsided. A firm belief in predestination reconciles the Hindu to every event in life, however calamitous. It was so decreed by the gods, therefore it has happened—such was the thought that allayed Govinda's grief. For a whole month Govinda was in mourning, and subjected himself to privations similar to those which he had endured at the time of his father's death. The mourning ended with the performance of a religious ceremony. Govinda, like all orthodox Hindus and dutiful Hindu sons, performed the ceremony with suitable pomp. He gave to every Bráhman of the village a priestly fee of four annas. He gave a feast to all his caste-men living at Kánchanpur and in the surrounding villages. And lastly, he had to give both rice and pice to hundreds of poor men, beggars, and religious mendicants, who on such occasions crowd to the houses of all classes of Hindus. All this entailed considerable expense; and as Govinda's exchequer was seldom solvent, he had again to consign himself to the tender mercies of the eternal blood-sucker, Golak Poddár. The English reader may exclaim, "Govinda must have been a fool to spend money on such an occasion, especially as he had no money." Fool or no fool, he had to spend it. Whether he had money or not is beside the point. Spend he must, whether he had it or not. The customs of the country, the laws of Hindu society, the Hindu religion, all demand it. If Govinda had not made the usual presents and given the customary feasts, he would have lowered himself in the estimation of his caste-men. He would have been black-balled. There was therefore no help for it.

CHAPTER LXI.

THE END.

He calls for Famine, and the meagre fiend
Blows mildew from between his shrivelled lips,
And taints the golden ear.

The Task.

It is a trite saying that misfortunes never come singly; they always come in clusters. This was the case pre-eminently with our hero, Govinda Sámanta. Wave succeeded wave; after he had recovered from the shock of one, another was ready to overwhelm him. He had hitherto nobly kept his head above the waters, right manfully riding upon every wave that came rolling upon him in never-ending succession. But his strength had been exhausted by repeated exertions, and no wonder he succumbed at last under the terrible calamity of 1873.

Early in the beginning of that year the eagle eye of Sir George Campbell discovered from the watch-tower of Belvedere the approach of a formidable enemy in the north-western corner of the territories over which he bore sway. He looked at the sky, and behold, it was brass. He looked at the earth, and behold, it was flint. With characteristic energy he blew the note of alarm. The Viceroy, Lord Northbrook, who had been taking repose on the heights of Simla, after the harassing labours of the preceding twelvemonth, left the hills, and hurried to the capital. Consultations were held; accurate accounts of the state of the country were called for; the probable magnitude and extent of the threatened famine were estimated; and wise plans were adopted for alleviating, if not entirely averting, the impending calamity. Day after day, week after week, month after month, millions of the population looked up anxiously to the skies, to discover a cloud of the size even of a man's hand. But not a speck was seen in the blue canopy. The heavens had been completely shut up. When there was no doubt that famine would be sore in a part, at least, of Bengal, the supreme and the local Governments made extraordinary exertions to store up food for starving millions. Never did any Government in the world act, in the face of a great calamity, with such promptitude, such presence of mind, such energy, such considerate benevolence, as the Government of Lord Northbrook. And yet it is a singular fact, that there are people in India, both Englishmen and natives, who thought that the famine was a hoax, that it was "got up" by Sir George Campbell, and that the show was kept up by his able successor, Sir Richard Temple. Such people would have believed in the existence of the famine, only if they had seen myriads of the population die of starvation. The fact is, the paucity of deaths was owing, not to the slight character of the famine, but to the extraordinary energy of the Government, and to the splendid organization of relief, which was due chiefly to the high administrative ability of Sir Richard Temple.

Though the famine was not so sore in the district of Burdwan as it was in Behar, the population suffered greatly from an insufficient harvest.

Govinda's fields at Kánchanpur did not produce a fourth of the usual annual crop. As he had no other means of support than the produce of his fields, he was in great distress. He had food for himself and his family for three months; what was he to do for the remaining nine months? He could not get work as a day-labourer in the village, as most of his fellow-villagers were in equal distress with himself. There was therefore nothing left for him but to go to Burdwan, where Máharájáh Mahtáp Chánd Bahádur—the greatest landholder in Bengal—was with characteristic benevolence creating work for about two thousand labourers every day, with a view only to give them relief. It was with a heavy heart, and with tears in his eyes, that Govinda left his home, and wended his way towards Burdwan. He had never in his life hired himself out as a day-labourer. He had always tilled his paternal acres, and lived upon their produce. But now, in mature life, he had to stoop to the degradation of becoming a coolie. This thought dried up his life's blood. Like other labourers, he certainly worked on the Máharájáh's relief works, and got his daily wages. But the thought of his degradation haunted him by day and by night. It preyed upon his spirits. He wept day and night over his wretched lot. His health visibly declined. He was reduced to a skeleton. His heart was broken. And one morning he was found dead in his miserable hovel, far from his home and from those he loved. His son, on hearing the mournful news, hastened to Burdwan, put the remains of his father on the funeral pile, and reduced them to ashes. Thus was Govinda delivered from all his troubles.

THE END.

GLOSSARY OF INDIAN TERMS.

Aibara-bhát.—Literally, bachelor's rice; the dinners given to a man shortly before his marriage.

Alakta.—Lac; leaves or flimsy paper saturated with lac.

Áman.—The principal crop of rice; winter rice.

Ámra.—The hog-plum; Spondias magnifera.

Andarmahal.—The inner part of a house; that is, the women's apartments.

Annaprásana.—The ceremony of giving rice for food to an infant for the first time, generally performed when the child is six months old.

Anirhabhojana.—Same as *Aibara-bhat.*

Arhar.—A kind of pulse (Cytisus cajan).

Áske.—A sort of cake made of pounded rice.

Asoucha.—Ceremonial uncleanness consequent on a death in a family.

Asvatha.—Ficus religiosa.

Átapa.—Rice of unboiled paddy.

Átkouriyá.—A ceremony so called from there being used in it *eight* sorts of fried pulse and cowries.

Auksálá, or Ikshusálá.—A temporary hut raised for expressing the juice of the sugar-cane and turning it into molasses.

Aus.—Spring rice; literally, ripening in a short time.

Báblá.—The babool tree (Acacia Arabica).

Bágde.—A low-caste Hindu.

Bainchi.—A shrub and its fruit (Flacourtia sapida).

Bakula.—Mimusops Elengi.

Bálá.—Ornament for the wrist.

Bandhu.—A friend.

Bara-ghar.—The big room.

Barbati.—A sort of pulse (Embelia basaal).

Bari.—Little balls made of mashed pulse, dried in the sun, and used in curry, or fried separately.

Bat.—Ficus indica.

Bátásá.—A light cake of sugar.

Beri.—A pair of tongs for taking down a pot from the hearth.

Bhát.—Boiled rice.

Bhujno.—Same as *Annaprásana.*

Bhuta.—A ghost.

Bhutanath.—Lord of ghosts: a name of the god Siva.

Bhutariya.—An expeller of ghosts from a person possessed: an exorcist.

Bibi.—A lady; applied by Hindus especially to a European lady.

Bidhátá, or Vidhátá.—Purusha. The Creator.

Bigha.—About a third part of an acre.

Bishuti.—A stinging plant (Tragia involucrata).

Bonti.—A sickle placed erect on a wooden frame for chopping.

Bouti.—An ornament for the arm.

Brahmadaitya.—A Brahman ghost.

Burkundáz.—A police constable.

Chádar.—A sheet or scarf for the body.

Chandimandap.—Literally the house of the goddess Chandi or Durga; but it usually means a sitting-room in the outer yard of a house.

Chandrahár.—An ornament for the neck.

Charitámrita.—Literally, the nectar of biography—a biographical memoir of the Bengali reformer, Chaitanya, is so-called.

Charká.—Spinning-wheel.

Chásá.—Husbandman.

Chaturdola.—A litter used for carrying a bridegroom or bride.

Chhálnátalá.—An awning under which the marriage ceremony is performed.

Chhari.—A stick.

Chhenchki.—A hodge-podge of vegetables.

Chhoto-bahu.—The wife of a younger brother.

Chichinga.—Snake gourd (Trichosanthes anguina).

Chira.—Flattened rice.

Chongá.—A piece of bamboo, between two joints, used as a phial for oil.

Dá.—A bill-hook; a husbandman's knife.

Dadhi.—Curds.

Daivajna.—An astrologer.

Dál.—Pulse.

Dán.—Gift; presents.

Danda.—The sixtieth part of one day and night, that is, twenty-four minutes.

Dándá-guli.—The bat and ball used by Bengalis.

Dhenki.—The pedal; instrument for husking corn.

Dhol.—A sort of drum; tom-tom.

Dhuti.—The lower garment of a Bengali, usually a piece of cloth five yards long, and a yard and a half broad. The dhuti of the lower classes is shorter and narrower.

Dighi or dirghiká.—An oblong shallow pond.

Dom.—A low caste Hindu, especially engaged in making baskets of wickerwork.

Duli.—A litter for conveying women chiefly.

Durgápuja.—The annual celebration of the worship of the goddess Durgá.

Gamasta.—Agent of a zamindár.

Gámchhá.—Bathing towel.

Gaya asvatha.—A species of Ficus cordifolia.

Ghát.—Landing-place of a tank or river.

Ghatak.—A professional matchmaker.

Ghati.—Waterpot.

Ghi.—Clarified butter.

Ginni (Grihini).—House-mother.

Godá.—A large baboon.

Godhuli.—Literally, *cow's dust*, twilight so-called, from cows returning from the fields in the evening, and kicking up the dust.

Gopála.—Neatherd; a name of the god Krishna.

Gosálá.—Cow-house.

Gosvámi.—Literally the lord of cows, a spiritual director.

Got.—An ornament for the waist.

Gotama.—Founder of the Indian system of logic.

Gotra.—Race, tribe.

Guru.—Spiritual director.

Gurumahásaya.—Schoolmaster.

Háṇḍi.—Earthen pot, generally used in cooking food.

Hári.—The sweeper-caste.

Haridra.—Turmeric (Curcuma longa).

Hari-lut. — Literally, Hari's plunder, a ceremony at childbirth.

Hát.—Market.

Hát.—The hand.

Hátá.—An iron ladle or spoon.

Hátchhari.—Striking on the palm of the hand by a cane.

Háte.—In the hand.

Huká.—Smoking apparatus, hookah.

Indra.—One of the Hindoo gods, king of Heaven.

Jagajhampa.—A sort of drum, so called from its sound.

Jám.—A tree and its fruit (Eugenia jambos).

Jhámp.—A mat-door, a screen made of palmyra leaves and split bamboo.

Jhumko.—An ornament for the ear.

Kabuliyat.—Counterpart to a pátá, written agreement given by a raiyat to a zamindar, assenting to the conditions on which he holds land.

Kachu.—Arum indicum.

Kachhari.—Cutcherry, court-house,

Kadmá.—A kind of sweetmeat.

Kalam.—Reed for writing, calamus.

Kalai.—A sort of pulse.

Kalasi.—A water-pot.

Kalki.—Tobacco-bowl for the huka.

Kamádeva.—God of love.

Kamarsálá.—Smithy.

Kanchi.—A bamboo twig.

Kánsi.—A musical instrument in the form of a metallic plate, also the player on it.

Kánthala.—Jack tree and its fruit.

Kanyá.—Daughter, bride.

Kanyá-Sampradána.—The giving away of a daughter in marriage.

Kapála.—The forehead.

Karaniya.—Reckoning by karis or shells.

Karánja.—A tree and its fruit (Pongamia glabra).

Kári.—Cowries, small shells.

Kartikeya.—God of war and of beauty.

Káste.—Sickle.

Kátári.—A bill-hook, a husbandman's knife.

Katbel.—A tree and its fruit (Feronia elephantium).

Káthá.—A measure of land about four cubits square, or six feet long.

Káthákáli.—Measurement of land.

Kaviráj.—A physician.

Káyastha.—The highest Sudra caste, the writer caste.

Keutiyá.—A species of *Cobra de capello.*

Khábár.—Food.

Khadi.—Fried paddy.

Khágrá.—Species of reed (Saccharum spontaneum).

Khaichur.—A kind of sweetmeat; literally, pounded fried paddy.

Khájá.—A kind of sweetmeat.

Khájná.—Land rent.

Khali.—Mustard oil-cake.

Khari.—Chalk; ochre.

Khát.—A bedstead with tester-frames and posts for mosquito curtains.

Khenki.—An ill-natured, snarling woman.

Khoka.—A male infant.

Khonrá.—Lame.

Khud.—Broken rice.

Kodáli.—Hoe; spade.

Kulin.—High in rank.

Kuputra.—An unworthy son.

Kurul.—Axe.

Lagna.—Auspicious time, astrologically speaking.

Lákhráj.—Rent-free land.

Lakshmi.—Goddess of wealth and beauty.

Láru.—Sweetmeat, especially in the shape of balls.

Lavanga-latá.—A scandent shrub (Limonia scandens).

Lekhá-pará.—Reading and writing; education.

Lotá.—A brass pot.

Maharir.—Writer; clerk.

Mahásaya.—Schoolmaster.

Mal.—Silver rings for the ankles.

Mál.—Snake-catcher, or charmer.

Máldkar. — Florist; dealer in flowers.

Mamdo.—A Muhammadan ghost.

Man.—Forty seers, or 80 lbs. avoirdupois.

Manasá-Devi.—The goddess of snakes.

Mandal.—Head-man of a village.

Mankasha.—Working of a sum (in arithmetic) in *man*.

Mantra.—Prayer; incantation.

Marai.—Storehouse of paddy.

Masál.—A torch, usually made of rags soaked in oil.

Mitá.—A friend.

Moá.—A kind of sweetmeat.

Mudi.—A grocer.

Muga.—A species of pulse (Phaseolus aureus).

Muri.—Parched rice.

Murki.—Parched rice soaked in treacle.

Nath.—Ring for the nose.

Navánna.—Literally, new rice; the festival of first fruits.

Nándá.—A large earthen vessel.

Nápit.—A barber.

Nápitni.—A barber's wife.

Nisi.—Night.

Nousádar.—Sal ammoniac.

Ojhá.—One who cures persons possessed, or bitten by serpents.

Olá.—A kind of sweetmeat.

Padre.—A clergyman; father.

Págri.—Head-dress.

Painchhá.—Bracelet.

Páká.—Ripe; complete.

Palákánti.—A string of coral beads for the wrist.

Palása.—Butea frondosa.

Pálki.—A conveyance carried on the shoulders of four people, palanqueen.

Pánchan.—Bamboo stick.

Panchánan.—The Five-faced, a god with five faces and fifteen eyes.

Pán.—Betel-leaf.

Pandit.—A learned man.

Paniphal.—An aquatic plant and its fruit (Trapa bicornis).

Papaya.—A tree and its fruit (Carica papaya).

Pásá.—Ornament for the ear.

Pátá.—A document given by a zamindár to a ráiyat specifying the conditions on which land is held.

Patal.—A cucurbitaceous fruit (Trichosanthes dioica).

Pátáli.—A cake of molasses.

Páthsálá.—School, school-house.

Pausha.—Half of December and half of January.

Petni.—A dirty female ghost.

Phálgun.—Half of February and half of March.

Phalsá.—A tree and its fruit (Grewia Asiatica).

Phánrá.—Misfortune or accident as recorded in a horoscope.

Phánri.—A subordinate police station.

Phánridár.—A constable in charge of a phanri.

Phuthalai.—Fried peas.

Pimri.—A low stool.

Pithá.—Cake made of pounded rice.

Poá.—Half-pound.

Prahara.—Eighth part of day and night, that is, three hours.

Prajápati.—Creator, the god that presides over marriages.

Purohita.—Priest.

Ráiyat.—A cultivator.

Rákhál.—Cowherd, shepherd.

Rahtakamala.—The red water-lily (Nelumbium speciosum).

Rámkhari.—A sort of chalk.

Rangmasál.—Bengal light.

Rárhi.—Belonging to the country of Rarh, the districts on the western side of the river Bhagirathi.

Rasanchauki.—A sort of musical instrument.

Rasagolla.—A kind of sweetmeat.

Rásináma.—The zodiacal, or astronomical name of a person.

Ráyabághini.—A tigress, metaphorically used for a termagant.

Rishi.—A Hindu saint.

Rohita.—A species of fish (Cyprinus denticulatus).

Sábásh.—Well-done!

Sadgopa.—The agricultural caste.

Saheb.—A European.

Saheb-lok.—Europeans.

Sál.—A tree (Shorea robusta).

Sándi.—Flute; flute-player.

Sángát.—Friend.

Sankhachurni. / *Sankhachinni.* —Female ghosts of white complexion.

Sankshipta-sára.—A treatise on Sanskrit Grammar, used in Western Bengal.

Sara.—A species of reed (Saccharum sara).

Sardár-poro.—Senior scholars in a village school.

Saresvati.—Goddess of wisdom.

Sári.—A piece of cloth about five yards long and one yard broad, worn by women.

Sarkár.—An agent; a writer.

Saruchakli.—A thin sort of cake made of pounded rice.

Satya-yuga.—The true or golden age.

Satranja.—A coarse Indian cotton carpet.

Sayyátoláni.—Fee exacted by the friends of the bride from the friends of the bridegroom in the Vásarghar.

Ser.—One pound avoirdupois.

Serkashá.—Working of a sum in *sers.*

Sidá.—A gift of rice, pulse, vegetables, oil, &c.

Sil.—Curry-stone.

Siva.—A Hindu god.

Skandakátá.—Headless ghosts.

Sloka.—A couplet in poetry.

Solá.—The Indian cork-plant (Æschynomene paludosa).

Sráddha.—Funeral ceremonies.

Sriphal.—A tree and its fruit (Cratæva marmelos).

Srotriya.—A class of Brahmans.

Subhankara.—An eminent Indian arithmetician.

Sudhkashá.—Interest in arithmetic.

Suktárá.—Venus, or the morning star.

Sutiká-griha.—The lying-in-room.

Sutra.—Aphorisms.

Suvarna-Vanik.—The banker caste.

Tábij.—Ornament for the arm.

Taktaposh.—A wooden frame used for sitting on or sleeping.

Tál.—Borassus flabelliformis.

Tanpurá.—A musical instrument.

Tarkári.—Curry.

Tejpatra.—A leaf (Laurus cassia) put in curry to give flavour.

Tol.—A Sanskrit school.

Tolá.—Cess, fee, exaction.

Topiwálá.—Hat-man, a person wearing a beaver hat, that is to say, a European.

Tulasi.—The sacred basil (Ocymum sanctum).

Uchhe.—A vegetable (Momordica muricata).

Ugra-kshatriya.—A Sudra caste engaged chiefly in husbandry.

Ulu.—An exclamation of joy made by women at the time of marriage.

Uthan.—The open yard of a house.

Vágdán.—Betrothal.

Vaidya.—The medical caste.

Vairági.—A mendicant.

Vaishnava.—A follower of Vishnu, especially in the form of Chaitanya.

Vásarghar.—The room in which a married couple spend their first night.

Vedantism.—A system of Hindu pantheism.

Vijaganita.—Algebra.

Vijamantra.—The seed-prayer, the essence of prayer supposed to be expressed in certain unmeaning sounds.

Viná.—A musical instrument.

Visvakarma.—The Creator, the Indian Vulcan.

Yaksha.—Fabulous beings in Hindu mythology.

Yama.—The Indian Pluto.

Yánti.—Betel-nut-cracker.

Zilla.—District.

Published by

Facsimile Publisher
Ashok Vihar, Delhi-110052 (India)
Website: www.facsimilepublisher.com

Distributed by

Gyan Books Pvt. Ltd.
5, Ansari Road, Daryaganj, New Delhi-110002 (India)
E-mail: books@gyanbooks.com, Website: www.gyanbooks.com

2 222000 010652